Comparative Children's Literature

Children's literature has transcended linguistic and cultural borders since books and magazines for young readers were first produced, and popular children's books have been translated throughout the world.

Emer O'Sullivan traces the history of comparative children's literature studies, from the enthusiastic internationalism of the post-war period – which set out from the idea of a supra-national world republic of childhood – to modern comparative criticism. Drawing on the scholarship and children's literature of many cultures and languages, she outlines the constituent areas that structure the field, including contact and transfer studies, intertextuality studies, intermediality studies and image studies. In doing so, she provides the first comprehensive overview of this exciting new research area. *Comparative Children's Literature* also links the fields of narratology and translation studies, to develop an original and highly valuable communicative model of translation.

Taking in issues of children's classics, the canon and world literature for children, *Comparative Children's Literature* reveals that this branch of literature is not as genuinely international as it is often fondly assumed to be. The book is essential reading for those interested in the consequences of globalization for children's literature and culture.

Emer O'Sullivan is Professor of English at the University of Lüneburg, Germany. Her book *Kinderliterarische Komparatistik*, on which this book is based, won the International Research Society for Children's Literature Award for outstanding research in 2001.

Comparative Children's Literature

Emer O'Sullivan

Based on her book,
Kinderliterarische Komparatistik

Translation by Anthea Bell

 Routledge
Taylor & Francis Group

LONDON AND NEW YORK

First published 2005
by Routledge
2 Park Square, Milton Park, Abingdon, Oxon, OX14 4RN

Simultaneously published in the USA and Canada
by Routledge
270 Madison Ave., New York, NY 10016

Routledge is an imprint of the Taylor & Francis Group

Transferred to Digital Printing 2006

Typeset in Baskerville by Taylor & Francis Books

British Library Cataloguing in Publication Data
A catalogue record for this book is available from the British Library

Library of Congress Cataloging in Publication Data
O'Sullivan, Emer.
Comparative children's literature / Emer O'Sullivan.
p. cm.
Includes bibliographical references and index.
1. Children's literature–History and criticism. 2. Children–Books and
reading. 3. Literature, Comparative. I. Title.
PN1009.A1O77 2005
809'.89282–dc22
2004015163

ISBN 0–415–30551–9

Printed and bound by Antony Rowe Ltd, Eastbourne

For my parents
Maurice and Mairéad O'Sullivan

Contents

Figures

Preface

This book first saw the light of day as a *Habilitation*, a post-doctoral thesis in the German academic system as qualification for a professorship. Published as *Kinderliterarische Komparatistik* by the Universitätsverlag C. Winter in Heidelberg, it received, in 2001, the biennial IRSCL Award for outstanding research.

Preparing an edition for publication in English has in itself been a comparative exercise, taking into account the different traditions and conventions of academic discourse in German and English. The result is not only significantly shorter (a lengthy chapter on the German translations and reception of *Alice in Wonderland* was excluded), but this revised and updated version has also reduced the myriad footnotes characteristic of a German academic tome. Assisting this transition from one discourse to another was the translator Anthea Bell, with whom it was an honour and delight to work. The correspondence accompanying her translation was full of enlightening reflections often reaching far beyond any specific matter in question, as well as entertaining anecdotes from her experience as a translator.

Children's literature studies in English is mainly a monolingual phenomenon, mostly dealing with the wealth of children's literature in the English-speaking countries and referring to critical material written in English. Researchers who do not write in that language generally remain internationally unnoticed. In this book, readers will encounter many names of scholars hitherto unquoted in the English language context, likewise primary texts from different languages. The quotes have all been translated into English, with the original passages, in the case of primary texts, given in the footnotes. If one of the effects of this book is that readers reach for hitherto unknown primary or secondary texts in languages other than English, then it will have succeeded in one of its aims: to make children's literature research itself more comparative and more aware of developments outside the English-speaking countries.

Acknowledgements

I am grateful to colleagues at the Institut für Jugendbuchforschung at the Johann Wolfgang Goethe-Universität in Frankfurt for their active interest and helpful discussions while I was writing the German book upon which this is based, with special thanks to Hans-Heino Ewers, the director of the institute, and to my colleagues Bernd Dolle-Weinkauff, Gabriele von Glasenapp and Ute Dettmar. I am also grateful for the assistance and support of numerous colleagues and friends, experts on children's literature and other areas, only a few of whom can be named here: Klaus Doderer, Göte Klingberg and Walter Scherf, three pioneers of children's literature research, Nancy Chambers, Valerie Coughlan, Robert Dunbar, Jeffrey Garrett, Harald Husemann, Gillian Lathey, Joep Leersen, Gertrud Lehnert, Myriam Mieles, Kimberley Reynolds, Verena Rutschmann, Reinbert Tabbert, J.D. Stahl, Rüdiger Steinlein, Elisabeth Stuck, Anna Katharina Ulrich, Anne de Vries and Gina Weinkauff. I was gratified to have such an illustrious and intelligent translator as Anthea Bell working on my book. A small grant from the *Vereinigung von Freunden und Förderern der J.W. Goethe-Universität* [Association of Friends and Supporters of Frankfurt University] helped to finance assistance with the bibliography and the index. My sincere thanks are due to the International Research Society for Children's Literature for honouring my book with the biennial Award, an honour which was instrumental in generating interest in an English version. Without the love and support of my husband, Dietmar Rösler, there wouldn't even have been a German version.

I wish to thank the following for permission to reprint copyright material: Axel Scheffler for the illustration from *A Squash and a Squeeze* and for the drawing 'The Scissors of International Coproduction' published in *Die Zeit*, Daniel Maja and Hachette Jeunesse for the illustration from *Émile et les détectives*, Michel Gay and l'école des loisirs for the double illustration from *Papa Vroum* and John Burningham and Jonathan Cape for illustrations from *Granpa*. Every effort has been made to trace and contact copyright holders. The publishers would be pleased to hear from any copyright holders not acknowledged here.

Introduction

After the Second World War the notion that children's literature could promote international understanding became a credo: children's literature, crossing all borders with ease, was expected to give rise to a Utopian 'universal republic of childhood'. Since the late twentieth century we have been experiencing a different type of internationalism, this time not as an idealistic postulate but as the result of global market forces; it is generated by multinational media companies which manufacture products for children all over the world. Neither the idealistic postulate of a 'universal republic of childhood' nor commercial globalism, however, alters the fact that books for children have always been written by real authors at real places in different languages, and that they have been and still are read, in translations into other languages, in other parts of the world.

Children's literature studies, too, has often set out from the idea of an international corpus of books for children, assuming texts by authors from different linguistic and cultural areas to be part of a single concept of children's literature and overlooking the fact that this also includes translated works which have been adapted to the readers' cultures, sometimes deviating extensively from the source texts. Children's literature has transcended linguistic and cultural borders since books and magazines specifically intended for young readers were first produced on a significant scale in eighteenth-century Europe. In many countries it includes a high proportion of translations and thus provides an interesting field for comparative research. But children's literature, not traditionally regarded as meriting serious scholarship, has hitherto flown under the radar of comparative literature, the discipline generally responsible for researching cross-cultural phenomena. Consequently, we have a situation in which comparative literature largely ignores children's books, and children's literature studies too seldom works with comparative methods.

This book argues that children's literature studies that neglects the comparative dimension is approaching significant areas in a questionable manner, and that, if it sets out from the idea of an international corpus of children's literature, it is not only subscribing to a north-west European and American fiction, but also neglecting to adequately describe and explain the crossing of linguistic and cultural borders. I do not propose here that we have only to apply general comparative methods to a previously disregarded literary field. Instead, the main characteristics distinguishing children's literature from general literature – in particular the fact that it is written or adapted specifically for children by adults, and the asymmetry of communication between the parties involved which arises from this assignment of texts by adults to children – call for a comparative approach specific to children's literature which differs in certain areas from mainstream comparative literature. Since comparative approaches to children's literature have so far occurred in isolation, and the field lacks a consolidated body of knowledge, this book is a first attempt to lay the foundations of the field.

Chapters 1 and 2 take stock of those studies that do exist. A brief historical survey of this area of research, from the enthusiastic internationalism of the post-war period, which set out from the idea of a supra-national world republic of childhood, through analytical studies of translation and reception to the comparative essays of the last thirty years, is provided by means of a critical summary. An outline of nine constituent areas in Chapter 2 will help to structure the field of comparative children's literature: the general theory of children's literature, contact and transfer studies, comparative poetics, intertextuality studies, intermediality studies, image studies, comparative genre studies, the comparative historiography of children's literature and the comparative history of children's literature studies. In describing these areas, I shall also discuss questions of methodology and assess existing contributions to the subject. That many comparative issues can and must inevitably be approached from various perspectives is illustrated on a small scale at the end of Chapter 2, taking the adolescent novel as an example. At the end of the book, the concepts of children's classics, the canon and world literature for children will be discussed in more detail, showing how such phenomena can only be adequately addressed using a complex approach from multiple viewpoints. The consideration of fundamental theoretical questions pertaining to children's literature in Chapter 2 is the prerequisite for a later investigation of the way in which it crosses borders: only by first addressing the nature of narrative communication in children's literature generally, for instance, can we go on to provide a differentiated analysis of the translation process in children's books in the following chapters.

Chapter 3 deals with three basic questions of comparative children's literature: the conditions in which literature for young people develops, its culture-specific status and its international exchange. Among other points made in this chapter, an analysis of the different courses taken by the development of children's literature in various parts of the world will refute the assumed universal validity of a model based solely on books for young people in the north-west European industrialized countries. The international exchange of children's literature will be examined in the light of the distribution of children's literature and the economic dimension, and will be shown not to be as international as it may appear.

While Chapters 1 to 3 will organize and describe the field of comparative children's literature both historically and by outlining its areas of operation, Chapters 4 to 6 will offer an in-depth study of translation and reception, areas central to comparative study. Positions and theories from general translation studies will be discussed in Chapter 4, as well as scholarly work in the area of the translation of children's literature. Analysis of the norms and values of the target culture communicated in translated children's literature, and of adaptations made during the translation process on the grounds of what translators assume to be the child reader's receptive abilities and requirements, will show why translated books can be considered a particularly clear indicator of concepts of children's literature, and indeed of childhood itself, that are specific to a given time and culture, and why practice can differ so widely in the fields of translation for children and adults.

Linking the fields of narratology and translation studies, Chapter 5 will develop a theoretical and analytical tool, a communicative model of translation, using a category analogous to that of the implied author – the implied translator. The implied translator will be identified as perceptible on two planes of discourse: as 'the translator' in paratextual observations, and as the narrator of the translation in the narrative text itself. The identification of this second manifestation is particularly useful in the analysis of translated children's books, and textual analyses will show how and why the narrator of the translation can intervene in the structure of the translated text, even to the point of drowning out the narrator of the source text.

Finally, in Chapter 6, I shall address the concepts of *Weltliteratur*, world literature for children, the canon in mainstream and in children's literature and children's classics, a term which is used to denote both works of historical importance and best-selling popular books. I shall investigate the origins of texts generally regarded as children's classics together with explanations for their selection, evaluation and preservation, and examine their transmission in translation and in various media adaptations. Taking Carlo Collodi's *Pinocchio* as a test case, and its reception in Germany, the USA and in mass culture, I will examine the independent life that classics can develop in translated and adapted form and reflect on the consequences of children's literature and culture in the age of globalization. Analysis of the concept of classics of children's literature will be shown to draw together various areas of comparative children's literature addressed throughout this study.

1 Comparative literature and children's literature

The comparative context

The development of a global economy, accompanied by modern communications and information technology, the fall of political borders, increasing voluntary mobility and emigration as a result of war, poverty or political persecution are all factors that have far-reaching consequences for our approach to cultural products, forcing us to rethink cultural identities beyond traditional national paradigms. The study of transnational cultural products lies at the heart of comparative literature, which was established in the universities of the nineteenth century as a counter-discipline to studies of national language and literature. This opposition determined the subject of comparative literature: whereas 'national' philologies concentrated exclusively on literature within the political borders of the nations concerned, comparative literature, as a kind of corrective measure, dealt with so-called *Weltliteratur* or 'world literature'. The subject of comparative study goes beyond a single literature; it is what different literatures have in common, as well as the peculiarities and individual features of the various literatures which come to light only when they are seen in relation to others. Its subject traditionally derives from several languages, thus distinguishing it from the study of single literatures.

In view of the fact that individual disciplines of language and literature could no longer be understood as solely national, criticism of the traditional idea of comparative literature was voiced from the late 1980s onwards, to the effect that it needed to be complemented. Critics called for an extension of the subject beyond an exclusive focus on linguistic differences, insisting that cultural differences should become an object of comparative studies of literatures in the same language – for instance, the comparison of Spanish and Latin American literature, or the literatures of the various German-speaking countries. At the same time, under the influence of systems theory and constructivism, new poststructuralist disciplines such as translation studies, gender studies, cultural studies and alterity studies developed which applied new theories and methods to areas on which comparative literature thought it had the monopoly. Analyses of border-crossing phenomena come to the fore in such interdisciplinary studies of literature and culture as New Historicism, a discipline '[which] has given scholars new opportunities to cross the boundaries separating history, anthropology, art, politics, literature and economics' (Veeser 1989a: ix). In particular, the development of the concept of postcolonialism not only proved to be methodologically productive as a way of opening up the subject, but also contributed to the new and further development of comparative literature as a discipline in Asia, Africa and South America, one that, characterized by a shift of perspective, departed from the Eurocentric perspective and its system of values (see Bassnett 1993: 6).

Recently, European and American comparative literature, too, has adopted methods and subjects developed in other disciplines. A predominantly literary tendency in investigating the connections between individual texts (usually European or North American), authors, genres, periods and national literatures has been replaced by an interdisciplinary cultural studies approach. In 1993 leading scholars in the American Comparative Literature Association published a report proposing a new, comprehensive definition of comparative literature:

> The space of comparison today involves comparisons between artistic productions usually studied by different disciplines; between various cultural constructions of those disciplines; between Western cultural traditions, both high and popular, and those of non-Western cultures; between the pre- and postcontact cultural productions of colonized peoples; between gender constructions defined as feminine and those defined as masculine, or between sexual orientations defined as straight and those defined as gay; between racial and ethnic modes of signifying; between hermeneutic articulations of meaning and materialist analysis of its modes of production and circulation; and much more.
>
> (Bernheimer *et al.* 1995: 41f.)

Comparative literature today, being situated on the interface between national philologies as well as between literary studies and such disciplines as philosophy, history of art, psychoanalysis, anthropology, sociology, film studies, theatre studies and so on, is, according to Hans Ulrich Gumbrecht, 'generally and normally recognized as the name for an intellectual and institutional space not where literatures [are] actually compared, but rather where experimental thinking relevant for the future of the Humanities [can] take place' (1995: 401).

For those working in traditional comparative literature, children's literature was not a subject to be taken seriously. But even in more recent comparative studies, some of which deal with the extensions of the field mentioned above and focus on literatures usually banished to the periphery of cultural discussion, children's literature is hardly ever mentioned. From the viewpoint of children's literature studies, the lack of a comparative dimension has occasionally – but repeatedly – been seen as a deficiency. Scholars have emphasized the fact that an adequate survey of children's literature which 'evolves from international, rather than national paradigms' (Bouckaert-Ghesquière 1992: 93) can really only be carried out if approached with comparative methods, but for a long time no one went any further than pointing out that this would be desirable. When Mary Ørvig (1981: 229) complained: 'It is a deplorable fact that the entire international children's book field is lacking in comparative studies', she was taking her place in a tradition which runs from Mary Thwaite (1963) and Göte Klingberg (1967a), to be continued in the 1980s and 1990s by such writers as Margaret Kinnell (1987), Gertrud Lehnert (1988) and Anne Pellowski (1996). However, some of those who point out that such a dimension is desirable have persuasively contributed to it, and in the context of early interest in the internationalism of children's literature first steps towards comparative studies were taken, showing the way forward to a genuinely comparative approach to children's literature that has, albeit hesitantly, been developing in recent years.

Paul Hazard: a comparatist turns to children's literature

With Paul Hazard's *Les livres, les enfants et les hommes* [Books, children and men] (1932), a book on children's literature was published by a leading figure in the field of comparative studies at a time when children's literature hardly existed as far as comparative literature and academic literary criticism were concerned.[1] However, Hazard did not regard his study as a first step in a new branch of scholarship but as a plea for the right of children to appropriate, imaginative, non-didactic books, and for a literary education through reading texts of high aesthetic quality, which he ascribes to a series of European children's classics. He combines his regard for literary education with a comparative account of the history of various European traditions in children's literature, and an attempt to do justice to their respective national strengths. Hazard sets out from an image of childhood which owes much to the Romantic myth. He puts the emphasis on imagination as the child's strongest urge, and on the distance between the childhood and adult realms, linking the former with the archaic. Children, he says, need a kind of literature that reifies the nature of childhood in order to achieve a free, childish identity. In one of the most frequently quoted passages of the book, he has children appealing to adults:

> 'Give us books,' say the children; 'give us wings. You who are powerful and strong, help us to escape into the faraway. Build us azure palaces in the midst of enchanted gardens. Show us fairies strolling about in the moonlight. We are willing to learn everything that we are taught at school, but, please, let us keep our dreams.'
>
> (Hazard 1944: 4)

Hazard also writes about the part children's literature plays in the construction of a specific cultural or national identity. As he sees it, children's literature forms the soul of a nation and preserves its characteristic features. In a controversial section of the work headed 'Superiority of the North over the South', he compares the achievements in children's literature of several European countries. He dismisses Spain entirely and points out that the two Italian masterpieces – *Pinocchio* and *Cuore* – were belated. He sets the generally poor tradition of the South against that of the North with its English nursery rhymes, school stories such as *Tom Brown's Schooldays*, authors of the calibre of Sir Walter Scott, Robert Louis Stevenson, Kipling, Twain, Pushkin, Gogol and Hans Christian Andersen. Hazard sees Andersen as supreme not just in the North but in all children's literature because 'Andersen is unique in his capacity for entering into the very soul of beings and of things' (ibid.: 96). He offers two explanations for the superiority of the North. The first tries to account for the specific development and nature of the imagination using the old – and discredited – theory of climate to explain the character of nations. Speaking of Andersen, he says:

> How conscious we are in all this of the powerful imagination of the North, instinct with sensitiveness! How different it is from the imagination of the South which etches everything sharply under the direct brilliance of the sun! Beneath this sky laden with mists, where the light remains timid and gray even on the fairest days, we grasp the significance of doubts and confusions. There the sharpness of a too clear vision will not belie the man who sees grimacing faces in the tree roots, who peoples the sea with phantoms delicately traced on its grayish expanse.
>
> (ibid.: 99f.)

Hazard's second explanation addresses a question of central importance for a comparative study of the development of children's literature: the different concepts of childhood in different cultures. In contrast to the educational ideals of the Romance-language areas, he claims, childhood exists in its own right in northern European cultures: 'For the Latins, children have never been anything but future men. The Nordics have understood better this truer truth, that men are only grown-up children' (ibid.: 110).

Although his approach may have been questionable, Hazard none the less addressed comparative aspects of the subject such as differing concepts of childhood, different traditions of children's literature specific to certain nations, and different mentalities. However, his work does deviate in some surprising ways from the methods of comparative study. Hazard insists that children simply took what they needed from the treasury of adult literature – the novels of Defoe, Swift and so on. This is a romantic idea which will not stand up to either the literary theory of the relationship between children's and adult literature, or an examination of the conditions of literary production and international transfer. Hazard takes little notice anyway of the processes of actual cultural exchange; he does not reflect on the procedures of translation and adaptation, but sets out by assuming that children's literature communicates across all borders. This point leads us to the aspect of the book which has proved most durable: although Hazard recognizes national features in the literatures of various groups and ascribes significance to them, he imagines a place of childhood which transcends all political and linguistic boundaries:

> Children's books keep alive a sense of nationality; but they also keep alive a sense of humanity. They describe their native land lovingly, but they also describe faraway lands where unknown brothers live. They understand the essential quality of their own race; but each of them is a messenger that goes beyond mountains and rivers, beyond the seas, to the very ends of the world in search of new friendships. Every country gives and every country receives – innumerable are the exchanges – and so it comes about that in our first impressionable years the universal republic of childhood is born.
>
> (Hazard 1944: 146)

The wide international appreciation of Hazard's work on children's literature after the Second World War (the American translation appeared in 1944, the German translation in 1952, translations into Swedish, Czech and other languages followed) confined itself mainly to the idea of the humanizing function of books in the universal republic of childhood, a Utopia of international understanding. In the post-war period the idea of the universal republic of childhood became a repository for the traumatic experiences of adults. Bertha E. Mahony writes in her foreword to the translation of Hazard that appeared in 1944:

> Today it seems likely that humanity's longing for a world commonwealth of nations, which shall move towards the abolishment of periodic wholesale destruction and make the brotherhood of men more possible, will express itself in a second attempt at such an organisation. Paul Hazard reminds us in words which can scarcely be bettered that the world republic of childhood already exists.
>
> (Mahony 1944: vii)

But the concept of universal childhood is a Romantic abstraction which ignores the real conditions of children's communication across borders. There is no 'world republic of childhood' in which the conditions are in any way on a par with one another. Many children in developing countries are excluded from all but the most basic education, while their counterparts in wealthy countries are afforded a comparatively protracted and protected childhood and education. While the former might probably never see or be able to read a children's book, most of the latter have access to unlimited books and other media which cater for their age groups and leisure habits. 'The child' can't be spoken about as a singular entity; class, ethnic origin, gender, geopolitical location and economic circumstances are all elements which create differences between real children in real places.

The vision of the universal child, the same the world over, refuses to acknowledge difficulties and contradictions in relation to childhood, offering in their place a glorification of the child, cast in the role of innocent saviour of mankind in a tradition which reaches back to Rousseau's *Émile* with its creed that with every child humankind receives another chance for positive renewal. Children's literature conceived in this spirit serves as a site on which adult difficulties are addressed and often placated; it is about promises which the adults' generations could not keep, amongst them international understanding and world peace.

However, criticism of the enthusiastic over-estimation of the potential beneficial effects of children's literature should not make us forget that post-war measures to foster literary exchange in the cause of international understanding did encourage a generally open-minded attitude towards the literatures of other nations. This is particularly clear from the work of the International Youth Library (IYL) and its founder Jella Lepman. In 1946 Lepman turned to twenty nations, most of which had been at war with Germany only a year before, asking for donations to set up an international exhibition of children's literature in Munich. Her appeal ran: 'Bit by bit ... let us set this upside down world right again by starting with the children. They will show the grown-ups the way to go' (Lepman 2002: 33). In her work at the IYL Lepman tried to put the ideal of international understanding through children's literature into practice by means of many activities, and by her part in the founding of IBBY (the International Board on Books for Young People) in 1953.[2]

Approaches to comparative children's literature

An approach which emphasizes the internationalism of children's literature tends to be characteristic of the important monographs published in the 1950s – see, for instance, Bettina Hürlimann's major survey of European children's literature, *Europäische Kinderbücher aus drei Jahrhunderten* [Three centuries of European children's books] (1959), Luigi Santucci's study *Letteratura Infantile* [Children's literature] (1958), which takes up Hazard's ideas by presenting fantasy as the literary genre best suited to children, and Mary Thwaite's *From Primer to Pleasure in Reading* (1963). In 1968 Anne Pellowski, founder of the Information Center on Children's Cultures, published a ground-breaking work in the form of an extensive annotated bibliography, *The World of Children's Literature*. Its aim was to provide 'the information (or the means to it) which would lead to an accurate picture of the development of children's literature in every country where it presently exists, even in the most formative stages' (Pellowski 1968: 1). She intended this work to be the basis for comparative study of the subject.

The 1960s and 1970s saw the beginning of an interest in translations, and with translation questions of adaptation and reception emerge for the first time. Three names are pre-eminent: those of Richard Bamberger, for many years director of the Internationales Institut für Jugendliteratur und Leseforschung [International Institute for Children's Literature and Reading Research] in Vienna, Walter Scherf, Lepman's successor at the IYL, and Göte Klingberg, co-founder in 1970 of the International Research Society for Children's Literature

(IRSCL). Bamberger's observations on the importance of translations (1961) are among the first to be found in any critical writing on children's literature. Scherf wrote many articles on reciprocal influences in children's literature – for instance, the influence of Spain and Great Britain on children's literature in Germany (1976). A growing interest in the translation of children's literature is indicated by the third IRSCL conference organized by Göte Klingberg and Mary Ørvig in 1976, which was devoted to that subject (see Klingberg, Ørvig and Amor 1978). In his book *Children's Fiction in the Hands of the Translators* (1986) Klingberg systematically studied the different ways in which references in the source texts were adapted in translation. Klingberg's major contribution to the comparative study of children's literature, together with his theoretical writings, consist in the production of complete annotated bibliographies of all children's books published in Sweden, including translated books;[3] using these, scholars could embark on studies of the distribution and reception in Sweden of literature from various other countries. One such study was his own *Das deutsche Kinder- und Jugendbuch im schwedischen Raum* [German books for children and young people in the Swedish area] (Klingberg 1973). These writers, working on comparative aspects of children's literature at quite an early stage, recognized that methods of comparative literary studies should be employed in research on children's literature (see Bamberger 1978: 13). As early as 1967, in the programme he drew up for the historical study of children's literature, Klingberg pointed to the necessity of a comparative history of European literature for children and young people (see Klingberg 1967a: 330). Twenty-seven years later, in an article of 1994, he repeated that demand; it had not yet been met.

A fruitful extension of the discussion of children's literature in comparative terms came in the 1980s, particularly with the adoption of systems theory and through links with translation studies. The theory drawn up by the Israeli semiotician Zohar Shavit (see Shavit 1986) which sees children's literature as part of the literary polysystem, to be analysed in its connections and its modes of functioning over and beyond any aesthetic or educational evaluations,[4] gave new impetus to the theory of children's literature. Such an analysis, says Shavit, offers the prospect of drawing paradigmatic conclusions, since children's literature belongs at the same time to the literary, social and educational systems. From the comparative viewpoint, the problem with this approach is that, by setting out from systemic definitions of, for instance, the development of children's literature in different cultures, it puts forward a theory of cultural conditions that claims universal validity (see Chapter 3).

The growing interest in comparative aspects of children's literature is illustrated by a series of publications since the 1990s, many of them deriving from international conferences on the subject – they include Perrot and Bruno (1993), Ewers, Lehnert and O'Sullivan (1994), Webb (2000) and Neubauer (2002). A number of established journals have also dedicated special issues to comparative aspects of children's literature in the last two decades, for instance *Poetics Today* 13:1 (1992), *Compar(a)ison* 2 (1995) and *New Comparison* 20 (1995). The most recent addition was a special double issue in 2003 of *META* 48: 1–2 on translating children's literature. The cultural turn in literary studies has also led to an inter-disciplinary opening in children's literature, resulting in studies which, while not strictly comparative in that they deal with the literature of one cultural/linguistic context only, take account of historical, social and ideological factors, applying psychoanalytical theory, gender-studies approaches and poststructuralist criticism. Postcolonial theoretical approaches especially have flourished in countries such as Australia (see Bradford 2001) and the United States and Canada (see McGillis 1999) through a growing awareness of the cultural and territorial rights of their First Nation inhabitants, but also through addressing contemporary multieth-nicity. In European children's literature studies topics such as migration and cultural minorities are receiving increased attention (see Müller 2001).

Despite the progress in the discussion of comparative subjects in children's literature studies, the prevailing concept of this literature is still predominantly internationalistic. Foreign texts are often read in their translations into German, English, etc., and then discussed as if they had originally been written in those languages. The lack of awareness of the nature of literary translation leads, in academic practice, to interpretations difficult to imagine in the study of adult literature. For instance, Charles Frey and John Griffith, in their interpretation of the *Geschichte vom Suppenkasper* [The story of Augustus] from Heinrich Hoffmann's *Struwwelpeter* [Shock-headed Peter], dwell on an aspect to be found only in the English translation (missing from their bibliography) and quote the author ('says Hoffmann') as saying that it was 'a *sin* / To make himself so pale and thin' (1987: 57; emphasis added). The mention of sin introduces an important religious element not present at all in Hoffmann's original, which contains neither the idea of a transcendental judge nor any reproof: 'O weh und ach! / wie ist der Kaspar dünn und schwach!' [literally: 'Oh woe, alas! How thin and weak Kaspar is!']. The interpretation of a text on the basis of the unthinking use of a transla-tion can thus lead to statements that will not survive a glance at the original.

Furthermore, theoretical works on children's literature very seldom cross linguistic borders. In Peter Hunt's *International Companion Encyclopedia of Children's Literature* (1996) all the articles on the theory, criticism, genres and context of children's literature are contributed by British, American, Australian and Canadian writers. As a result, this 'international' encyclopedia is in the nature of an anthology of contemporary children's literature studies in the English-speaking world, since most of the entries do not mention theories from other linguistic areas or recommend them for further reading. In her introduction Margaret Meek claims: 'This volume is its [children's literature's] first avowed encyclopedia' (1996: 1). It says much about the situation that a highly regarded and well-read British critic like Meek overlooks Klaus Doderer's four-volume *Lexikon der Kinder- und Jugendliteratur* [Encyclopedia of children's literature] published twenty years earlier (1975–82), the first comprehensive and truly international reference book on the subject. However, and this too is a heart-ening indication of the spread of a comparative awareness, a revised edition of the encyclopedia will shortly be published which promises to address many of the shortcomings listed here.

2 Constituent areas of comparative children's literature

Today we can no longer speak of a fixed number of 'pillars upholding the edifice of Comparative Literature's subject matter' (trans. from Weisstein 1968: 107). The contemporary discussion of the organization of the subject and the definition of borders and hierarchies within it, some of which were given in Chapter 1, is of such variety as to defy summary.[1] The 'pillars' named by Ulrich Weisstein in his Introduction of 1968 – literary epochs, periods and movements, genres, the history of subjects and motifs and the mutual elucidation of the arts – now give way to an 'uncertainty of category' (Koelb and Noakes 1988: 11), with comparative literature today considered 'to be less a set of practices ... and more a shared perspective that sees literary activity as involved in a complex web of cultural relations' (ibid.). Despite this tendency to uncertainty in comparative literature, I would like to put forward a structural proposition for the evolving discipline of comparative children's literature. It will divide up the field and delineate its areas of study. It is the first proposal of its kind and can only be enhanced by future discussion and modification.

Comparative children's literature must concern itself with general theoretical issues in children's literature, especially questions pertaining to the system itself, its particular structure of communication, and the social, economic and cultural conditions which have to prevail in order for a children's literature to develop. A central preoccupation has to be with what is characteristic, distinctive and exclusive to individual children's literatures, which emerges, as do their commonalities, only when different traditions are contrasted with each other. It has to deal with forms of children's literature in the different cultural areas, and with their respective functions in those areas. Furthermore, comparative children's literature must address all relevant intercultural phenomena, such as contact and transfer between literatures, and the representation of self-images and images of other cultures in the literature of a given language. Comparative children's literature, like mainstream comparative literature, must consider those phenomena that cross the borders of a particular literature in order to see them in their respective linguistic, cultural, social and literary contexts. However, it would not be adequate to adopt methods and issues from general comparative literature and simply apply them to texts written for children. The particularities of children's literature demand the formulation of specific questions distinct from those of mainstream comparative literature. This is manifest in some areas, less clearly so in others.

In this chapter, comparative children's literature will be divided into nine areas. They are:

1 Theory of children's literature
2 Contact and transfer studies
3 Comparative poetics
4 Intertextuality studies
5 Intermediality studies
6 Image studies
7 Comparative genre studies
8 Comparative historiography of children's literature
9 Comparative history of children's literature studies

Depending on the nature of the questions involved, these subject areas, isolated here for the purpose of my proposed structure of the field, can overlap, and several questions should and must inevitably be approached from more than one angle. To illustrate this, the adolescent novel is taken as a brief example at the end of this chapter. The following pages will name questions relevant to each area, in many cases referring back to studies already undertaken, and will, in most cases, sketch examples. The accounts of the areas do not claim to be exhaustive, some of them offer no more than a taster; it remains the task of future scholars to put more flesh on the bones of the discipline.

1 Theory of children's literature

Is a children's book a book written by children or for children? Is a book written for children still a children's book if it is (only) read by adults? What of adult books read also by children – are they children's literature? These questions posed by Karín Lesnik-Oberstein (1996) have been asked in countless variations by scholars attempting to define children's literature. Should it be defined by its intended or by its actual audience? The key difference between children's and adult literature lies in the fact that the former is written or adapted specifically for children by adults. Belonging firmly within 'the domain of cultural practices which exist for the purpose of socializing their target audience' (Stephens 1992: 8), it is a body of literature into which the dominant social, cultural and educational norms are inscribed. This aspect is particularly relevant when studying forms of transfer of children's literature to ask, for instance, to what degree norms of the source text influence or even prohibit translation. In what follows, I will take a brief look at aspects of children's literature theory which address key areas of difference between it and mainstream literature, going on to examine the narrative communication in children's fiction, the addressees of children's literature and its general status.

Children's literature is seen, in a system-theory based approach (see Shavit 1986 and Ewers 2000), as a specific and distinct segment of the general literary system requiring a theory of its own. It has its own fields of activity in marketing, publishing, libraries, teaching, criticism, etc., which distinguish it from adult literature. According to this theory, the definition of children's literature is determined not on the level of the text itself, that is to say in the form of specific textual features, but on the level of the actions and actors involved: texts are identified by various social authorities as suitable for children and young people. These include educational institutions both ecclesiastical and secular, figures active in the literary market (publishers, distributors, etc.) and those who produce the books (editors, authors, etc.). Adults, therefore, assign texts to children and, in the process, transmit dominant morals, values and ideals.

The asymmetry of communication between the partners involved which arises from this assignment by adults of texts to children and young people is a constituent element in children's literature, and many of the essential differences between children's and adult literature derive from it. It recurs at all levels of the children's literature system. Production, publication and marketing by authors and publishing houses, the part played by critics, librarians, booksellers, teachers and others as intermediaries – at every stage of literary communication we find adults acting *for* children. However, that should not be seen as a negative factor *per se*, since without adult authors, publishers, intermediaries and so forth, there would be no communication; children cannot act independently in the literary market. Asymmetrical communication, which is addressed as a central issue in children's literature theory, manifests itself initially outside the text. The principles of communication between the adult author and the child reader are unequal in terms of their command of language, their experience of the world, and their positions in society, an inequality that decreases in the course of the young reader's development. Children's literature is thus regarded as literature that must adapt to the requirements and capabilities of its readers. It tries to bridge the communicatory distance between the unequal partners involved by adapting language, subject-matter and formal and thematic features to correspond to the children's stage of development and the repertory of skills they have already acquired. Göte Klingberg (1986: 10) defines this adaptation as 'the consideration of ... the supposed interests, needs, reactions, knowledge, reading ability and so on of the intended readers'. The German author Kirsten Boie formulated the corresponding questions a writer for children asks as follows:

> What *can* I expect of children whose understanding of language is not yet nearly as well developed as my own adult linguistic skills, without asking too much of them? What *ought* I to expect of children without contravening educational, psychological, moral and aesthetic requirements, particularly since it is not always easy to bring those four into line with each other? And the third question, unfortunately, is: what does the market allow me, want me or forbid me to do in a rapidly developing media society?
>
> (trans. from Boie 1995: 4f.; emphasis in the original)

The asymmetry that characterizes children's literature not only has a bearing on the discussion of its status within the literary polysystem, it also affects all aspects

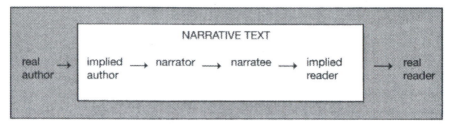

Figure 2.1 Six-part model of narrative communication

of the transfer of children's literature across linguistic borders, as the discussions and examples in the following chapters will show.

Narrative communication[2]

In the quotation above Kirsten Boie asks as a real author, one who physically writes texts for young readers, how she should approach the task. As narrative theory has shown, the author does not communicate directly with the reader, rather the communication takes place between agencies within the narrative text.

In the basic narrative structure proposed by Seymour Chatman in *Story and Discourse* (1978) (see Fig. 2.1), six different parties form three pairs. The narrative text – indicated by the box in the middle – is the message transmitted from the *real author* to the *real reader*, from the one who physically wrote the text of the book to the one who actually reads it. These are not to be found within the book itself, nor does the real author communicate directly with the real reader; the real author, according to Chatman, 'retires from the text as soon as the book is printed and sold', what remains in the text are 'the principles of invention and intent' (1990: 75). The source of the work's invention, the locus of its intent is the *implied author*, whom Chatman calls a silent instructor, the 'agency within the narrative fiction itself which guides any reading of it' (ibid.). The implied author, an agency contained in every fiction, is the all-informing authorial presence, the idea of the author carried away by the real reader after reading the book. The *implied reader* is the implied author's counterpart, 'the audience presupposed by the narrative itself' (Chatman 1978: 149f.), the reader generated by the implied author and inscribed in the text. The asymmetrical nature of the communication in children's literature is reflected in this model as follows: an adult implied author creates an implied reader based on (culturally determined) presuppositions as to the interests, propensities and capabilities of readers at a certain stage of their development. The implied author is thus *the* agency in children's literature which has to bridge the distance between 'adult' and 'child'.

The next, innermost, pair in the model comprises the *narrator* and the *narratee*. The narrator is the one who tells the story, the narratee, in the words of Barbara Wall, is 'the more or less shadowy being within the story whom … the narrator addresses' (1991: 4). The narrator is not always sensed as a persona in the text; Chatman distinguishes between the 'overt' and 'covert' type. Overt are the narrators who feature as figures in the narrative, an example being Oswald Bastable in Edith Nesbit's *The Treasure Seekers*:

> There are some things I must tell before I begin to tell about the treasure-seeking, because I have read books myself, and I know how beastly it is when a story begins, 'Alas!' said Hildegarde with a deep sigh, 'we must look our last on this ancestral home'.
>
> (Nesbit 1899: 3f.)

Another example is Christopher Robin's father, who tells the stories and features in the frame in A.A. Milne's *Winnie-the-Pooh* (1926). Equally overt are narrators who don't feature as characters but as an authorial presence in the text, such as the one who declares in Nesbit's *The Enchanted Castle*: 'the sensible habit of having boys and girls in the same school is not yet as common as I hope it will be some day' (Nesbit 1907: 7). The overt narrator has become less common in children's literature over the past few decades but, even without saying 'I', may be no less revealing of character and attitude, as evident in the mimicking opening of *Harry Potter and the Philosopher's Stone*: 'Mr and Mrs Dursley, of number four, Privet Drive, were proud to say that they were perfectly normal, thank you very much.' (Rowling 1997: 7).

The narratee, too, can be a character in the novel – Christopher Robin in *Winnie-the-Pooh* is an obvious example, or the social worker for whom Hal writes the account of his story in Aidan Chambers' *Dance on My Grave* (1982); more often the narratee isn't actually portrayed but evoked. The overt first-person, authorial narrator occasionally addresses the narratees with questions or appeals such as 'You know the kind of house, don't you?' or 'You may imagine their feelings' (Nesbit 1907: 7). The narrator is created by the implied author and is not to be confused with that agency. Similarly, the narratee should not be identified with the implied reader, although in some cases there will be some overlap. Again taking *Winnie-the-Pooh* as an example: Christopher Robin of the frame is the narratee, but the implied reader or rather implied readers include older children and adults reading the story to children. There are elements in the text which appeal to and can be understood only by them, indeed which are written specifically with an older audience in mind.

The addressees of children's literature

The audience for children's literature includes adults as well as children – adults in their capacity as intermediaries (who buy, give and recommend books) reading with the child in mind, adults reading aloud to children, and adults who read children's literature for their own pleasure. Some of the readers' roles they adopt are inscribed in the texts themselves and so can be inferred from the textual structure. More than one implied reader can be discerned in certain children's books which address both child and adult readers. Zohar Shavit classified these as 'ambivalent' texts, formally belonging to one system (children's literature) but read by members of another (adult literature) (see Shavit 1986: 37). She links her classification of 'ambivalent' texts in the literary polysystem with problematic assumptions about the authors' intentions, claiming that authors of ambivalent texts use the supposed child narratees only as an excuse to locate a text within the children's system, when it is really meant to please adults alone: 'The child ... is much more an excuse for the text rather than its genuine addressee' (ibid.: 71).[4] So-called ambivalent texts, however, should not be classified solely on the basis of their position in the literary polysystem. This classification must take place in the context of an analysis of the narrative communication in children's literature, whose structure has altered greatly over the course of time. In children's literature of the eighteenth and nineteenth centuries, adult intermediaries were informed explicitly by authors, in forewords or afterwords intended especially for them, that the work in question was a children's book. This form of communication in separate paratexts has gradually gone out of fashion; it now takes place more indirectly in the body of the text and can, for instance, be conveyed by the choice of certain topics (these 'signals to intermediaries' are discussed in Ewers 2000).

Setting out from the question of how the narrator speaks to the narratee – and the image of the spoken word is important here – Barbara Wall traces the development from the early nineteenth century, when adults were addressed, to the simple address to children that has been dominant in English-language children's literature since the early twentieth century. She points out the self-conscious tone in which adults have spoken to children, well aware that other adults were listening in, and the difficulty for authors of developing an honest narrative voice which takes children seriously and speaks expressly to them, rather than speaking over their heads to other adults. She distinguishes between 'double address' and 'single address'. In literature using the double address system, of which Barrie's *Peter Pan* may be considered a typical example,

> narrators will address child narratees overtly and self-consciously, and will also address adults, either overtly, as the implied author's attention shifts away from the implied child reader to a different older audience, or covertly, as the narrator deliberately exploits the ignorance of the implied child reader and attempts to entertain an implied adult reader by making jokes which are funny primarily because children will not understand them.
>
> (Wall 1991: 35)

As Wall sees it, the time when 'children's books were written almost as much for adults as they were for children' (ibid.: 147) ended in the early twentieth century, giving way to the 'single address' in which 'narrators ... address child narratees, overt or covert, straightforwardly, showing no consciousness that adults too might read the work. Concern for children's interests dominates their stories' (ibid.: 35). Wall names as the precursor of this approach – with no immediate successors – Carroll's *Alice's Adventures in Wonderland* (1865), although this book is regarded by many people as a prime example of 'double address'. Pioneers of the 'single address' now predominant in children's literature were such writers as E. Nesbit, Beatrix Potter and Frances Hodgson Burnett.

As well as the modes of address and implied readers' roles inscribed in the text, there is a wide variety of ways in which a text can be read. We must distinguish between how the implied author speaks to the imagined readers and the actual reception of the text, between a text with double address and a text to which adult readers may also be drawn, although no such approach is inscribed in the text itself. Only too often a book that appeals to adults – such as *Alice in Wonderland* – is assumed to be addressed to them, although there are few stylistic or structural features in the text to back that assumption. Wall therefore rightly contrasts 'double address' with a 'dual audience', a feature especially characteristic of a text that appeals to adults although it is not addressed to them. She cites Beatrix Potter as an example:

> although she commands a dual audience, [she] uses single not double address. There are no jokes in Potter's work whose purpose is to amuse adults, or even the author, while children pass them by, although in almost every story there are parts which will yield up much more meaning to adults than to children.
>
> (Wall 1991: 165)

The concept of dual or double address risks reducing the possible diversity of readers' roles in children's literature due to the dichotomy involved in simply viewing 'adults' and 'children' as narratees. Although it is unavoidable to speak of 'adults' and 'children' as readers, it should be made clear that these two groups of readers are nothing more than constructs. Since its beginning, psychoanalysis has insisted 'that childhood is something in which we continue to be implicated and which is never simply left behind' (Rose 1994: 12). Most texts display elements which appeal to a variety of readers at different stages of development and at different ages. More appropriate to the description or analysis of inscribed readers or addressees would be the image of a sliding scale rather than two poles. It would therefore seem preferable to speak of multiple address, which of course includes double and dual address.

Premature identification of the nature of the address in a text also ignores the fact that there are various different 'adult' ways of reading children's literature. An adult may read aloud, read on behalf of the child, or read children's books for their own sake, as if they were peer texts. In addition, the adult reader may adopt the role of an implied child reader. This role, in my own view, has at least two variants: one is regressive, in which adult readers revert to a remembered or imagined childhood while they read, aiming to take a childlike pleasure in the text and excluding 'adult' reflections; in the other, adults, aware of their adult status, long for or look back to an idealized childhood, at the same time knowing how impossible it is to realize this longing. The fact that a certain book for children also appeals to adult readers is not on its own sufficient for us to assume double or multiple address. Textual analysis must establish whether different possible ways of reading are involved, or whether there are traces of address to an audience of adults as well as children.

Status

A feature distinguishing children's literature from adult literature is that its origins are to be found both in the literary and the educational systems. This dual reference, with simultaneous poetic and pedagogic criteria, has far-reaching consequences for the status of children's literature, of which comparative children's literature must be critically aware. Comparative study of children's literature must look at its specific conditions and developments in various cultures, and at its respective status in the literary system of different linguistic and cultural communities. That is to say, it must look on the one hand at the cultural status of children's literature, which may be partly determined by the proportion of texts with double address and by the degree of literary development it has undergone, and on the other hand at the educational status, which is related to the pedagogic value and functions of children's books in the broadest sense. The general status of children's literature also depends on the relationship between the cultural and educational systems, which can vary greatly within a culture from epoch to epoch. Status is thus influenced by factors as diverse as the nature of the texts themselves and the general assessment of childhood and its status at a given point in time within a given cultural area. For instance, a general cultural underestimation of children's literature has been the norm in Germany at least since the beginning of the nineteenth century (see Ewers 1996a: 852), and Germany is not exceptional in this respect. According to Shavit, the low status of children's literature in the polysystem means that higher status can be achieved not through any internal workings of the literature itself but only through higher-ranking systems; hence, 'the children's writer [is] perhaps the only one who is asked to address one particular audience and at the same time appeal to another' (Shavit 1986: 37). As already mentioned, Shavit applies the term 'ambivalent texts' to those books that aspire to be appreciated by readers of the more highly regarded system of adult literature; they then enjoy higher status. At the other end of the scale are texts that do not appeal to adult readers at all – for instance, series by Enid Blyton and Carolyn Keene. But, we have to ask, why is the status of Enid Blyton, hugely popular with children, so low in the adult literary system?

In his study of Blyton, David Rudd argues that critics have constantly belittled her simply because they employ the wrong tools. Instead of using those designed to analyse canonical literature, they should be looking at the characteristics of oral transmission, the tradition into which the tales of the storyteller Blyton more readily fit. The elements of the oral tradition include formulaic language, schematic and derivative characters, stories which change to suit the circumstances of time and audience, and its open form. These contrast with the qualities of 'literature', in which style is paramount, the work is thematically integrated, character is rounded, and originality at a premium (see Rudd 2000:

155ff.). A similar point was put forward by Hans-Heino Ewers (1990), who, setting out from structuralist folklore theory which draws a distinction between 'folklore' or oral culture and 'literature', proposes a descriptive model in which the determining factors are modes of transmission and uses of literature. He uses the term 'written folklore', coined by Alieda Assmann in 1983, to describe literature of a functional character which draws on a basic stock of subjects, motifs, characters and plots (it would be perhaps more apt to speak of 'written oral transmission'). Since the different textual practices are of different cultural standing, and since the less highly esteemed textual types of 'written folklore' (or written oral transmission) and popular literature dominate children's literature, they bear much responsibility for its low status. Children's literature, to a considerable extent, is functional literature; in particular, texts written for very young readers are occasional in character – lullabies, jog-along knee songs, bedtime stories, birthday stories, and so on. Since the criteria of literary criticism observe the rules of the most highly regarded and valued kind of textual practice, Ewers claims that higher status for children's literature can be achieved only at the price of making it increasingly 'literary' (see Ewers 1990: 86).

An indication of the low status of children's literature is evident in, for instance, the choice of titles included in bibliographies of translated literature. Patrick O'Neill's (1981) English-language bibliography of translations from the German, includes Erich Kästner's works for adults but none of his children's books, which have not only been translated several times over but which today, far more than his adult texts, account for his international fame (see Dolle-Weinkauff and Ewers 2002). The only children's book in the bibliography is a translation of Peter Bichsel's *Kindergeschichten* [Children's stories] (1969), a book awarded a prize by the *Gruppe 47* [Group 47] German cultural movement (and thus approved by the adult literary system), listed by O'Neill in a version entitled *There's No Such Place as America* (Bichsel 1970) by the acclaimed translator Michael Hamburger.

One of the subjects for a comparative analysis of the status of children's literature is the question of the general and culture-specific degree of its openness in relation to other literary areas, for instance the canon of adult literature. Works for adults have been (and still are) more commonly read by children and particularly young people than, conversely, children's books have been accepted into mainstream literature. Among those that have found acceptance are Tolkien's *The Hobbit* (1937), Michael Ende's *Momo* (1973), Peter Pohl's début novel *Janne min vän* [Johnny, my friend] (1985), Jostein Gaarder's *Sofies verden* [Sophie's world] (1991) and, most recently and famously, J.K. Rowling's *Harry Potter* novels (from 1997). Children reading works that were not intended for a young public can influence the development of children's literature, in that those working in it may react by changing the goods on offer. Examples of the significant import of entire genres from adult into children's literature, in reaction to the popularity of certain texts, are the stories deriving from *Robinson Crusoe*, known as 'Robinsonnades', on the continent of Europe in the late eighteenth century. The same kind of reaction is perceptible in the adoption of novels of adolescence, hitherto exclusively for adults, into young adult novel fiction in the second half of the twentieth century (see section 10).

Another factor important for comparative studies is the question of the culture-specific classification of works by individual authors or whole genres as being for children, for young adults or for adults. Definition of the boundaries between these areas is influenced by social attitudes to children and the status of children's literature in general. The degree of ease with which the border can be crossed indicates the breadth or otherwise of the culture-specific system in question. Sometimes, although not frequently, stories published for children in one country appear in translation on an adult list in another without any indication of their original readership, for instance the German translations of Luigi Malerba's children's stories (see Schultz 1994). Such changes in the classification of texts can indicate the attitude to children in the countries concerned and their estimation of children's reading capabilities and needs.

The features of children's literature mentioned in this section that distinguish it from adult literature – its definition as texts assigned by adults to the group of readers comprising children and young people, the asymmetry of communication in children's literature, and its belonging to both the literary and educational realms – can be regarded as universal, as features of all children's literature. Consideration of questions of a general theoretical nature relating to children's literature is a prerequisite for any comparative study of the subject, since without attention to such peculiarities as the specific structures of communication and the status of children's literature in the entire literary system of a linguistic and cultural community, no adequate study can be made, for instance, of the contact between children's literatures or the comparative poetics of children's literature.

2 Contact and transfer studies

Comparative studies of translation, reception and influence, for which I prefer the more comprehensive term of contact and transfer studies, are concerned with every form of cultural exchange – translation, reception, multilateral influences, etc. – between literatures from different countries, languages and cultures. These range from comparison of cases in which contact or influence between individual writers is reflected in their work, to typological comparison, which looks at similarities and parallels in literatures that have arisen independently and without contact through analogous conditions of production or reception, to intertextual procedures such as allusion, quotation and parody. The methodological spectrum runs from hermeneutical analysis carried out in a study of intertextuality to a semiotic investigation of social, cultural or aesthetic affinities.

Chapters 4 to 6 will show, through an extensive discussion of selected aspects of contact and transfer studies, especially translation, how the specific features of texts for children call for a distinctive approach in comparative children's literature. Here I shall sketch a broad general outline of the areas of contact and transfer studies in children's literature. These are:

- contact, transfer and reception,
- international mediators,
- specifics of the translation of children's literature,
- non-translation and delayed reception and
- cross-cultural development of literary traditions.

Intertextuality, belonging both here and to the study of comparative poetics, will be discussed separately in section 4.

Contact, transfer and reception

Studies of all forms of the influence of a work, an author or a whole national literature on other authors, literatures, etc. have long enjoyed particular popularity in comparative literature. This branch of study includes exploration of possible points of contact between literatures, through the reception by individual authors of works from cultural or linguistic areas outside their own, studies of different forms of literary contact (for instance, in letters written by authors to other authors across linguistic borders, or studies of the sources in an author's 'foreign' reading), and the question of the possible influence or effect of reception on the work of individual writers. In the older type of comparative study of influences, a tendency to attribute similarities in different literary traditions to mechanical influence, and to give only quantitative enumerations without placing them in a wider social, historical and cultural context, led to accusations of unthinking positivism and gave this field of study a poor reputation. None the less, the study of contacts, reception and analogy proves to be an area that still plays an important part within comparative literature. Major impulses that have contributed to its methodology derive from reception theory, theories of intertextuality, and systems theory. Contact studies today no longer look for cause and effect but focus on dynamic processes of exchange between cultures; these studies are a point of departure for questioning the particularities of a given work and its function in that specific historical and cultural situation.

In the field of children's literature Walter Scherf's comment as long ago as 1976, in an essay on the influence of Spanish literature on German children's literature, still holds true:

> The history of the multilateral influences in the field of children's literature has not yet been written. Except for a few single attempts to give a survey of the adaptations and translations the one or other literary work has gone through, nobody has ever tried to make a comprehensive analysis from the very beginning portraying not only the factual exchange between two national children's literatures, but giving also the documentation on how the translations have been accepted, how readers, critics, book selectors evaluated them – and how the function of the texts were [sic] changed by adaptation and translation tendencies, how their reading and their influence have been reflected in memoirs and biographies.
>
> (Scherf 1976: 62)

Several studies deal with the cross-cultural reception of individual works and authors in other cultural areas, for instance the reception of *Pinocchio* in the German-speaking countries (Marx 1987), the French reception of *Heidi* (Mooser 1993), Enid Blyton in Germany (Prieger 1982), the *Biggles* books in Sweden (Mählqvist 1983), *Robinson Crusoe* in Germany (Stach 1996) or Karl May in Poland (Honsza and Kunicki 1987). And to date a few works have been written on aspects of bilateral and multilateral literary connections in children's literature, such as those between France and Germany (Baumgärtner 1992), between French and Italian children's literature in the nineteenth century (Colin 1995), between Dutch and other literary traditions (Duijx 1994), on German–Turkish literary relations (see the essays in the journal *Diyalog* 1, 1992) or on international influence on Finnish children's literature in the nineteenth century (Kuivasmäki 1995). One of the areas most thoroughly researched so far is that of the literary connections between Sweden and Germany (see Klingberg 1973, who casts light on educational as well as literary influences). However, there is not yet any systematic analysis of the dynamics of bilingual, multilingual and cultural literary relationships that explores, for instance, the translations and literary traditions which have functioned as a model for a given literature.[5]

International mediators

Mediators, *agents littéraires* between the literatures of different countries, are traditionally recruited from various groups: publishers, authors and translators are the best known, but travellers, diplomats and scientists have played, in the past, an active part too. Today this area is dominated by literary agents, scouts, editors and, above all, the licensing departments of publishing houses. Institutions in children's literature such as IBBY and the International Youth Library (IYL)[6] expressly act as intermediaries and promote translations by providing information about foreign texts worth translating and, in the case of IBBY, giving awards to translators. But other institutions and those who run them also promote or have promoted translation activity.[7]

   In the context of contact studies in children's literature we must ask how, by whom, in what way and on what level contacts are made, who reads foreign children's literature, who conveys it across borders, who translates it (when and how), and how the international mediation of children's literature differs from that of adult literature. The question of the interaction between works translated and those authored by one and the same person must also be explored in comparative terms. An unusually high number of German translators of children's books are also writers themselves, and an above-average number of writers also translate. They include James Krüss and Josef Guggenmos,[8] who deserve praise for having imported nonsense literature into the German-speaking countries, Paul Maar and above all Mirjam Pressler, who has made Israeli and Dutch/Flemish literature available to German readers and has won major prizes both for her own novels and for translations.

The fact that so many authors also work as translators, however, should not lead us to conclude that writers of children's literature read more children's books than most people. Far more than their counterparts in other areas of the literary world, their reception of literature is generally outside the field in which they are working. Often they may read little or no children's literature,[9] and apart from their own literary activities may remain entirely outside the discourse of this branch of literature.

Specifics of the translation of children's literature

Over and above general issues of translation, a theory relating to children's literature must concern itself with aspects specific only to this area. The particular, asymmetrical communication in children's literature, which can lead to the coexistence of different reader's roles in the texts, makes it necessary to ask to what degree translators take account of which roles. The actual receptive ability of child readers, and the ability that intermediaries assume them to have, must be studied as factors with considerable bearing on decisions made in translation. The notion that children's literature is indivisible and international is in part sustained by the fact that in the translation process works are commonly adapted with the aim of avoiding intrusively 'foreign' elements. These characteristics of the translation of children's literature will be discussed at length in Chapters 4 and 5.

Among the other specifics of the translation of children's books is the readability of the text. Picture books and some books for small children offer anyone reading them aloud the opportunity to put on a dramatic performance. The sensual dimension of the spoken word is part of that performance. As Riitta Oittinen writes: 'The text should live, roll, taste good on the reading adult's tongue' (1990: 77). Related to this is the typographical design of the text, such as words printed in italics, capital letters and so on, which stage-direct the spoken language, indicating intonation, tone, tempo, pauses, emphasis, etc. So far there have been few analyses of translation for children investigating its specific stylistic acceptability to children and its suitability for reading aloud.[10]

A future, major task for the study of translations of children's literature would be for each culture to set translations into their language in context, constructing a systematic and historical survey of the various strategies, tendencies, criteria of selection and methods employed. Such a project is far from realization at present, as even the bare bibliographical details of the translations made into different languages have not yet been documented in most languages. The survey of translations in Swedish children's literature is still uniquely comprehensive.[11]

Non-translation and delayed reception

Comparative children's literature must also look into why a book is not translated, or is translated only after a long delay. Sometimes the reasons are obvious. In Germany, for instance, the denigration of other literatures under National Socialism led to a decrease in activity in the field of translation. The events of the years 1933–45 and the cultural isolation that went with them led to a need in post-war Germany to catch up with the translation of books published earlier. Re-education, and in particular the issuing of licences to publish children's books from the countries of the administrators of the post-war zones, gave new impetus to delayed reception after the Second World War, resulting in an enormous number of translations of children's classics and the re-establishing of contact with the evolution of genres in other literatures.

But obvious political rifts do not alone explain all delayed reception. Another reason for delay before a book is translated could be that it is still too unfamiliar for the target culture. Records of individual cases suggest that a book will be accepted for translation only when it shows similarities with a work that is already available (and above all is successful). Maria Nikolajeva claims exactly the opposite, believing that once a particular 'semiotic space' is occupied by one author, similar authors in translation will be rejected (Nikolajeva 1996: 37). However, examples show that this is not necessarily the case. For instance, the IYL vigorously campaigned for the German translation of Maria Gripe's *Glasblåsarns barn* (1964; Ger. *Die Kinder des Glasbläsers* 1977, Engl. *The Glassblower's Children* 1976) from the year of its first publication, but in vain. Scherf 1978 explained that this book, a 'fable' illustrating 'the intellectual desolation of our time, an age of conspicuous consumption, beneath a camouflage of surreal magic' (trans. from ibid.), was acceptable to German readers and critics only after the success of Michael Ende's thematically similar *Momo* (1973).

A further possible reason for delayed translation, or for the fact that a book is not translated at all, can be found in the absence of analogous social or literary interests and developments in the target culture. Thematically significant American books for young people dealing with the subject of violence, for instance Warren Miller's *The Cool World* (1959), didn't reach the German book market until twenty years after its appearance in the USA. The different pace taken by social and cultural developments in the USA and the Federal Republic of Germany anchored these subjects in the public mind at different points in time (see Isensee 1993). The general issue of non-translation as a reflection of the international balance of power in the world of children's literature will be discussed in detail in Chapter 3.

Comparative analysis of the reception of a children's book from another linguistic area may not always take the date of translation as its point of departure. Many books – particularly in English – have been widely received in Germany in the original.[12] Studies of the reception of texts must also reflect which languages were taught using what texts,[13] where the foreign governesses employed by better-off families came from,[14] what books they brought with them, and so on.

Cross-cultural development of literary traditions

Besides looking at questions of delayed reception and translation or the failure of a work to be translated at all, comparative children's literature must pay particular attention to the complexities resulting from the adoption and further development of literary traditions. I will illustrate the point here with a very brief sketch of cross-cultural development of the genre of fantasy for children.

In 1816 E.T.A. Hoffmann's 'Nussknacker und Mausekönig' [Nutcracker and mouse-king] appeared. As Mary Thwaite remarked appreciatively:

> It was in this land of Teutonic thoroughness and purpose that imagination in children's reading first found true expression, and a magic light from a realm unknown to rationalism penetrated into their books. The Romantic movement at the end of the eighteenth century affected children's books in Germany earlier than elsewhere.
>
> (Thwaite 1972: 257)

This pioneering German literary fairy tale for children (as well as adults) depicted, for the first time, a realistic modern setting instead of the other-worldliness of fairy stories. The heroine's belief in the wondrous – she is a psychologically realistic child figure – is satisfied only when she can experience another, fantastic world. Hoffmann is giving 'precise literary expression to his precarious situation, finding himself as he did in a world alien to his own cast of mind' (trans. from Ewers 1996a: 866). With this work he became the founding father of children's fantasy, although the tradition was not immediately carried on in his country. Hans-Heino Ewers speaks of the squandering of the heritage of the Romantic reforms in German children's literature in the nineteenth and early twentieth century, which rather followed the Brothers Grimm and an anti-modern children's literature of traditional fairy tales (see Ewers 1996b: 738). After Hoffmann, fantasy for children continued to be written mainly outside Germany, first by Hans Christian Andersen, later and most notably in Victorian England, where it saw its heyday with Lewis Carroll, George MacDonald and a little later Edith Nesbit. Only by way of England in the middle and late years of the nineteenth century, and through the creative appreciation of works of the 'Golden Age' of English fantasy in Sweden (particularly by Astrid Lindgren), did fantasy in children's literature finally find its way back to Germany after the Second World War (ibid.). The publication and reception of *Pippi Longstocking* in Germany thus paved the way for the (delayed) reception of many works by the classic English fantasy writers, and so a tradition that originated in Germany but had no immediate sequel there returned to its birthplace en route from England and Sweden.

3   Comparative poetics

The poetics of children's literature addresses aesthetic elements and literary forms of this branch of literature without necessarily noting linguistic borders. However, a series of culture-specific poetological questions can be fruitfully pursued, for instance a survey of the aesthetic development of children's literature and the way it changes its forms and functions in different cultures. Within this area, comparative children's literature must consider children's literature in terms of both general and comparative poetological questions: the ways in which it is organized, its narrative methods, structural features (motifs and themes), dialogic elements such as intertextuality and metafictionality, and aesthetic categories such as humour. It has to examine the forms of children's literature between different 'types of textual uses' (trans. from Assmann 1983) with their respective modes of transmission: oral folklore, written folklore (or written oral transmission), popular literature and highbrow literature.

An important study which addresses comparative aspects of the poetics of children's literature,[15] citing various European traditions (most notably Swedish, Norwegian, British and Russian), is Maria Nikolajeva's *Children's Literature Comes of Age* (1996).[16] The title itself suggests the author's evolutionary model: her touchstone of quality is the complex literary work. She believes that 'children's literature in all countries and language areas has gone through more or less ... four stages' of development (Nikolajeva 1996: 95), namely: 1. Adaptations of existing adult literature and of folklore; 2. Didactic, educational stories written directly for children; 3. Canonical children's literature (in Lotman's sense of the term), with clear generic forms and gender-specific address, whose characteristic feature is the typical epic narrative structure, and, finally, 4. Polyphonic, or multivoiced, children's literature, 'a convergence of genres which brings children's literature closer to what is generally labelled modern or post-modern literature' (ibid.: 9).

Children's literature is, without doubt, becoming more aesthetically elaborate – especially in those countries where it has had the longest time to develop. But the singular noun 'children's literature' denotes a simultaneous coexistence of a plurality of textual manifestations and of all the types of literature – literary, didactic, formulaic, retellings and folklore – named by Nikolajeva. To see children's literature in terms of stages of development to be overcome, of didactic and formulaic texts being cast off to make way for the exclusively elaborate, to claim that 'the evolution of modern children's literature leads towards a state in which traditional epic narratives are gradually replaced by new structures which ... I call polyphonic' (Nikolajeva 1996: 9), is deterministic and ultimately impoverishing. The majority of works of children's literature belong to the less literary genres and are necessary for the socialization of children and their acquisition of literary skills, besides having the important function of entertaining. To privilege one of the many forms of children's literature, the elaborately aesthetic, at the expense of all others and to imply that they will simply become extinct in the course of evolution is to negate the various functions that this literature will always continue to serve and to ignore its rich and necessary diversity.

A (comparative) poetics of children's literature must acknowledge the coexistence and interaction of all forms – from the new, 'literary' children's literature to the baby's concept book and formula fiction (see Chapter 3 for a critique of assumed universal patterns of development for children's literature on which models such as Nikolajeva's are based).

Literary children's literature

The complexity of contemporary 'literary' children's literature, a term borrowed from the German discussion (see Ewers 2000), or what Nikolajeva calls the 'sophisticated children's book' (1996: 127) reflects fundamental transformations during the past decades in the child's everyday world: changes in society and above all changes in the structure of the family and patterns of family interaction. These altered childhood worlds make new demands on children's literature, bringing forth new forms. Children's literature studies has noted the increasing introduction into children's books of the literary techniques of the modern psychological novel: abandonment of overt and controlling narrative voices in favour of single and multiple focalizations, changes of perspective, montage effects, internal monologues, stream-of-consciousness and other forms of psycho-narration. This new literary children's literature is distinguished by insecurity and ambivalence instead of certainty, linear rather than circular narratives and diversity instead of simplicity. Experimental forms and metafiction, characteristics of a distinctly artistic form of literature that constantly reflects on its own literary nature, go beyond what used to be thought of as the limits of the expected or acceptable in children's books. A poetics of children's literature must ask to what degree metafictional elements such as parody and intertextuality featured in children's literature even before this new 'literary' development – for children's books have often been particularly notable for a high degree of dialogue with texts written earlier[17] – or whether they should be seen exclusively, as in Nikolayeva (1996: 153ff.), as the result of writers adopting postmodern tendencies.

An increase in the literary complexity of children's books in Germany has been perceptible since about 1970 (see Ewers 1995) and is seen as corresponding to the increase in children's rights in that society, as somehow equating the receptive capacities of children and adults, and as an element of cultural modernization. Nikolayeva (1996) identifies these changes in English children's literature from the 1950s onwards and in Swedish children's literature after the end of the 1960s. Interesting from the comparative viewpoint is the way this kind of poetic children's literature is introduced, accepted and developed in different linguistic and cultural areas.

Humour

Laughter, as a physiological phenomenon, an inborn human capability, is considered as universal as humour: 'There is no society in which humour has not been reported to exist' (Ziv 1988: ix). Humour as 'a social message intended to produce laughter or smiling' (ibid.) fulfils certain social and psychic functions. However, the techniques employed, the comic situations and above all the themes or subjects of humour can be culture-specific. Relevant questions to be asked about humour in children's literature from a comparative viewpoint include the following: are there any universal aspects of humour for children?

Do the genres regarded as particularly amusing differ from one culture to another? Are certain methods and forms of humour preferred in different cultures, or are certain forms of humour to be seen as culture-specific? Visual and graphic forms of humour are predominant in some literatures (in Spain or France, for instance), while in others, such as Turkey, the humour of the puppet theatre enjoys pre-eminence. Black humour, to take another example, is not well represented in children's literature as a whole and occurs mainly in British children's literature, in works by such authors as Roald Dahl or Joan Aiken. In Germany many educationalists are 'reluctant to entertain children by making their blood run cold, considering it tasteless or even dangerous' (trans. from Grützmacher 1985: 4). How do modes and techniques of humour differ in children's literatures, and at what periods? Do some literatures contain more humour than others? What kinds of humour, from slapstick to satire, are admitted in which traditions of children's literature (and when)? Where and to which periods do more domesticated forms of humour belong? Where and when did the grotesque carnivalesque humour of bodily functions and excess as identified by Bakhtin become acceptable in children's literature? When do which paraliterary genres become 'a refuge for forbidden laughter' for children (trans. from Feuerhahn 1992: 40)? Is humour an obstacle to translation? How is humour translated, and how is it adapted in translation to the norms of the target culture?

Themes and motifs

A poetological and comparative study of themes and motifs found in children's literature must be clearly distinguished from a positivist compilation of lists which fails to investigate the thematic elements of a book in relation to their aesthetic functions, compositional elements, modes of representation, intertextual relations, etc. I would like to give a brief outline here of the way in which the comparative study of themes and motifs is distinct from the mere collection of occurrences, taking the treatment of death as my example.

Educational and therapeutic aspects, as well as thematic stock-taking, are dominant among the various approaches to this subject. However, an analysis of the different ways in which death is depicted and of its changing function in children's literature is of cultural as well as literary interest. As Kimberley Reynolds writes of English children's literature in the nineteenth century: 'Through the mingling of spiritual, social and aesthetic discourses, literary representations of dead and dying children became multivalent signifiers' (2000: 169). Poetological functions attributed to dying in these texts range from the use of death for educational purposes as an element in cautionary tales and verses of the eighteenth and nineteenth centuries, to the psychologically sensitive guidance on saying goodbye and coming to terms with death found in the realistic children's literature of Scandinavia and Germany after the late 1960s.

The portrayal of death is motivated by religious and educational factors in the early nineteenth-century story *The History of the Fairchild Family* (Sherwood

1818–47), in which two chapters depict the different deaths of two children. In 'Fatal Effects of Disobedience to Parents', a vain, disobedient girl causes her own agonizing death by burning, an end which is described in detail and in analogy to the fire of hell; in 'A Happy Death', the joyous death for which a pious boy has been longing comes after a time of infirmity as the result of an unidentified illness.[18] The children of the Fairchild family (and the child readers), other than being urged to piety, also receive graphic moral admonishment on leading an upright life by being shown criminals mouldering on the gallows. The uninhibited treatment of death in this novel, not to mention the fact that it was regarded as a suitable subject for children's literature, shows how acceptable the theme was at the beginning of the nineteenth century. Apart from religious instruction, this and similar novels of the period also contained direction on correct social conduct, for instance at a funeral.

From the later years of that century onwards death was ousted from realistic children's literature in Europe, subsequently only to be found in the context of fantasy, such as *At the Back of the North Wind* (MacDonald 1871) or *Peter Pan* (Barrie 1904/1911). Of British children's literature in the first half of the twentieth century, Naomi Lewis writes that it 'obey[s] the time's unspoken codes for junior reading: no deaths, disasters, poverty; no great emotions, no stern moral lessons – none of those features that gave such force to nineteenth-century fiction' (1989: vii). In this, it parallels social developments. As a result of dramatic advances in medicine, the decrease in infant mortality and higher life expectation, death becomes a forbidden subject in the second half of the nineteenth century (see Ariès 1975). The active participation of children in the ritual of death ends around this time too, whereas from the sixteenth until well into the nineteenth century they had played an important part in such ceremonies. In the nineteenth century, for instance, German children were given the day off school to accompany a condemned man to the place of execution, singing hymns to comfort him (see Rutschky 1983: 98f.).

Death returns to realistic children's literature with a different function in the late 1960s in Scandinavia, in books such as *Malena och glädjen* [Malena and her joy] (Lindquist 1969), *Så var det när Olas farfar dog* [When grandad died] (Gydal and Danielsson 1973) or *I stripete genser* [In a striped jumper] (Breen 1975), and in the 1970s in Germany, in books such as *Oma* [Grandma] (Härtling 1975) or the award-winning *Servus Opa, sagte ich leise* [Goodbye grandad, I said softly] (Donnelly 1977), in reaction to the social taboo on the subject and to the idyllic children's literature of the post-war period that avoided social realism. A matter-of-fact and educational approach to death and its presentation in realistic and didactic children's literature occurs at this time, and the former religious content of the subject is superseded by psychologically determined plots and modes of representation.

Study of motifs in the field of comparative children's literature should analyse the symbolic techniques developed in children's literature to enable writers to present death itself. They include fantasy, in which human death is distanced by the device of using animal characters, as in Susan Varley's *Badger's Parting Gifts*

(1984), or the gradual disappearance of a character, as in Gordon Sheppard and Jacques Rozier's *The Man Who Gave Himself Away* (1971). The novel *Corda Bamba* [Tightrope] (Bojunga-Nunes 1979) successfully combines psychological under-standing with a choice of literary theme in its presentation of death: in an imaginary dwelling in the young protagonist Maria's mind, which she can reach only along a tightrope, she visits separate rooms and witnesses successive episodes from her and her parents' past, events which she has suppressed since the accidental death of her tightrope-walking parents.

Other investigations of the motif of death in children's literature could examine how, in fantasy, it can feature as a way of overcoming time and space, for instance as a gateway to fantastic adventures in Astrid Lindgren's *Bröderna Lejonhjärta* [The Brothers Lionheart] (1973), or how it combines the aesthetic and the erotic, especially in the death of young girls. Death becomes the prettily staged literary fate of girls who will never grow up – or never be allowed to grow up – to become women. Female sexuality is not permitted to develop and its repression mingles with the eroticism expressed in the extinction of the budding woman thus rendered permanently chaste and safe from violation, age and corruption (see Reynolds 2000: 185): nothing can be purer than a girl who dies a virgin. The link between death fantasies and erotic desire is evident in stories such as Johanna Spyri's *Wo Gritlis Kinder hingekommen sind* [Gritli's children] (1883), in which an old nurse acts as a kind of go-between, presenting death as desirable in poems and stories, while two girls have 'forbidden', intimate conver-sations about dying. Nineteenth-century British fantasies for children, too, are pervaded by 'the presentation of death as seductive and desirable' (Reynolds 2000: 176).

Discussion of the subject of death in children's literature also touches on analysis of children who never grow up, including classic characters from J.M. Barrie's *Peter Pan* (1904/1911), Antoine de Saint-Exupéry's *Le petit prince* [The little prince] (1943) and Astrid Lindgren's *Pippi Långstrump* [Pippi Longstocking] (1945). Whether they die young or live for ever, the children in such stories remain symbolically immortal, since they are not subject to the wear and tear of time, unlike the immortal, and miserable, Struldbruggs in Swift's *Gulliver's Travels* (1726).

Accounts of the death of children in nineteenth-century literature played an important part in establishing the idea of children's literature in general, since they recorded the transience of childhood:

> The nineteenth-century way of killing a child makes childhood more real than any other period of life. ... Legitimizing childhood transience – both the ordinary transience of growing up and the extraordinary transience of the short life abruptly truncated – was one of the enabling conditions for the confident creation of major children's literature.
>
> (Plotz 1995: 17)

The representation of death and the acceptability of the theme in various cultures at various times have repercussions on the translation of children's literature,[19] and poetological and comparative studies of the subjects and motifs of children's literature must also take account of these aspects. The translator Anthea Bell considered in 1985 that, in comparison with their British colleagues, European publishers seemed more willing to confront quite young children with the theme of death. She described the difficulties she had in the translation of a picture book by Janosch, a retelling of the Grimms' tale of the hedgehog and the hare. The publisher (not the translator) was uneasy about the death of the hare and the tombstone shown on the last double spread. He explained to Janosch the 'difficulty of rendering Death an acceptable subject for the very young. No problem, says author [sic], I'll write you a new ending for the English version' (Bell 1985a: 10). In the new version, altered by Janosch for the English market (Janosch 1985), the hare does not die but ends up in hospital with a broken leg.

4   Intertextuality studies

Some of the earliest children's books – such as *Robinson Crusoe* and *Gulliver's Travels* – were adaptations of existing ones for adults. Children's literature has from its inception been a thoroughly intertextual literature of adaptations and retellings (see McCallum and Stephens 1998). Retellings, parodies, cross-cultural references, simple as well as subtle and complex forms of interaction between literatures from different languages and cultures are amongst the subjects of intertextuality studies. Intertextuality as an aesthetic procedure is investigated in literary studies in separate languages and, when it crosses linguistic and cultural borders and media (see the next section), in comparative literature. Although this relates only to one small part of the broader intertextuality theories of Julia Kristeva (1969) and Mikhail Bakhtin (1984a), the focus of intertextual analysis is mainly on the integration of allusions in a text, on different intertextual procedures such as quotation, imitation, parody and an examination of the dynamic located in the communication between texts themselves and readers. Central to the study of intertextuality in children's literature are the communication structures on which the process is based, the interrelationship between the components of intertextuality, 'of writer/text/reader – text/reader/context' (Wilkie 1996: 132). What can authors presuppose in their writing for children? Or, as Christine Wilkie puts it: 'What does [a piece of writing] assume, what must it assume to take on significance?' (ibid.).

In the discussion of intertextuality in children's literature to date, one point of emphasis from the viewpoint of reader-response theory has been on decentralization and openness. Breaks in the narrative such as intertextual references are seen as a playful destabilization of the young readers' security, as a challenge to their notions of what constitutes a fictional text, which encourages them to adopt an active, reflective attitude to reading (see Moss 1992: 58). John Stephens, exploiting the homonymy of the English noun 'subject' and the verb 'to subject', explains the difference between the assumption of active and passive positions as follows: 'The subject can signify not only the role of one who acts, but also one who is subjected to the authority of the texts' (1992: 6). Stephens sees intertextuality primarily as a critical potential that can militate against a self-contained, passive subject position:

> Intertextuality encourages self-conscious subjectivity because it is structurally similar to intersubjectivity, because it keeps visible the processes of narrative discourse and representation, and because its play of differences functions as a critique of social values.
>
> (ibid.)

Intertextuality in children's literature is not, as one might perhaps conclude, confined to texts for readers at the more advanced stages of their development. It is being increasingly used playfully, in the form of quotations from literature, fairy tales and nursery rhymes in literature for very young readers or picture books for children who cannot yet read, such as *The Jolly Postman* (1986) or *Each Peach Pear Plum* (1987) by the picture-book authors Janet and Allan Ahlberg:

> Because the primary audience is very young and has a limited grasp of the narrative and graphic codes for decoding picture books, artists have used the playfulness of this audience to produce works which are at the limits of children's literature.
>
> (Moss 1992: 55)[20]

The study of intertextuality in children's literature must reveal the various functions of intertextual references, which can serve to characterize figures in a story,[21] as well as making a plea for reading in general, such as in Roald Dahl's *Matilda* (1989). Reference to earlier works is evidence of the authors' awareness of a literary tradition and their (aspiring, declared or felt) participation in this tradition; the dialogue in which a connection is established between texts can show where an author stands.

The difference between intertextuality for adults and for children lies in the nature and cogency of the intertextual relations between pre-text and intertext and the degree to which texts for children sometimes have a need to be overreferential (Wilkie 1996: 136). The most frequent context for intertextuality in children's literature is comedy: references to something already known are funny because of the element of surprise (something familiar appears in an unfamiliar context) or incongruity, for instance through a change of perspective, as in Paul Maar's story of 1968 *Die Geschichte vom bösen Hänsel, der bösen Gretel und der Hexe* [The tale of wicked Hansel, wicked Gretel and the witch], told from the witch's point of view, or in *Ten in a Bed* (Ahlberg and Amstutz 1983), where the girl Dinah finds the bears from *Goldilocks and the Three Bears* in her bed, smiling mischievously at her because they are well aware that she and they have swapped roles. Intertextual references may be rather superficial in children's literature, with the playful element to the fore; it is more usual to find broad, extensive intertextuality drawing on many pre-texts than one which exhausts the potential resonances of the references concerned. The cogency of intertextual relations is generally slight in children's books, while in literature for young adults, particularly the adolescent novel (see section 10), inter-textuality of a higher degree may be found. However, there are some examples of intensive preoccupation with a pre-text in books for children, for instance in the novel *Das Wildpferd unterm Kachelofen. Ein schönes dickes Buch von Jakob Borg und seinen Freunden* [The wild horse under the stove],[22] a creative reception across linguistic, cultural and temporal borders of *Winnie-the-Pooh* (Milne 1926).

In Christoph Hein's novel, published in the German Democratic Republic (GDR) in 1984, toys come to life in tales shared by a man and a boy in a framework story. Each of the toys, the boy's constant companions, has a distinctive character; one of them is an animal of very little brain whose answer to the question 'two plus one?' is 'I'm sure it's not more than four or five ..., I know exactly how many it is, I just can't remember at the moment. Two, maybe?' (trans. from Hein 1984: 17), and who, always hungry, brings along a suitable container when going for a walk in the woods, just in case he finds something edible. The boy and his toys meet up in the woods and go on picnics or on a treasure hunt, even though they aren't entirely sure what it is they are looking for or where exactly they may find it. Someone's birthday is forgotten, the wood is flooded after days of rain, balloons are used as a means of transport and two of their party hunt a fearsome animal.

Das Wildpferd was composed for Hein's son Jakob, just as the *Pooh* books originated in stories told by Milne to his son Christopher Robin. It echoes *Winnie-the-Pooh* on the structural level, in elements of the plot, in characterization and in the themes of friendship and imagination. Before moving on to note the peculiarities of Hein's intertextual reworking of some of Milne's themes to present his vision of childhood for his own specific historical and cultural situation, we should briefly examine the interrelationship between the components of intertextuality, of writer/text/reader – text/reader/context, to ask about *Winnie-the-Pooh* in the GDR, about Hein's knowledge of the text and whether the intertextual references could possibly have been recognized by Hein's readers.

The first and obvious question is: was *Winnie-the-Pooh* known and read in the GDR? The first German translation by E.L. Shiffer, which was published in 1928 but enjoyed nothing like the enthusiastic reception in Britain and the USA (one reason surely being because it erased the elements specifically addressed to the adult reader of *Winnie-the-Pooh* – see O'Sullivan 1993), was reissued once in the GDR in 1960 with a relatively small print-run of 5,000 copies. *Winnie-the-Pooh* was not alone in this; many international classics could not be found on the East German market because the royalties for them had to be paid in hard currency (see Thomson-Wohlgemuth 2003). No new translation of Milne's book appeared in the GDR; the second, more successful German translation of *Winnie-the-Pooh* by Harry Rowohlt, appreciated by both children and adults alike, was published in the Federal Republic of Germany in 1987, three years after Hein's *Wildpferd*. Karin Richter, an expert on children's literature in the GDR, called Milne's *Winnie-the-Pooh* an example of the kind of fantasy for children widely unknown in the GDR (see Richter 1992: 135).

Did Hein know *Winnie-the-Pooh* in either German or English? The textual evidence states that he must have. Establishing such certainties was the main task of the old school of influence studies, of which S.S. Prawer said that Virginia Woolf 'only has to say of a character in *To the Lighthouse* that he is "working on the influence of something on somebody" for us to know that he is remote and ineffectual and that his work is arid' (Prawer 1973: 60). When questioned by his English publisher Klaus Flugge, Hein insisted that any resemblance to *Pooh* was coincidental, although a careful reading of his novel makes this seem unlikely. However, the specific facts of Milne's influence on Hein are of less interest here than the questions which follow: why and how did Hein rework elements of Milne's narrative into his own?

Could Hein's readers – child or adult – have picked up the allusions to Milne? The intertextuality is unmarked, no names from *Pooh* are cited, no passages quoted; neither the title of the pre-text nor the name of the author is mentioned. Could his readers none the less have recognized them? As *Winnie-the-Pooh* was not widely known to readers in the GDR, it is unlikely that the intertextual relationship between *Wildpferd* and *Pooh* would have been realized. Even if the references had been marked, it would not necessarily have led to a dialogic, intertextual reading. So we can assume that the intertextual references went widely unnoticed in the GDR.[23]

What can be said about Hein's intertextuality? What does *Winnie-the-Pooh* as pre-text lend to an East German children's novel of the late twentieth century? The resonances listed above of *Winnie-the-Pooh* in *Das Wildpferd unterm Kachelofen* serve to underline the basic differences between the two novels in theme and in their approach to childhood itself. Where Milne's Utopian vision, an amalgam of a pre-industrial Golden Age and the lost paradise of childhood, is only clouded at the very end by Christopher Robin starting school and thus having to leave the enchanted Hundred Acre Wood for ever, Jakob's difficulties in school and with the adult world generally are neither excluded from the fantasy stories he tells nor from the frame; these experiences are, rather, the negative motive force for his imagination. The conditions of childhood in the late twentieth century are not romanticized, the boy's perspective of his place in society is portrayed with psychological realism, in keeping with the general tenor of European children's literature since the 1970s.

The most significant divergence is the reversal of the adult–child roles. Milne's adult narrator not only has access to the world of imaginary childhood, it is he who presents it in story form to the child. The storyteller in Hein's novel is the boy, Jakob Borg ('borgen' in German means 'to lend'); he 'lends' his stories to the adult who desperately wants to hear them. Here the child is the guardian of the imagination, he believes in miracles and is capable of producing them in his everyday life: ' "Wondrous things often happen to us," said Jakob, "indeed, the world is full of marvels" ' (trans. from Hein 1984: 70). Imagination, the child's gift, is shown to be lacking in the adult world. In Hein's novel only the adult who has the capacity to listen to and understand the stories he is told as the privileged narratee of a child narrator may regain access.

A further dimension of the relationship between the texts can be found in the official East German 'position' towards Milne's novel. When the republication of *Winnie-the-Pooh* was under consideration by the authorities in 1959, a number of reports on it had to be submitted to the censorship authority within the Ministry of Culture (this was, as Gabriele Thomson-Wohlgemuth reminds us (2003: 247), the case for each book published in the GDR). The content of one of the reports, which she cites, indicates the differences between classical fantasy and the postulated norms of East German children's literature:

> *Winnie the Pooh* is exclusively about fantasy, happiness and child's play. Certainly our children are not less imaginative in their play, but it cannot be denied that the fantasy of our children moves in another direction. Our time is not so much about a single child with his toys on his own – and if this does prevail in a child, it is not desired and does not match our didactic ideals.
>
> (ibid.: 248)

Although writing his novel over twenty years after this report, his orientation towards fantasy such as Milne's, even if it was unconscious, was none the less a clear statement by Hein on the kind of literature he found more rewarding, and perhaps more relevant, for children. Through what can be read as a reinterpretation of *Winnie-the-Pooh*, Hein would seem to signal his admiration for Milne's book as a model of children's literature in contrast to that of the GDR, which was characterized throughout 'by its aim of integrating the recipient into the socialist order' (Dolle-Weinkauff 1996: 746). At the same time, by realigning the relationship between child and adult in a reversal of the roles found in Milne's novel, Hein demands more respect for and admiration of the individual child.

This example of productive reception, of intertextuality across language, space and time, takes us to the core of comparative children's literature to observe and analyse phenomena involving literature transcending linguistic and cultural borders, and to identify patterns of connections between them. It is not cause and effect that is of interest here when examining the particularities of a work in its specific historical and cultural situation, but the dynamic processes of exchange between cultures.

5 Intermediality studies

Comparative literature, as an interdiscipline, was never exclusively concerned with the relationship between (national) literatures but focused also on that between literature and other aesthetic forms; study of different cultural codes (in the visual arts, dance, music, cinema, the theatre) has always been one of its traditional subject areas. Children's literature, by virtue of the way in which it engages with mass culture, is perhaps even more markedly distinguished by forms of intermediality than adult literature.

In the contemporary era of major technological change, as Margaret Mackey notes, 'we can see stories shifting and altering their borders even as the world of make-believe expands beyond anything our ancestors might have imagined' (1999: 16). Stories and characters that originally appeared in print form are adapted into films, videos, DVDs and CD-ROMS, are reworked into audio and website forms, are transmuted into text-based toys and commodities (china and clothing showing characters from favourite books, etc.) and appear as (electronic) playmates in theme parks, making the boundaries of the possible worlds of fiction ever more nebulous. The recent '*Harry Potter* phenomenon', the global marketing of book, film and merchandise, provides an instance of the resituation of children's literature into a broad, global domain. At the same time, as Mackey notes, 'the vocabulary for describing new hybrid forms of story that cross media boundaries and variously impinge on our daily lives is surprisingly limited' (ibid.). Mackey, one of the leading researchers on intermediality in children's culture, uses the example of *The Tale of Peter Rabbit* by Beatrix Potter and close to one hundred retellings in a variety of media to explore the impact of new media and technologies on how children learn about stories and reading, showing how new conventions and protocols of storytelling are emerging with attendant cultural emphasis on fragmentation, adaptation and reworking of texts.

Subjects to be addressed by intermediality studies are the dynamic relations between children's literature and the various media, including the adaptation processes: how have texts of children's literature been performed in various media? How are they reworked and transposed across media boundaries? How do the different social contexts and audiences come into play? How are these texts, media and commodities marketed? How do commercial as well as techno-logical changes affect the ways in which children engage with fictions? What is the role of the marketplace in framing children's developing understanding of narra-tive? What will be the consequences, if proven true, of Mackey's assumption that

> many children are learning to approach the world of literature with a certain leeriness, which may be entirely appropriate to the marketing tech-niques involved in the sale of that commodity, but which may have a deleterious effect on their interest in engaging with that world.
>
> (Mackey 1998: 143)

Some of these issues will be discussed more extensively in Chapter 6, when the global transformations of Carlo Collodi's *Pinocchio* are critically assessed.

6 Image studies

Image studies, or imagology, is traditionally concerned with intercultural relations in terms of mutual perceptions, images and self-images and their representation in literature. Unlike mere typological inventories of the ways in which other nations appear in literary texts ('The Chinese as represented in French literature'), it tries

> to understand the various forms of the relevant images appearing in the literary field, how they come into being, and their effects. It also aims to cast

light on the part such images play in various other ways of encountering individual cultures.

(trans. from Dyserinck 1980: 32)

The aim of image studies is to make examination of the literary image of another country, culture or ethnic group a legitimate field of study in literary criticism by proposing theoretical ideas on cultural and literary factors and their reciprocal relationships; it also investigates the role of images in the field of international literary relations and the conclusions they allow us to draw about those who produce them. Recent works on orientalism, postcolonialism, the study of alterity and the history of mentalities have moved literary representation of what is 'foreign' and 'Other' to the centre of cultural studies. Hand in hand with the general rise of interest in cultural stereotyping and identity constructs – indeed, image studies may be regarded as constructivism *avant la lettre* – goes a new interest in imagology itself. Leerssen (2000: 270) therefore describes 'the complex links between literary discourse on the one hand and national identity-constructs on the other' as a subject suitable for modern imagological investigation. It studies the textual ways in which an image and its historical context are expressed rather than its pretended reference to empirical reality and aims to observe the context of contemporary history as well as such conventions of discourse as intertextuality. Further, it aims to examine the genesis and reciprocal influence of images in different countries and cultures through binary image models as well as the general structural patterns of image complexes and their 'grammar' (see Leerssen 2000).

As cultural artefacts consumed at an early stage in the socialization process, children's books are a particularly valuable source for studying the various schemata, conventional national attributes and their counter-stereotypes which may be acquired at that stage. Such areas as the following can be productively addressed by image studies in children's literature:

- culture-specific topographies,
- the extra-textual function of images of another country,
- poetological aspects of the representation of 'foreigners' and
- constancy and change in the representation of other countries.

In addition, image studies might address the representation of domestic and foreign social organizations and cultural practices in children's literature, such as youth gangs, family structures, mother–child relationships, different forms of children's games, etc., as well as culture-specific image types such as those of the foreign governess. A further area of interest is the influence of images on the translation process – how the selection, translation and marketing of children's literature from a particular country is determined by the images of that country in the target literature (see Seifert forthcoming). Image studies can also examine such aspects as how different nations are gendered in children's literature or how national stereotypes can be utilized in books for girls and boys to impart the currently appropriate gender-specific modes of thought and behaviour (see the examples in O'Sullivan 2002a).

Culture-specific topographies

Research in this area has so far focused mainly on images of home and how textual representations of cultural, national or regional identity are linked with landscape. Reinbert Tabbert (1991b and 1995) has analysed the dominance and significance of certain aspects of the environment in the children's literature of different cultures: they include the forest in German children's books, the garden in English books, the Alps in Swiss books and the outback in Australian children's literature. While Tabbert focuses specifically on auto-images, a further aspect is the recourse to topographies regarded as typical in the representation of foreign landscapes (on the German fairy-tale forest in British children's literature with a German theme see O'Sullivan 1990).

According to John Stephens in his taxonomy of the landscapes of Australian picture books, the aspect that most clearly differentiates the literature of one country from that of another is 'a sense of place' (1995: 97). Representations of landscape can function as metonyms for social significance or cultural heritage. What is depicted can be regarded as a 'correspondence between external and internal realities as perceived by a society at a particular cultural moment, with the further implication that consumers will internalise the representation and its accompanying myths' (ibid.: 99). This relationship between topography and ideology has been highlighted by others who have investigated the extra-textual function of images of another country.

The extra-textual function of images

Extra-textual functions of images, which range from instilling a sense of national identity in the process of socialization to extreme forms such as propaganda, are usually produced by means of contrast. The foreign element acts as a foil against which the writer's own nation appears more clearly, with the familiar image and the foreign image contrasted in order to reinforce awareness of the readers' own cultural identity or to criticize factors of the self-image perceived as undesirable. The function of self-images in historical novels for young people in Switzerland was studied by Verena Rutschmann (1994), who showed how they promoted national consciousness beyond the boundaries of the four linguistic areas of the country, as well as the virtues of citizenship and economy. Marieluise Christadler (1978) showed how images of 'otherness' in the children's literature of France and Germany were used as tools for purposes of wartime propaganda.

Poetological aspects of the representation of foreigners

National stereotypes, familiar images of certain nations, are among the 'common frames' and 'intertextual frames' (Eco 1979: 20f) in literature.

Intertextually recognizable, they are a kind of 'literary shorthand' (O'Sullivan 1989: 57) which triggers an extensively preprogrammed actualization of associations, thus investing them with a special aesthetic potential. Although image studies has always acknowledged roles of the image that are immanent in the text, it has, to date, seldom directly addressed their literary function. National stereotypes are like a backdrop against which every description of another nation is written and read, and against which authors can realize the aesthetic potential of those stereotypes. They can bring them into play to fulfil expectations and affirm current stereotypes, they can use them to contradict predictions or deliberately omit them where they would have been anticipated; authors can make stereotypes thematic, subvert them in a playful manner, or give them an immanent narrative function in the work. An example of the latter can be found in Jan Needle's *Albeson and the Germans* (1977), in which the common Nazi stereotypes are functionalized to become an intrinsic part of the narrative (for further examples of literary functions of stereotypes see O'Sullivan 1989: 168–218 and 1990: 253–301). As the personified 'Other', a foreigner in literature can also act as the catalyst of change.

Of further relevance is the affinity between certain genres or literary themes and nationalities or cultures. In German (children's) literature, for instance, England is frequently used as the setting for ghost stories or detective stories, because by using such a background authors can trigger a wealth of schemata and associations. By portraying a pipe-smoking detective in fog-bound London, they can, with great economy of means, arouse readers' intertextual memories of other detective stories and films.

Constancy and change in the representation of other nations

Images can shift along with changing political circumstances, so analysis of changes in stereotypes and their use, both of which are dependent on the writer's time, is an important aspect of image studies. The image of the Germans in British children's literature since 1871, for instance, shows a clear development from characteristics like 'gentle', 'family-loving', 'benign', 'musical' or '*gemütlich*', attributed during the late nineteenth century, to the 'brutal', 'overpowering', 'cruel', 'loud' or 'unfeeling' traits of the threatening, Prussian German of the World Wars in books written from the end of the nineteenth century until the 1960s, thus mirroring one of the structural factors involved in national characterizations, that of *weak* vs. *strong* (see Leerssen 2000: 276f.). While during the early nineteenth century Germany had all the charms of a politically weak country, the same country of the Wilhelminian period had 'all the repulsive hallmarks of efficiency, power and ruthlessness' (ibid.). The shift in image is directly connected to the nation's rise in international stature. This alteration in German image from soft to hard, weak to strong, exotic to threatening can be traced by examining the adjustment of the valorization of the stereotype of 'the musical German' over a period of about a hundred years. What follows is a thumbnail sketch of changes which are documented in greater detail in *Friend and Foe* (O'Sullivan 1990), a study of the cultural history of Anglo-German relations from 1870 to 1985 as reflected in the medium of children's fiction.

The earliest mention of music in the corpus of British children's books with a German connection is in a story of a young boy who grows up to be a great poet, first published in 1862, in which the sensitivity of Germans to the arts in general is underlined. Music especially is 'innate in the German character' (Ewing 1912: 75). In a fairy tale by Julia Goddard, the 'Poor Musician' of the title acquires a magic violin (Goddard 1863), while in a story in Margaret Roberts' *Fair Else, Duke Ulrich, and Other Tales* (1877) a poor wandering minstrel gives up his travelling for the love of a woman and settles down to become a city musician. The musicality of the Germans is presented in these books – all of which were written prior to or during the 1870s before the Prussianization of Germany and England's reaction to it started to be reflected in children's literature – as exclusively positive.

The first discordant tones are to be heard in a story published in 1902, set during the Franco-Prussian War. The music here is loud and rowdy, produced by 'rough drunken' German soldiers with their 'shouts and songs and laughter' (Lucas 1902: 56f). This is the harbinger of portrayals which become increasingly negative. Music serves the purpose of illustrating the uncouthness and arrogance of members of the German army in books written and set during and just after the First World War. In Captain Charles Gilson's *A Motor-Scout in Flanders*, for instance, drunken Pomeranian soldiers sing 'a very raucous interpretation of "Deutschland über alles" ' (Gilson 1915: 49); during the Second World War British pilots who look down from their planes on a show parade in Germany see men in Nazi uniform goose-stepping and 'a typical German Band, blowing and swaggering' (Dupont n.d.).

What happens to the aggressive musicality of the Germans after the war? As is well known, swaggering Nazis have become an important stock character in British comedy, escape stories and the like. However, around the end of the 1960s, a positive shift took place in the portrayal of the German in British children's literature. In these books, set during the periods of the World Wars, recourse is taken to the familiar stereotype of musicality, but here its favourable properties are used as redeeming features of individual 'positive' Germans. The semantic core 'music' remains the same, but the interpretation has changed. The drunken, loud, nasty, raucous music gives way to a recurrence of the gentle, sensitive musicality found in the earlier books, making the character endowed with the gift (usually a prisoner of war) almost exclusively positive. A cluster of this type of book appeared in the 1970s, for example Robert Westall's *The Machine-Gunners* (1975), David Rees' *The Missing German* (1976) or Gabriel Alington's *Willow's Luck* (1977), to name but three. The dark side of Germany during the period portrayed is not excluded from these books, but the overall positive power of an individual German character dominates, with music being used to denote his non-military side. The machine-gunner in Robert Westall's book teaches his English child-captors to sing the song 'Ich hatt' einen Kameraden!': 'The children took up the words of the sad old soldiers' song.

They sang so sweetly that Rudi was close to tears. What was happening to him? He grew less like a soldier every day; more like a *lehrer* in some kindergarten' (Westall 1975: 132). In Elsie McCutcheon's *Summer of the Zeppelin* Elvira is told that her father has been reported missing in action. Almost immediately afterwards she hears music being played on the church organ. The rector tells her that the piece, *Jesu, Joy of Man's Desiring*, was composed 'by a German musician called Bach. And you won't often hear it played as superbly as that' (McCutcheon 1983: 53). The organist is a German prisoner of war. These positive Germans must be seen as an apparent attempt, thirty years after the end of the Second World War, with Germany now a political ally and the Cold War enemy lying further east, to show young British readers that, despite the image in British popular culture, Germans should not exclusively be associated with warmongering.

The attribution of binary opposites (active/passive, rational/irrational), a central mechanism in the construction of gender, can be seen in the example provided here to apply similarly to the construction of national images in literature, with the shift from traditionally 'female' characteristics attributed during the late nineteenth century (family-loving, gentle, benign) to the traditionally 'male' characteristics (loud, overpowering, unfeeling, cruel) of the Prussian German of the World Wars in literature written from the end of the nineteenth century until the 1960s, when the 'gentle' valorization re-emerges. The reconstruction in British texts of a textual stereotype such as the musicality of the Germans relates that stereotype to the state of political, economic or cultural relations between Great Britain and Germany and shows how such a feature, although its semantic kernel remains constant, can be positive or negative in its valorization, depending on the time in which the texts were written.

7 Comparative genre studies

The kind of issues to be addressed in the area of comparative genre studies will be sketched here using examples from one particular genre, girls' stories, as an illustration. One early form of the girls' story, the doll story, developed as a genre in France, where it was very popular from 1800 onwards.[24] According to Susanne Barth (1998: 30) it appeared in two forms: as a story of the doll's education, in which it is 'brought up' by the girl and they playfully enact together stages in a girl's childhood and future (marriage, etc.), and as an (auto)biographical doll story, a narrative of individual development and an early forerunner of the story for teenage girls. This genre became established in Germany in the 1830s partly in translations from the French, partly through imitations. In the imitations the genre was 'Germanified'; by comparison with the French texts, says Barth, the moralizing element in the self-reflection is stronger, there is none of the occasional ' "ambiguity" which sometimes counters the manifest intention of the text' (ibid: 34), and the educational aspect is made more systematic. The author of a German version of a French doll story for girls, *Memoiren einer Berliner Puppe* [Memoirs of a Berlin doll] (Winter 1840), adapts it to the middle-class

German model of education; the aristocratically elegant atmosphere of the French original is turned into a solidly bourgeois environment. The 'Frenchified and courtly patterns of thinking and acting' (trans. from Barth 1998: 40) that deviate from German moral standards and were sharply criticized in children's literature after the eighteenth century, become such German virtues as industry, good conduct and piety. The aesthetic innovations of the French model, with its entertaining mixture of narrative, reflection and direct speech, are also rejected by the German imitations in favour of older, familiar narrative patterns. Doll stories adapted to German tastes rather than books simply translated from the French dominated the field until the 1860s. Only after around 1865 did ideological reservations relax in the wake of progressive adaptation to an aristocratic lifestyle in prosperous middle-class circles, and it was only then that 'tastes in reading changed so much that the sophisticated French doll story was now felt to be an entertaining and liberating pleasure to read' (ibid.: 42).

An account of the development of this sub-genre of girls' stories in one culture begins, as so often, comparatively, by looking at predecessors from another culture from which the sub-genre was transferred. However, a comparative study of a genre such as girls' stories cannot confine itself to that approach alone. It must also reveal the genre's varying distance from its parallels in other literary traditions. A comparison of characters and perspectives, for instance, will illustrate the differences between girls' books in different cultures. Arguably the most important American novel written for girls in the nineteenth century, Louisa May Alcott's *Little Women* (1868), which celebrates family life and gives pride of place to family solidarity, is more like a family story than a girls' one. Indeed, it inspired a whole family-story genre in the USA (see for instance Susan Coolidge's *What Katy Did* (1873)). In Germany, on the other hand, girls' stories written at about the same time as *Little Women* are tales of individual development, with such titles as *Backfischens Leiden und Freuden* [The joys and sorrows of a teenage girl] (Helm 1863) and *Der Trotzkopf* [The defiant girl] (von Rhoden 1885). The course of the girl's development from child to adult, often ending with marriage, is frequently the story of integration into the social and family environment and, after her initial rejection of it, her acceptance of the predestined female role in society. In terms of the history of modernization, this aspect of German girls' books as stories of individual development makes them appear more progressive than the American family story.

Comparative genre studies could also, to stay with our example of girls' books, include research into the reasons for their increased production in many European countries and the USA after the middle of the nineteenth century,[25] the century in which scientific discourse on sexuality was developing, as well as into the changing status of this branch of literature. While 'those works recognized as having literary merit' (Reynolds 1990: xvi) were considered 'high fiction' in late nineteenth-century Great Britain – they included 'boys' adventure and school stories, depictions of bourgeois family life and a hybrid of fantasy and riddle à la *Alice in Wonderland* or Lear's "nonsense books" ' (ibid.) – girls' books, independently of the quality of the texts or the social class of the readers to whom they were addressed, were classified as 'low fiction' (ibid.) along with 'bloods' or comics. Similarly, it was said of 'Backfischliteratur' – books for teenage girls – written in Germany at the same time: 'To this day, it seems likely that no area of literature for children and young people has been so disparaged by literary criticism and in educational literature as the traditional genre of girls' stories known as "Backfischliteratur" ' (trans. from Wilkending 1996: 105).

It would also be a rewarding comparative task to look into the reciprocal relations between the women's movement in the late nineteenth and early twentieth centuries in Europe and the USA and the constructions of girlhood and womanhood in the books written especially for girls in those parts of the world. Gisela Wilkending (1996) has shown how attacks on teenage literature at the end of the nineteenth century in Germany were aimed at women's emancipation. In parallel, as Kimberley Reynolds revealed, authors and publishers of girls' fiction in England tried not only to control the pace of social change, 'but actually to reverse its progress' (Reynolds 1990: 109).

8   Comparative historiography of children's literature

Comparative historiography is interested in the development of children's literature research in different countries, and the criteria according to which histories and accounts of the various children's literature are written. It calls for fundamental discussion of the cultural, social, economic and educational conditions in which literature for children developed. There is still no comparative study of children's literatures from different cultures which takes account of these aspects. Even a comparative history confined to European children's literature,[26] let alone one of all the children's literatures in the world, could not be realized by a single writer (see the over-ambitious one-woman project by Carmen Bravo-Villasante, *Historia de la literatura infantil universal* [International history of children's literature] (1971)). Ganna Ottevaere-van Praag undertook with *La littérature pour la jeunesse en Europe occidentale (1750–1925)*, published in 1987, the most extensive attempt so far to write a history of Western European children's literature from the mid-eighteenth to the twentieth century. In this knowledgeable study, which was awarded the first international 'Pinocchio Prize' of the *Fondazione Nazionale 'Carlo Collodi'*, the author compares the historical context and development of children's literature in England, France, the Netherlands, Germany and Italy, establishing similarities and differences. Less illuminating is her account of the connections between the literatures of those countries – the actual transfer of texts across borders, translations, the reception of works and their influence on the development of the literatures concerned. The study is primarily a comparative history of European children's literature in the context of the socio-historical developments, chiefly underscoring the changing ideologies of childhood. Ottevaere-van Praag thought that, in view of the far-reaching changes in the sociological conditions of childhood after the First World War, together with changes in the form and status of children's literature, to continue the task for the years after 1925 'was a job for a whole team of critics rather than a single historian' (trans. from Ottevaere-van

Praag 1987: 29). This was undoubtedly a correct assessment, but placed in the introduction to a history of children's literature in Western Europe covering almost two hundred years, from the origins of the specific literatures studied in the book to the First World War, it must make us wonder whether it does not also apply to the author's own project.

Problems for the comparative historiography of children's literature arise partly from the different state of its documentation in individual countries or linguistic areas, which in turn is connected with the state of research, and that again depends on the status of children's literature in that area. The histories of children's literature that do exist, whether national or international, are only too often accounts of what children read, or mere positivist enumerations of the most 'important' or successful authors. Even in the *International Companion Encyclopedia of Children's Literature* (Hunt 1996), the widely differing methods of presentation and horizons of the articles on separate countries will hardly allow comparisons to be made, ranging as they do from histories of important authors and works without any interpretation of developments, to a few studies of changes in the form and function of children's literature in the area described.

The comparative historiography of children's literature faces a series of open questions. How should historical accounts be organized: by genres or periods, by countries, linguistic areas or regions? What is the basis of periodization – the same as that in the corresponding adult literature? That, however, is often of only limited relevance to children's literature, since socio-historical developments, for instance in the field of education, have constantly influenced the distinct evolution of literature for children. How can a useful framework be constructed for writing about the phases of development and the changes in the form and function of children's literature while still maintaining a balance between empirical description and theoretical reflections? Comparative historical studies of children's literatures produced under similar conditions could lead to a closer understanding of the circumstances that encourage or hinder the development of these literatures. Much might be learned, for instance, from a study of cultural colonization within Europe by comparing books in Flemish, where the literature of the Netherlands was an obstacle to the development of an independent and innovative Flemish children's literature in Belgium (see Bouckaert-Ghesquière 1992: 88), and English-language children's literature of Ireland, which had to contend with a similar situation (see Chapter 3).

Comparative historiography should ask whether certain historical periods, for instance the Enlightenment, can perhaps be fully understood only from the comparative angle, as periods of intense, lively international exchange in the field of children's literature. The influence of Rousseau on the educational philosophies and children's literatures of north-west Europe has been adequately documented. Among the activities involving translation and reception in children's literature at the end of the eighteenth century was the production of Christian Felix Weisse's magazine *Der Kinderfreund* [The children's friend] (1776–82), modelled on the English weekly magazines of the time. Weisse in turn inspired Arnaud Berquin to found his monthly journal *L'Ami des Enfants*

[The children's friend] (1782–3). Berquin was translated into English, and the translation gave rise to a series of imitations (see Thwaite 1972: 67). What Germany still lacked at that time was, according to Köberle (trans. from 1972: 17), 'already available in France and England' and was taken over from those countries.

The normative and restrictive category of 'national literature', like other such identity constructs, has lost ground today to concepts of hybrid identities and literatures, and to cultures of the diaspora. Multilingual and multicultural authors such as Elias Cannetti, Joseph Conrad, Salman Rushdie, Kazuo Ishiguro or Rafik Schami cannot be placed in any national literary category. José Lambert, calling for new 'literary world maps', thinks that, if it still seems at all useful to employ national categories, we should no longer speak of 'German literature', 'Indian literature', and so on, but of 'literature in Germany', 'literature in India', etc. (see Lambert 1991). Such categories naturally include translated literature as well as all literature by migrants and literatures of the diaspora, regardless of the language in which it is written and the passport held by its author.

The development of any children's literature cannot be adequately described or understood, if its interactions with other literatures are ignored. Not only comparative historiography but also the historical study of various children's literatures ('in France', 'in Japan', etc.) must look at the books chosen for translation, asking such questions as: what was translated when, and from which languages? When were certain texts or literatures translated (and if it was only after a lapse of time, what are the reasons for that delay)? How were they received, and how popular were they? Did they appear on lists of recommended reading? Some recent historical works have developed an awareness of influences from other literatures and cultures.[27] Ernst Seibert's work on Austrian literature for young people during the transition from the Josephine period to the Restoration (1770–1835), for instance, devotes a chapter to 'The dominance of French educational writing and books for young people in Vienna around 1800' (see Seibert 1987).

9 Comparative history of children's literature studies

The metacritical dimension of comparative children's literature, like comparative literature in general, must 'recognize both the culture-specific (national) and intercultural (international) character of theories' (trans. from Zima 1992: 62). It involves looking at culture-specific aspects of the study of children's literature, which in turn are influenced by how the subject is institutionally established in different cultures. It should also take account of the theoretical approaches and historiographical writings developing from that institutional situation, and the connection between the theory and the actual production of literature for young people.

In Germany until the 1960s, discussion of children's literature was almost entirely confined to the didactic context, in relation to teacher training. In the late 1960s James Fadimann identified the level of institutional development, together with a primarily educational interest in children's literature, as the aspects distinguishing research in Germany. The much-cited paradigm change in literary studies in Germany after the late 1960s which opened the area to fields other than 'high' literature, combined with new approaches such as structuralism and reception aesthetics, allowed children's literature to develop as an academic subject. The first chair for the subject was established in Frankfurt in 1964. The first university chair for children's literature in France (at the University of Bordeaux III in 1974) was devoted to 'Littérature populaire et pour la jeunesse'. The study of children's literature was thus placed in the context of popular or para-literature. In England, on the other hand, there was no professorial chair for children's literature studies until the end of the 1990s; for a long time children's literature featured at tertiary level predominantly in the training of librarians. These contextual situations of children's literature influence the way in which it is studied, whether theoretically and historically or with a more 'applied' approach.

Where children's literature is approached as a genuine literary and cultural subject in academic institutions, it is, as a rule, studied and taught as part of the national literature of the country concerned – that is to say, in England by scholars of English language and literature, in Germany by Germanists, etc. – even if they do not entirely ignore its international aspect, through the use of translations, etc. Since children's literature is still regarded as being on the borderline of literary studies, scholars of foreign languages and literatures are usually unable or unwilling to 'waste' resources on it.[28]

A comparative history of children's literature studies must describe the relation between the institutional situation, the level of research and international influence. Ruth Bottigheimer sees American children's literature studies 'far more influenced by developments in Germany [than] by scholarship in England', since German children's literature studies had a better institutional basis,[29] and such a basis is 'paramount in the creation of influence' (1993: 91f.). In fact, in the 1970s parallels could be traced between American and German children's literature studies as the focus in America started to shift in the course of the 1970s to scholarly works which tried 'to study the instrumental motivation of children's literature and its socio-political as well as its psychological effects' (Zipes 1994: 205). This development runs parallel to the first critical and revisionist studies in German children's literature.

Among aspects to be considered in a comparative history of children's literature studies is the status of research into children's literature and its historiography. In 1914 an entry on children's literature appeared in Britain in the *Cambridge History of English Literature* (Darton 1914), a rare early example of the recognition of the importance of this branch of literature in the context of general literary discourse. Nationally specific focuses of research are also relevant to comparative studies, as illustrated by the striking interest shown in historical children's literature research by a generation of researchers in Germany who wrote their doctoral and *Habilitation* theses in the 1970s and 1980s on the children's literature of the Enlightenment, looking at it from the socio-historical and psycho-historical angle. This interest can be partly explained by the wish

> to find out and explain how members of a highly developed culture could become Nazi hangmen and (bureaucratic) torturers, or alternatively fellow-travellers who looked away from the crimes of the Nazis and later tried to suppress what had happened.
>
> (trans. from Steinlein 1996: 252)

This made the history of children's literature in Germany an 'essential organ of the critical appraisal of bourgeois socialization and those "evil" consequences of it that induced ideological blindness' (ibid.).

A comparative study might also examine the key critical texts of children's literature in different cultures. For instance, it would be illuminating to take Hazard's monograph *Les livres, les enfants et les hommes*, which appeared in 1932 and was widely read internationally after the Second World War, and compare it in detail with a work published in the same year, *Children's Books in England: Five Centuries of Social Life*, by F. J. Harvey Darton, the first major historical study of British children's literature. Hazard's work, as shown in Chapter 1, is a passionate plea for literature tailored to children's requirements, imaginative and not didactic. It is deeply felt, partisan and selective. In the rarefied heights of his discourse about the essence of all children and the flow of human sympathy crossing borders created by international children's literature, Hazard does not turn to pragmatic questions of production or cultural exchange. The notion that children's literature is also a commercial product is far from the spirit of *Les livres, les enfants et les hommes*. Not so with the aims and organization of *Children's Books in England* by Harvey Darton, a bibliophile publisher, journalist, editor, and the great-great-great-grandson of the founder of the important children's book publishing firm of Darton. Darton wrote a soundly based, critical and pragmatic account of British children's literature, including all its commercial and bibliographical detail, also mentioning (at least sporadically) the significance of translated literature for the development of English children's literature. He showed himself a perceptive and intelligent literary critic, whose socio-historical approach and evaluations of individual works are still quoted today in British literary discussion.

Comparison of the nationally specific interests and tendencies of these key texts on the subject of children's literature in France and England reads like an embodiment of national stereotypes. On the one hand, we have a sophisticated academic writing a very general work full of *esprit* on children and their literature; on the other, a 'gifted amateur', a pragmatist recording facts with sensitivity and historical awareness, who understands children's literature in terms not merely of literary but also of social history. If we add a German representative in the shape of the educationalist Heinrich Wolgast from a somewhat earlier period, with his reformist work *Das Elend unserer Jugendliteratur* [The miserable state of our children's literature] (1896), which rejects outright the idea of a specific literature for young people, we could see the three as standing for Johan Galtung's typology of the Anglo-Saxon, Gallic and Teutonic styles of scholarship (see Galtung 1983). A comparative history of children's literature must take critical note of culture-specific academic traditions and styles, and be aware of different systems of discourse in order to make a productive contribution to an intercultural communication of knowledge. Children's literature studies, which may be described as a discipline with an international subject but usually with monocultural horizons of research, is badly in need of such a dialogue.

10 The interlinking of different areas of comparative studies

Taking the adolescent novel as an example, this section will briefly demonstrate how subject areas in children's literature studies can often be usefully dealt with only by combinations of comparative questions, and approached by way of several of the areas of comparative children's literature outlined here.

Literature with the phase of life of adolescence or young adulthood as its subject, and literature actually addressed to adolescents, are eminently suitable subjects for comparative study, as evidenced by Peter Grotzer's two-volume work on adolescence in German, English, American and French literature, *Die zweite Geburt* [The second birth] (1991). The development of an extended phase of pre-adult life can be studied in terms of *cultural history* or the *history of mentalities*: in what cultural areas has a transitional period between childhood and adulthood been specially marked out as adolescence, and since when? If childhood as we know it today is largely the invention of eighteenth-century European bourgeois family culture, then young adulthood is a twentieth-century phenomenon connected with democratic societies. Young adulthood first appeared in America with the emergence of teenagers as a distinctive group, and the idea began to gain ground in Europe prior to the First World War in parallel with the 'Americanization' of European societies. Adolescence is recognized as having a central function within the ethno-psychoanalytical discussion of social change. To Mario Erdheim (1984), it is at the heart of all cultural change in the form of a 'second chance': only in and from adolescence can those impulses come that alter a society which is fundamentally inclined to preserve the *status quo*. A rewarding field for comparative study would be to contrast the idea and representation of adolescence in the literature of what the social anthropologist Claude Lévi-Strauss (1963) dubbed the 'hot' and 'cold' cultures, i.e. those called 'hot' because they warm quickly to the new and assimilate change and because their social structure allows progress, social elevation and rapid development through 'warming' (the example usually named is the USA), and those insular cultures called 'cold' because they are intent on 'freezing' social change and clinging to an established and rather schematic social structure (Japan is cited here as a traditional example).

Questions of the development of literature about and for young adults belong to the area of *literary history*. A tradition of writing about adolescence goes much further back than the special literature actually addressed to young adults, which developed only in the second half of the twentieth century and focuses on teenagers' search for identity and autonomy, their struggle against adult authorities in order to develop their own set of values. Adolescent novels differ from other forms of teenage fiction – issue novels, romance series, horror fiction – in their serious and explicit exploration of such themes as sexuality, spirituality and relationships, often using metafictive devices. Key authors include Aidan Chambers, Robert Cormier and Peter Pohl.

The adolescent phase has, on the other hand, been a popular subject in German literature since the eighteenth century – Goethe's *Die Leiden des jungen Werthers* [The sorrows of young Werther] (1774) and Karl Philipp Moritz's *Anton Reiser* (1785–90) are regarded as early examples of literature of adolescence. Around the beginning of the twentieth century the genre flourished again with such novels as *Freund Hein* [The grim reaper] by Emil Strauss (1902), Herman Hesse's *Unterm Rad* [Under the wheel] (1906) and Robert Musil's *Die Verwirrungen des Zöglings Törless* [The confusions of the pupil Törless] (1906). There is no doubt that these novels were widely read by young people, too. However, literary discourse on adolescence, which Hans-Heino Ewers calls 'probably the most difficult crisis in the personal development of modern man', was supposed to be conducted 'without the participation of those involved' (trans. from Ewers 1992: 292). Official literature for young people in Germany, at least until the middle of the twentieth century, was anti-*Werther* literature, which, unlike the novels named above, did not imaginatively reconstruct and empathize with the crisis of adolescence to the full. Only in the second half of the twentieth century did official literature for young people accept what was traditionally an adult literary genre, adopting its themes and narrative patterns.

The analysis of differences in the realization of those patterns in adult literature as well as in literature for young people is relevant from a *literary-theory* point of view. The transfer of novels that themselves are literary borderline cases across linguistic and cultural boundaries is particularly worth investigating; such novels may be published for adults in the culture in which they originate, but for young people in translation, an example being the novels *Breven till nattens drotting* [Letters to the queen of the night] (Edelfeldt 1985) and *Kamalas bok* [Kamala's book] (Edelfeldt 1986a) by Inger Edelfeldt, which were published for adults in Sweden and for young adults in Germany (see Edelfeldt 1986b and 1988). Such classifications can be traced back to the different boundaries drawn in allocating certain themes and texts to the different audiences, or to the breadth or narrowness of the literary areas concerned.

Analysis of elements and structures dealing with initiation rituals, or the temporally and culturally specific presentation of the conflict between generations, or of adolescents breaking free of the family, belongs to the area of *themes and motifs*. Matters relevant to the study of *gender-specific genres* include the handling of narrative patterns depending on the gender of the protagonists and whether a book is clearly addressed to a male or female reading public. If the dominant theme in the traditional adolescent novel with a male protagonist is his search for identity, with a usually autonomous finale, novels with female protagonists often have different narrative patterns, more often bearing greater resemblance to the family novel and the love story.

Of interest from a *poetological* perspective is the pronounced intertextuality and metafictionality of the adolescent novel, as witness even the titles of two famous specimens of the genre, J. D. Salinger's *The Catcher in the Rye* (1951) and Ulrich Plenzdorf's *Die neuen Leiden des jungen W.* [New sorrows of young W.] (1978). The first refers to a poem by Robert Burns, the interpretation of which is a key to the mental turmoil of the protagonist Holden Caulfield. The second title refers to Goethe's *Die Leiden des jungen Werthers* [The sorrows of young Werther], so that both implicitly and explicitly we have here a confrontation with the German 'literary heritage' and a dialogue with Goethe's earlier text. References to literature and other art forms often allow the protagonists to articulate their experiences and problems and express their self-absorption and sense of their own magnificence.

Comparative *translation and transfer studies* must ask which countries produce literature for adolescents at all, what books are translated where, which firms publish them (publishers of adult literature or children's literature?), and where such books are not readily accepted because of the lack of a comparable concept of adolescence. Anna Katharina Ulrich reminds us that some categories of books, such as adolescent novels, 'are not within the understanding of children's literature in non-European countries' (1998a: 127).

More compelling even than the example of adolescent literature, which allows a glimpse at how a complex approach from various comparative perspectives helps to refine our understanding of these novels, is the example of the central comparative concept of world literature. As will be shown in Chapter 6, only an approach from multiple viewpoints can adequately address this phenomenon as it manifests itself in children's literature.

3 The development, culture-specific status and international exchange of children's literatures

Among the central questions of comparative children's literature theory to be discussed in this chapter are the conditions of the development of children's literature, its culture-specific status, and its international exchange. Most descriptive models are based on developments in the industrialized countries of north-west Europe, the birthplace of children's literature, and are often presented as universal rather than culture-specific accounts of – for instance – German-language, English-language or West European children's literature. This idea of universal patterns in the development of children's literature will be criticized in the following pages by analysis of differences in the course of its development in different countries, in the light of their respective historical, political, economic and cultural situations.

That analysis is followed by an account of factors with a bearing on the esteem in which children's literature is held within a culture. They include the prevalent concept of childhood, personal experiences of childhood, and the status-relevant functions of children's literature. A culture's evaluation of its own literature for children has direct effects on its status internationally. That status will be discussed in the context of the international exchange of children's literature, which, as the analysis of the distribution of children's literature and the economic dimension of exchange shows, is not as international as is often assumed.

A model of the development of children's literature

It was established in Chapter 2, section 9, that there is still no comprehensive comparative study of the children's literatures of various cultures that takes account of the different conditions in which they arise and develop, and that many histories of individual children's literatures are merely accounts of what children read, or simply enumerate the most prominent authors. We lack not only accounts of the history of individual children's literatures that satisfy the demands of scholarship, but also, partly due to the long dominance of an internationalist concept of children's literature, comprehensive reconstructions of the exchange of children's literature across linguistic and cultural borders.

Furthermore, there is often little awareness of the potential differences in the development of children's literature in different cultures.

Through an analysis of the development of English children's literature, and of the later development of Hebrew children's literature that leaned heavily on the German model,[1] Zohar Shavit, in *Poetics of Children's Literature*, assumes a universalist approach to the development of children's literature: 'The issue at stake is ... the universal structural traits and patterns common to all children's literatures' (Shavit 1986: xi). She identifies the crucial factor in the development of children's literature to be the educational ideology of such intellectual movements as those of the 'Puritans in England and America, or the followers of the Jewish Enlightenment in Germany 150 years later' (ibid.: 134). Irrespective of their ideological differences, both shared the view 'that in the process of their education, children needed books, and that those books must differ from adult books principally through their fundamental attachment to the educational system itself' (ibid.). Besides the primary frame of reference of the educational system from which the development of children's literature proceeds, Shavit saw the second driving force behind it in the rivalry between children's books accepted or sanctioned by the literary and education systems, and the chapbooks that were popular reading for children from the seventeenth century onwards. Commercial publishers recognized in this readership the potential for a new market and 'tried to produce children's books that would be as attractive as chapbooks, but would still be acceptable to parents and teachers' (ibid.: 159). Religious and moral educators, too, realized that the best way to combat the chapbooks, which they considered a corrupting influence, was to replace them with alternative reading material. Children's literature became stratified, says Shavit, in response to the need to fight popular literature. She thus regards children's literature as developing from what at first was a purely educational literature, which then branched out in reaction to the expansion and commercialization of the market. Based on her analysis of English literature, and seeing it confirmed by the development of its Hebrew counterpart, Shavit takes this to be a pattern which applies to every literature:

> I contend that the very same stages of development reappear in all children's literatures, regardless of when and where they begin to develop. That is to say, the historical patterns in the development of children's literature are basically the same in any literature, transcending national and even time boundaries. It does not matter whether two national systems began to develop at the same time, or if one developed a hundred or even two hundred years later (as with Hebrew, and later with Arabic and Japanese children's literatures). They all seem to pass through the very same stages of development without exception. Moreover, the same cultural factors and institutions are involved in their creation.
>
> (Shavit 1986: 133f.)

Models like these (and that of Maria Nikolajeva discussed in Chapter 2, section 3) are problematic from the point of view of comparative literary studies because, above and beyond a useful systemic view of the development of children's literature in specific (usually northern European)[2] cultures, they present a theory of cultural conditions which claims to be universally valid. However, a differentiating look at the conditions of the development of children's literatures in a variety of cultures in the light of their respective historical, political and economic situations will reveal that this is patently not the case. After a brief survey of the normative north-west European model, I will illustrate with two examples of the development of children's literature which deviate from that model how the theory of the universality of development in children's literatures is treading on very thin ice.

The north-west European model

The specific children's literatures of the north-west European countries arose from, and developed in parallel to, the far-reaching structural changes in all social areas in those countries in the eighteenth century. The rise and development of this branch of literature go hand in hand with the evolution of bourgeois society. Central factors are:

- on the social level, the formation of the middle classes and the establishment of modern society;
- on the economic level, the change in the literary market as an important stage in the emergence of the bourgeois public in the eighteenth century, the rise of educational children's literature being one of the elements involved (see Wild 1987: 3ff.), and the development of purely commercial children's literature that soon followed;
- on the level of the family, the differentiated development of the middle-class family and middle-class childhood, that is to say the separation of family and work and the liberation of children from working life, the emergence of the nuclear family and the growing intimacy of family connections, the perception of childhood as a phase of life differing fundamentally from adult existence and the definition of children as objects of serious responsibility in need of protection and education; and
- on the level of education, the introduction of compulsory school attendance for all, the building up of the school system, and the development of (literary) educational discourse.

These factors are the prerequisites for the development of children's literature in large parts of Europe, and, depending on the pace of their realization, individual children's literatures developed at different times. In Italy, for instance, specific children's literature developed about fifty years later than in Germany. In the south of Italy, in particular, the 'traditional conditions of socialization of the old, pre-bourgeois society' (trans. from D. Richter 1996: 34) predominated for longer, as did those of 'pre-literacy', in which children learned by watching and imitating, a knowledge of books being as unnecessary for them as for the majority of adults. Not until compulsory school attendance was introduced in the second half of the 1870s, with the concomitant advances in literacy, were the prerequisites for the development of a specific children's literature in place. It is no coincidence that the two great novels at the beginning of the development of Italian children's literature, Carlo Collodi's *Pinocchio* (1881–3) and Edmondo de Amicis' *Cuore* [Heart] (1886), are stories of the acquisition of literacy that emphasize the importance of schooling and learning to read. Delayed development in Italy can in fact be accounted for using Shavit's universal model for children's literature, but that model comes up against its limitations when, as in the two following examples, the influence of colonialism is felt.

Contravening the standard model (I): Black Africa

To talk about the development of children's literature in 'Black Africa' is to generalize; Africa is not a homogeneous country but a vibrant heterogeneous continent. As Osayimwense Osa reminds us in his survey of African children's literature: 'Just as there is no language called "African", so there is really no one culture that cuts across the whole continent' (1995: xiii). None the less, many of the following points can be backed up by reports from different African countries.

The early stages of the development of (printed) children's literature in Black Africa were determined by colonial rule. In constructing an educational system based on their own system at home, the colonialists and missionaries imported literature that aimed to promote Christianity and 'civilization' (see Schmidt 1981: 23). With English and French school primers extolling the benefits of European life and values, literature was a foreign phenomenon imposed on the indigenous population from outside. In the postcolonial period, reactions are divided towards the book, something developed far away as the product of a different social model. The main reaction is a wish to develop an indigenous printed children's literature, reflecting and encouraging the country's own (oral) culture. Another reaction at least contemplates rejecting the book altogether:

> some African countries have even considered ejecting that imported idea the 'book' (and the library) to return to their long-established oral tradition. ... According to Adolphe Amadi, the dominant ethos of African society is at variance with the aims of libraries.
>
> (Heale 1996: 795)

Parallel with attitudes to the printed word and to reading,[3] attitudes to childhood and the child's position in society enter into the discussion, as do attitudes to the necessity or desirability of a literature conceived for this special group. A fundamental question that arises in many African countries runs: 'Do we want a "childhood" and a "youth" which needs its own form of literature?' (Dankert

1991: 23). An account of attitudes to children and their social position corresponds to what, from a European vantage point, is seen as a 'traditional' or 'pre-modern' form of society:

> African concepts of the child's personality, psychology, family relationships and place in society differ profoundly from those of the Western world. Traditionally, children are taught by their mothers in their early years. In rural areas they are expected to contribute to the family income and join in adult social life. In this context, in the rare cases where the book is present, it represents a form of individual and 'anonymous' communication which does not fit easily into a culture where the oral tradition is strong and there is a keen sense of collectivity.
>
> (Laurentin 1996: 802)

Thus products of modern, industrialized societies have been introduced into countries where childhood, literacy and the reading of books have different connotations.

A country's literature does not develop in isolation. The contribution made by any literature influencing it depends on its own stage of development and strength. In the case of Hebrew literature, which, as Shavit (1986) has shown, leaned on the German model, works that seemed valuable to Hebrew literature were selected and translated and, because it already had a highly developed written culture, the imported German literature was easily integrated into the target literature. In the former colonies, however, the language of books is still mainly that of the former colonial powers, and the majority of books on the market – in English or French – are directly imported without being in any way linguistically or culturally integrated, unlike the German literature translated into Hebrew. In such cases the market is dominated by 'foreign' literature, with an inhibiting effect on the establishment of an indigenous book industry and literature. Gloria Dillsworth described the children's book scene in Sierra Leone in 1988 as follows: 'A wide range of fiction can be found in the children's library and the most popular authors are Enid Blyton, Susan Coolidge, Louisa May Alcott, Richmal Crompton, Franklyn W. Dixon, Carolyn Keene, Capt. W.E. Johns' (Dillsworth 1988: 19). She does mention two authors from Sierra Leone, Clifford Fyle and Thomas Decker, but adds: 'There are only a few children's books written by Sierra Leoneans and those which are in print can be found in the children's library though not in adequate numbers' (ibid.).

In Shavit's developmental model, the market plays no part until the moment when, in the wake of the wider distribution of children's literature, it begins to broaden to include the mass production of 'popular' literature. As a rule the indigenous market in postcolonial societies is dominated by foreign products. The economic situation is notable, due to the low literacy rate, for the relatively small number of buyers, the lack of purchasing power in potential buyers, and the lack of investment in the publishing industry:

The considerable potential writing talent in Africa is being frustrated by a totally depressed publishing industry owing to a lack of foreign exchange to buy printing paper, machinery, film, chemicals, plates, spare parts. Financial institutions in most African countries do not as yet consider publishing a viable industry to which to lend money.

(Tötemeyer 1994: 410)

This situation does not permit expansion of the indigenous market for literature in the way foreseen by Shavit's model; in fact, the market is largely dependent on the educational context: 'Only in countries whose education system guarantees sufficient sales does local publishing thrive. ... This results in the oft-repeated cliché that in Africa books = school' (Heale 1996: 797).[4] Consequently, there is no comparable development of the numerous forms of popular print literature such as broadsheets, chapbooks or penny theatres that were common in Europe in the centuries after the invention of printing (see Pellowski 1996: 670). In addition, there is the problem of linguistic diversity within political structures that function as single economic units, with, for instance, some 395 languages in Nigeria alone.

We must ask how a children's literature can develop in a traditional, largely illiterate society that, without having gone through early stages of its own book production, finds itself in the middle of an increasingly globalized culture with omnipresent mass media in the big cities at least, in which to some extent a direct 'non-Western' connection is established between oral and audiovisual communication, neither of which uses written language.

The development of children's literature in the African countries therefore involves such factors as the consequences of colonialism; concepts of the family and childhood; the influence of 'developed' literatures; the influence of the mass media; literacy and illiteracy; linguistic diversity; and economic questions pertaining to the market and distribution. None of these are considered in Shavit's model. This point does not invalidate her analysis of the way in which Hebrew and English children's literature developed, or her important contribution to the systems theory of children's literature, but it does show how problematic it is to make universalist generalizations on the basis of the analysis of two developments which, by international criteria, are relatively similar.[5]

That criticism cannot be refuted by saying that the colonization of Africa makes it a special case. The indications of similarities in the development of literature in certain Asian countries show that the African situation is not without its parallels.[6] We can also see how little claim Shavit's universalist approach really has to general validity by looking at children's literature in a north-west European culture, albeit not in one of the leading industrialized regions.

Contravening the standard model (II): Ireland

Irish children's literature in English is an example of a development influenced by conditions other than those crucial to most other European children's literatures.[7]

The most important development in Irish children's literature in the twentieth century arose not from any political, educational or ideological programme, but from institutional changes, particularly in the publishing industry; it is only since the 1980s that publishing in English for a youth audience has happened to any significant extent in Ireland.[8]

There is scarcely another European literature whose level of involvement in the production of reading matter for its young was so slight as was Ireland's up until the 1980s. Before then children's literature was almost exclusively imported; Irish children's reading material was almost entirely British, even after independence in 1922 following centuries of British colonial rule. This situation hindered the establishment and development of a native book industry in the English language. (Children's books in Irish, on the other hand, have been produced since the 1920s by An Gúm, the Irish publications branch of the Department of Education.) Up until the 1980s, therefore, if Irish authors writing for children in English wanted to reach a purchasing public hardly existent in their own country, which until the end of the twentieth century was amongst the poorest in Europe, they had to publish in Britain (like Patricia Lynch or Eilis Dillon) or America, the country to which many key authors for children, such as Ella Young, James Stephens and Padraic Colum, emigrated at the beginning of the twentieth century.

The problem inherent in literature produced for a market abroad is that it is often forced to conform to 'foreign' images; expectations as to what an Irish children's book should be produced books following in the tradition of Irish legends and fairy tales, or else accounts of a poor, backward and rural country whose stage-Irish inhabitants were simple but happy.

Change on the cultural and institutional level started to take place in Ireland towards the end of the 1970s: 'expanding children's departments in bookshops, an excellent library service and tremendous interest in the schools in encouraging children to read' is how the author Tony Hickey characterized the situation, and yet there were 'hardly any children's books published in Ireland' (Hickey 1982: 36). But the improvement in the economic situation following Ireland's entry into the European Community in 1972, alterations in the school curriculum that placed more emphasis on project work and thus students' involvement with a greater range of literature, and last but not least, the large number of potential readers of children's books – approximately 50 per cent of the population of Ireland was then under the age of 25 – all combined to bring about change. A significant factor supporting this new development was the decision, in 1980, by the (state-funded) Arts Council to support the production of Irish children's literature in English. In 1981 the first two subsidized children's books were published by the newly founded Children's Press.

How radically the situation changed during the 1980s was illustrated by a survey, *The Book Market in the Republic of Ireland*, undertaken by the Irish Books Marketing Group in 1987, which showed that children's books were one of the most successful branches of Irish publishing overall – less than ten years after the founding of the first children's book imprint. And production continued to increase, peaking in the mid-1990s when seven publishing houses were regularly issuing books for young people.[9] These changes were accompanied by the setting up of promotional bodies and support groups. The *Youth Library Group of the Library Association of Ireland*, the *Children's Literature Association of Ireland* and the *Irish Children's Book Trust* were all established in the 1980s,[10] and the annual Children's Book Festival and the prestigious *Bisto Book of the Year Award* at the beginning of the 1990s. A number of universities now offer courses on children's literature; the amount of critical writing on the subject has risen over the past ten years, with the quarterly publication *Inis* providing a forum for commentary on and reviews of Irish and international publications; and the *Irish Society for the Study of Children's Literature* held its inaugural conference in 2003. The growth and expansion of children's literature in Ireland, the number of publishers now active in the area and the interest which it has generated are extraordinary when one considers that none of the organizations, activities or imprints named here was in existence before 1980. The development in Ireland demonstrates how the ownership of the means of production of an indigenous children's literature, coupled with the economic conditions which make publishing viable, enables the development of a literature of local interest and relevance rather than texts which have to adapt to the demands of global publishers.

Developments in postcolonial Africa and Ireland, different as they may be in respect of questions of literacy, linguistic diversity and economic factors, have in common the fact that they followed a different course from children's literatures in certain Western industrialized nations, for whose development universality has been claimed. None of the various factors set out here which had a formative influence on children's literature and its development in African countries and in Ireland are accounted for in Shavit's model, which cannot adequately address the question of how children's literature can develop under conditions which diverge significantly from those prevalent in Britain, Germany or France during the late eighteenth century. A genuinely comparative history of children's literature – as yet to be written – would examine the social, economic, political and cultural conditions which have to prevail for a children's literature to become established in the first place and would reveal how the histories of postcolonial children's literatures differ significantly from the postulated 'standard' model based on northern European countries. Instead of being regarded as a norm, that model would then be seen as just one that is applicable to a type of development in a given historical and socio-economic context.

The culture-specific status of children's literature

Going beyond the general aspects of the status of children's literature as a literary system, as discussed in Chapter 2, section 1, we may say that the regard in which it is held within a given culture is influenced by a number of factors, and they in turn partly determine the international status of that children's literature in the context of its exchange.

Two factors of special importance will be briefly discussed here: the prevailing concepts of childhood and the status-relevant functions of children's literature.

Concepts of childhood

The history of children's literature records the interdependence between prevailing ideas of childhood and the development of that branch of literature; the children's literature of Europe can be regarded as a product of the philosophical and poetic constructs of childhood developed during the Enlightenment and the Romantic periods. However, we should not assume that there is such a thing as a constant, ahistorical, European or North American idea of childhood. Hazard, although his own idea of childhood owed much to the myth of the child in European Romanticism with its emphasis on the childish imagination, pointed out the different attitudes to and concepts of childhood in the various countries of Europe, and saw them as a partial explanation for different kinds of children's literature and their development. In contrast to the ideal of upbringing in the Romance countries, the Anglo-Saxon world, he said, allowed children an existence of their own; youth there was of value in itself, and the journey was more important than the destination. Briefly, and in rather elevated terms, Hazard sums up his argument thus: 'For the Latins, children have never been anything but future men. The Nordics have understood better this truer truth, that men are only grown-up children' (Hazard 1944: 110).

The work of the American anthropologist Martha Wolfenstein may be read as confirmation of Hazard's remarks. In 1947 she observed French children and their parents in the park. She compares the French notion of childhood not, as Hazard did, to the British one, but to its American counterpart:

> If we compare Americans and French, it seems as though the relation between childhood and adulthood is almost completely opposite in the two cultures. In America we regard childhood as a very nearly ideal time, a time for enjoyment, an end in itself. The American image of the child ... is of a young person with great resources for enjoyment, whose present life is an end in itself. With the French ... it seems to be the other way around. Childhood is a period of probation, when everything is a means to an end, it is unenviable from the vantage point of adulthood.
>
> (Wolfenstein 1955: 115f.)

A concept of childhood that regards the human being as perfected only when civilized – seen here by Wolfenstein as characteristic of the French – is the opposite of Jean-Jacques Rousseau's idea of childhood as the better form of human existence, which prevails in the literature of the predominantly Protestant cultures of northern Europe and North America. These contrasting images of childhood, one Utopian and looking to the future, the other more mythical and looking to the past, are the basis for two fundamental types of children's literature:

educational literature and literature based on the idea of a 'Paradise lost' (see Pape 1981: 97).

Similarly, Dieter Richter divides what he calls novels of childhood, products of the nineteenth century, into novels of progression and novels of regression. Childhood novels of progression deal with a child who becomes an adult and describe the end of childhood; Carlo Collodi's *Pinocchio* is a prototype of this model. Childhood novels of regression, such as Lewis Carroll's *Alice's Adventures in Wonderland* and James M. Barrie's *Peter Pan*, try to retrace 'the lost world of childhood from which we are expelled, a dream childhood' (trans. from D. Richter 1996: 97). While novels of regression seem to dominate British children's literature from about the middle of the nineteenth century, stories of progression take the lead in the children's literatures of southern Europe. A comparative study of the animal picture books *L'Histoire de Babar, le petit éléphant* [The story of Babar the little elephant] (de Brunhoff 1931), *The Tale of Peter Rabbit* (Potter 1902) and *Die Häschenschule* [The school for hares] (Sixtus and Koch-Gotha 1924), each of them highly regarded in their respective French, English and German cultures, confirmed this when it contrasted, amongst other things, the civilizing effect of clothes in the French book with the constraint imposed by clothing in the English story: Peter's preference for wearing no clothes, says this study, is an expression of his proximity to nature (see Tabbert 1991b: 121).

Ariel Dorfman also sees the French view of children as potential adults reflected in the *Babar* stories. The adventures narrated in them always remain within the bounds of parental authority, 'in which universal bliss is assured by grown-up figures who never make mistakes … . The young … end up integrated into a world of adult values which are not to be questioned' (1983: 55). On the other hand, the carefree childhood of North America to which adults look back with nostalgia finds its most fitting expression, in Dorfman's opinion, in the films of Walt Disney, which are dominated by the 'infantilization of the adult' (ibid.: 55f.). Dorfman's assessment overlooks the fact that, parallel to the infantilization in popular culture, the maturing process is particularly central as a theme in the classics of American children's literature, not because of its civilizing effects but because it helps the individual to achieve independence and self-determination, even in opposition to society, as in the case of the outsider *Huckleberry Finn* (Twain 1884). Jerry Griswold claims to see an 'ur-story' (1992: xi) in the North American children's classics of the Golden Age of 1865–1914, in such books as *Little Women* (Alcott 1868), *The Adventures of Tom Sawyer* (Twain 1876), *The Wonderful Wizard of Oz* (Baum 1900) and *Rebecca of Sunnybrook Farm* (Wiggin 1903). In this 'ur-story' children symbolically overcome their parents and thus achieve independence. Childhood in general is of special cultural significance for the American self-image, according to Griswold, with Americans finding this archetypal childhood story, linked to the maturing process, particularly attractive due to their own political past:

> The recurring story of maturation in American children's books embodies and speaks directly to our own particular cultural experience and to

America's vision of itself: as a young country, always making itself anew, rebelling against authority, coming into its own, and establishing its own identity.

(ibid.: 242)

Comparative studies of the culture-specific nature of images of childhood entail the risk of presenting them as absolute, but they must always be related to changes in the history of a particular culture and to the simultaneous presence of different ideas of childhood. The concept of childhood in Germany, for instance, changed during the eighteenth century from the forward-looking, Utopian image of the Enlightenment to the backward-looking, mythologizing Romantic ideas critical of civilization. It cannot, however, be said that one tradition succeeded or eliminated the other: in their own way both concepts influenced the authors of subsequent generations. The twentieth-century author Erich Kästner, for instance, expressly saw himself as continuing in the Enlightenment tradition.

Status-relevant functions of children's literature

The educational status of children's literature, linked with the assessment of its socializing role, is particularly high at times when there are new values to be conveyed or old ones to be defended, as can be observed, for instance, in societies that find themselves in a phase of transition from traditional to modern. An example is the polarization of children's literature and literary criticism in Turkey, where two opposing factions compete for the attention of the children, the future of the nation. Zehra Ipsiroglu sees the strategies of one faction as a model for the other:

> Fundamentalist circles show us how literature for children and young people can be used for educational purposes. Individuals and groups seeking an alternative to fundamentalism and supporting modern education should proceed in a similar way, carefully choosing and offering to children thought-provoking works to provide motivation for emancipation and enlightened conduct.
>
> (trans. from Ipsiroglu 1992: 121)

In the struggle between educational concepts, translated children's literature plays an important part. The critical modernizers in Turkey want to see reforms introduced by means of modern, 'enlightened' children's literature, especially from Germany and Austria, while the fundamentalists, on the other hand, resist the excessive foreign influence of translations of children's classics, which make up over 80 per cent of the literature translated into Turkish. They want to see more books produced in Turkey itself to counter a takeover by other cultures.

Children's literature also gains esteem in pedagogical circles when it is enlisted to make a contribution to national education.[11] Children's literature in Hebrew rose in status at the beginning of the twentieth century because 'famous writers of literature for adults [saw] a national duty in the development of children's literature – an essential building block for the creation of the new nation in Palestine/Erez Israel – and [began] to write for that system themselves' (trans. from Shavit 1994: 14).

The most recent revaluation of children's literature in the culture of the Federal Republic of Germany was also connected with its function in society. The low opinion of children's literature that was the norm in Germany from the beginning of the nineteenth century was briefly raised at the end of the 1960s in the context of the student movement, with its sceptical attitude to the educational authorities, whom it identified as 'those chiefly responsible for the (re)production of authoritarian social structures by way of authoritarian character structures' (trans. from Steinlein 1996: 246). In the wake of this ideologically critical movement, there was an increased amount of discussion of education in general and children's literature specifically. The status of children's literature rose at this time not just in the realm of theory but also in the area of production, involving established and highly regarded creative figures and authors in the fields of adult culture and literature such as Heinrich Böll, Peter Hacks, Wolf Biermann and Peter Bichsel. Publishing houses that had never produced any books for children before founded children's lists and imprints. Children's culture and early forms of children's literature began to interest poets and anthologists such as Hans Magnus Enzensberger on both political and literary grounds (see his collection *Allerleirauh* [All sorts of things] (1961)). Christian Enzensberger published the first 'literary' translation of Lewis Carroll's *Alice's Adventures in Wonderland* in 1963, and the nonsense poet Edward Lear was discovered and translated by a number of German poets after a delay of almost a hundred years.[12] Thus, around 1968, children's books gained not only political but also a surprising amount of literary prestige. The avant-garde of '68, with its literary claims, revolutionized the understanding of the child reader in the German-speaking countries. Anna Katharina Ulrich wrote that they could do this 'only in their own, radical, non-didactic way, with an unpredictable short-circuit between the historical moment, their aesthetic programme and the child, which made "literature for children" appear a genuine area for topical, grown-up writing – a vessel for "adult literature" ' (trans. from Ulrich 1998a: 69).

What I have described here from a positive viewpoint – when authors from the more highly regarded system of adult literature turn to writing for children – can, in other circumstances, also indicate an absence of a specific children's literature with prestige of its own. The excessive public attention paid to those adult authors (or even celebrities) who have written a single children's book (and often not even a particularly good one)[13] frequently implies denigration of those authors who write 'only' children's literature.

In contexts where adult literature is strictly regulated, children's literature can appear in a new light, even acquiring a subversive function. Since it is a literary form subject to relatively little political censorship, it can become a forum for comments not tolerated in other areas, as two brief examples will show. To avoid the restrictions of the military government from 1964 onwards, Brazilian artists and intellectuals previously employed in radio, television, newspaper journalism, etc. but then barred as a result of censorship, found a new forum in the journal of children's literature *Recreio*, founded in 1969. They exploited the 'unfamiliar medium of the children's book to good effect' (trans. from Rutschmann 1992: 17). In the German Democratic Republic, too, children's literature offered many writers a freedom otherwise unavailable to them; it was not so closely observed by 'the Argus eyes of certain authorities ... which allowed it a certain licence and opened up a good deal of scope' (trans. from Peltsch 1990: 24). The first children's novel by the highly regarded writer, ornithologist and conservationist Wolf Spillner, for instance, *Gänse überm Reiherberg* [Geese over the Reiherberg] (Spillner 1977), developed from a newspaper article rejected for political reasons, about a local conflict between the conservation of greylag geese and economic interests. Reinbert Tabbert even speaks of the children's literature of the GDR as 'a kind of sanctuary for commitment to the ecological cause' (1992: 249).

At least in theory, the status accorded to children's literature in the Socialist countries of Europe was different from that in the capitalist societies. In a form of society where artistic literature, according to Karin Richter, was fundamentally understood 'as the organ of collective communication about social processes and individual stances' (trans. from 1996: 192), children's literature enjoyed equal rights as part of Socialist national literature. However, there was a rift between the declared and the real status of children's literature in public esteem. In 1956 the children's writer Alex Wedding pointed out the contradiction between the supposed parity of esteem, which was more in the nature of an official decree, and actual practice in the GDR, the main features of which were the lack of much literary criticism of children's books and the poor quality of what did exist, as well as the absence of any theory of children's literature. This assessment made in 1956 would, says Richter, 'still have been valid – in slightly modified form – in 1989' (ibid.: 196).

The development and promotion of children's literature depend on its educational and literary status in a given culture, and this domestic status can be of crucial importance for the international position of that literature beyond its own cultural borders. Joachim Heinrich Campe, Christian Felix Weisse and Christian Gotthilf Salzmann, leading children's authors of the German Enlightenment, at a time when the national prestige of children's literature was very high, formed a trio of writers who, in translation, influenced the development of other European children's literatures. Further internationally influential innovations in children's literature came from the pens of the Romantic authors Ludwig Tieck, Clemens Brentano and above all E.T.A. Hoffmann, whose literary fairy tales, a genre that consistently celebrated childhood and was thus in accord with the general literary developments of the time, also crossed the German-language border into other countries. None the less, according to Hans-Heino Ewers in his reconstruction of the lack of international attention paid to Germany after the early nineteenth century, one specifically German tradition steered the development of children's literature into a blind alley, a tradition that questioned, in principle, the necessity of a special literature for child readers (see Ewers 1997: 74). First formulated by the Grimm brothers, who saw traditional fairy tales as the ideal form of children's literature, it was later espoused by the educationalist Heinrich Wolgast who, with his reformist work *Das Elend unserer Jugendliteratur* [The miserable state of our children's literature] (1896), emphatically promoted, as suitable reading for children, a selected canon from adult literature. The result was the devaluation of a specific children's literature in German, with a consequent perceptible lowering of literary quality from the middle of the nineteenth century. The lost international prestige of German children's literature can be directly linked to this derogatory attitude towards a specific children's literature in Germany.

The international exchange of children's literature

Internationalism, international children's literature and international understanding through children's literature have been amongst the most important and widely used terms in children's literature discourse from the mid-1940s to the present day, but they frequently conceal the fact that there is no equal exchange of texts between all countries; rather, the border-crossing process is extremely imbalanced. Its direction is determined by political and economic factors as well as by the international status of the source language and culture. The following pages will take a closer look at geographical, cultural and economic aspects involved in the international exchange of children's literature.

According to Göte Klingberg, exchange between children's literatures occurs principally within groups of countries; he speaks of geographical regions of literature for children and young people within which a lively exchange takes place: 'Some of these regions have a long history behind them and are moulded by old political, economic and cultural links' (Klingberg 1986: 39). Shifts can occur: the partition of Germany, for instance, led to the fact that the GDR and the Federal Republic found themselves in different regions. Broadly, Klingberg divides Europe into 'a Western region, with exchanges between the English, German, French, Dutch and Scandinavian languages, and an Eastern region with exchanges between the Slavonic languages (especially Russian), Hungarian, and (East) German' (ibid.). He places the United States alongside Western Europe in the Western (or north-western) region, a classification confirmed by analysis of the origins of translations published in the USA.[14] Klingberg also speaks of a 'Southern European Romance language region' and a Far Eastern region, and maintains that the degree of 'foreignness' involved in exchange within the various regions is not so great as when there is exchange between regions.

Exchange between countries within the regions, however, is in fact as imbalanced as it is between the regions themselves. The international book trade is dominated by the north-west European and North American region. A glance at the countries of the Far Eastern region makes one wonder if it is appropriate to group them in one broad category. In Indonesia, for instance, since the country achieved independence in 1945 after centuries of Dutch colonial rule and the

Japanese occupation between 1942 and 1945, the development and expansion of the book market was made possible chiefly by American support, both financial and ideological. A glance at the languages from which books are translated shows English in the dominant position. The statistics provided by the UNESCO *Index Translationum* database[15] show that, of the top ten original languages translated into Indonesian since 1977, English leads with around 75 per cent, followed by Arabic (16 per cent), French (5.5 per cent), Dutch (5 per cent) and German (3.5 per cent). Only a single Asian language, Japanese, features on this list, representing fewer than 1 per cent of the translations; the category 'various languages', which might include other Asian ones, accounts for less than 0.5 per cent. With these figures in mind, one can hardly speak of Indonesia's belonging to a Far Eastern literary region of any kind, if intensive exchange is one of the criteria for membership. The absence of translations from one major Asian language can be explained politically: after 1965 all contact – including literary contact – with the People's Republic of China was broken off (as it was with all other Communist countries). Here membership of a political bloc takes precedence over a sense of belonging to a geographical and cultural region.

The situation in Japan also casts doubt on the validity of the thesis that exchange takes place mainly within regions. The statistics on translation provided by *Index Translationum* show that only two Asian languages feature in the list of top ten languages translated into Japanese since 1970, Chinese in fifth position and Korean in seventh. English tops the list, accounting for over 80 per cent, followed by French, German and Russian.[16] These imports from the West, however, are far from being reciprocated by translations from the Japanese in Western countries.

The economic dimension: a historic example

The exchange of children's books almost always goes hand in hand with economic factors; the status of a literature can often be described by reference to commercial and cultural links. If we were to trace these links in detail, we would need full documentation of all translated literature, something that at present exists only for Sweden, thanks to the work of Göte Klingberg and Ingar Bratt. In a study partly based on Klingberg's figures, the distribution of translated children's literature in Sweden for the period 1870 to 1950 was analysed by Lars Furuland (1978). In the 1970s, 75 per cent of all translated books for young people came from Britain and America. Children's literature in English, according to Furuland, became established as the leading source for translations in Sweden in the middle of the nineteenth century, thus taking over a position previously occupied by German-language children's literature. At that time, German was the language of most of the important religious children's books, and geographical proximity also played a part. The middle of the nineteenth century saw a sharp increase in literary production in Great Britain. A wide domestic reading public of both children and adults had developed, influenced by demographic growth and the extension of schooling. Technological developments which made paper and printing available at reasonable prices meant that reading material could be inexpensively produced. Other factors, such as the development and extension of the railway network from the 1840s onwards and the advent of the W.H. Smith station bookstalls, contributed to a massive expansion in the production of journals and novels. The expansion of the literary market led to works of literature – particularly novels – becoming goods for export.

In parallel with the increasing production of English children's literature, particularly fantasies, in the middle of the nineteenth century Swedish trade generally moved closer to that of Great Britain (see Furuland 1978). England became a major customer of the Swedish timber industry and played a not inconsiderable part in the industrialization of agrarian Sweden. The English novel of the nineteenth century, from Dickens to mass-market literature, was increasingly distributed among the middle classes of Sweden, and not there alone. From the mid-nineteenth century onwards, French and German publishing houses competing in the international market were only rarely able to challenge the domination of the Swedish market by literature in English (ibid.: 65). The dominant position of Great Britain in the literary export market, therefore, is connected with its early industrialization, which gave it a head start in literary production and brought with it the development of a mass-market reading public at home and, above all, the distribution of literature through trade channels.

Translations in Europe and the USA

The proportion of translations in developed children's literatures varies greatly, ranging from 1 per cent to around 80 per cent. Those countries that export the most also import the least: they are Great Britain and the USA, the mighty leaders in the production tables of children's literature. The proportion of translations published in Great Britain in recent years is between 2.5 and 4 per cent; it peaked in the 1970s at 5 per cent. It is estimated to be between 1 and 2 per cent in the USA.[17] In 1994 the publisher Klaus Flugge said regretfully of the situation in Great Britain:

> Over the last few years ... the British children's book market has changed. I feel the British have more or less turned their backs on foreign books for children and, to my regret, the number of translations I publish has diminished to one or two, in a list of at least forty titles a year. You may be surprised to know that this is more than most publishers. The reason for this is not so much that British editors or publishers don't read foreign languages or don't want to spend money on translations but simply that there is a lack of interest in this country in anything foreign.
>
> (Flugge 1994: 209f.)

The author Aidan Chambers, co-founder of the imprint Turton & Chambers in 1989, which specifically published translations and was unfortunately, and probably for that very reason, short-lived, writes about the resistance to translations in Britain and America. He cites the children's publisher Dorothy Briley, who remarked how the words 'Translated from the ...' on the title page of a book are 'code for "admire but don't buy it" ' (Chambers 2001: 114). In general, translated books are a greater publishing risk than books written by English-language authors. Chambers criticizes how 'the British are becoming more insular, less connected to others, less able to appreciate what other people produce and think and envision than they ever were' (quoted in Flugge 1994: 210), which is why, in his opinion, British children need greater exposure to translations, if this tendency is to be reversed. However, fewer translations than ever are being published. Most cultural commentators agree that the kind of cultural narrow-mindedness which leads to the exclusion of works translated from other languages in Britain and the USA 'is a form of cultural poverty and testifies to a lack of imagination in an information-rich world' (Stahl 1992: 19).[18]

The situation in Finland, with a proportion of translations of about 80 per cent, can be seen as the opposite of that in Great Britain; the proportion is also very high in the other Scandinavian countries. Figures in the Netherlands and Italy are both above 40 per cent, and in Germany around 30 per cent (in all these countries well over 80 per cent of translations are from English). Since Germany is the third-largest producer of literature for children, there are in absolute figures more translated titles from other languages in Germany than anywhere else, and consequently German has often been, and still is, an intermediate language through which authors writing in 'minority languages' have a better chance of gaining international recognition once they are translated.

How is it that the proportion of translations in children's literature can vary between 1 per cent and 80 per cent, even within the north-west European and American region? What factors influence whether and how much literature is translated into a specific language? One of these can be the state of development of children's literature. The proportion of translations is particularly high in cultures where a literary tradition is being established. The 80 per cent proportion of translations of children's literature in Finland has to do with the status and situation of a literature which cannot look back on a long tradition of writing in its own language. Modern Hebrew children's literature, which was beginning to develop in Palestine/Erez Israel at the beginning of the twentieth century (see Shavit 1994: 10), also endeavoured to enrich and extend itself by importing titles from other countries. However, the number of translations decreased there in proportion to indigenous literary development. In 1961, 700 titles were translated into Hebrew, in 1979 the number was 450, in 1983 it fell to 250 (ibid.). After the qualitative upswing and commercial success of Brazilian children's literature in the late 1970s, the number of translations also began to fall (see Rutschmann 1992: 17). This observation points to one of the factors which can be significant, but should not lead to the conclusion that the fledgling state of development of a literature is the exclusive explanation for the fact that it translates profusely. Literatures with a rich and long-standing tradition, such as the Swedish, can serve as a contrasting example.

Certain situations of need can also lead to a readiness to accept translations, for instance in post-war Germany, where, after more than a decade of cultural isolation, a special urge was felt to catch up with literary developments from abroad, and the internationalist spirit of the time there encouraged increased translation activity. Influential, too, are general marketing factors, which are led by factors such as how easy it is to sell the translated books and whether they fill gaps in the market or serve a special interest, and so on.

If we move from the openness or otherwise of the target literatures (into which the books are translated) to focus on the source literatures (from which the books originate), we can ask what determines the fact that books in a specific language are or are not translated. Here the following influential factors can be named:

- Knowledge of the *source language* among culturally creative figures in the target culture (translators, editors), and the presence and commitment of *scouts*, whose part as intermediaries cannot be overestimated. Hitomi Wakabayashi (1990) gave as the reason why hardly any Japanese children's books are translated into German that, while she could name over twenty Japanese translators of children's books from German, she knew of only one German translator working on Japanese children's literature. The problems, she thought, were first that few Germans knew any Japanese, and second the poor payment of literary translators. In addition, the translation of children's literature is even more poorly paid than the translation of adult literature, which again pays considerably less than the translation of technical texts. The comparatively small number of translators from the Japanese work in the better-paid commercial or technical field.

- *International relations* and *membership of political blocs*. Until recently these played a decisive part in exchange between the Socialist and non-Socialist states of Europe, for two reasons. Ideologically, Socialist children's literature was intended to serve the further development of society in the spirit of Socialist realism; suitable models could therefore come mainly from politically allied states. The other reason was economic: the Socialist states of Eastern Europe, as trading partners, engaged in an exchange of children's literature. Books from countries in the same bloc were more affordable than books from the capitalist countries, for which hard currency had to be paid. In the 1970s, therefore, the proportion of children's books translated from English in the children's literature of West Germany had its East German parallel in the shape of translated literature from the Soviet Union. While the preponderance of American and English books was followed in West Germany by books from the French and Dutch, Polish and Hungarian translations took second and third place among translations in the GDR.

- *Confessional aspects*, which in Europe now tend to be of solely historical significance. The historic opposition between Catholic and Protestant countries and cultures was reflected not only in the different treatment of religious material (saints' lives and little Catechisms for Catholics, Bible stories for

Protestant children), but also in different moral concepts and ideas of individual responsibility. In line with this, confessional aspects played a part in decisions on what should or should not be translated:

> The opposition of Catholicism and Protestantism ... has determined ... the policy of publishers and translation zones. ... The Spanish translated *Fabiola*, a novel by an English (but Catholic) cardinal, and the French gave a warm welcome to the many little stories by the very Catholic Canon Schmid. On the other hand, it is to a Swiss publisher (Mignot of Lausanne) that we owe the first French translation (1872) of *Little Women*, an American novel in the tradition of John Bunyan's *The Pilgrim's Progress*, that classic of English Protestant culture, before Hetzel, a 'lay' French publisher, himself translated the same novel in 1880 under the title of *Les Quatres filles du docteur March*.
>
> (trans. from Nières 1992:12)

- The *relationships between countries*. The influence of such connections is evident in the transfer of literature from Germany to Israel. Scarcely anything was translated from German into Hebrew in the four decades after the Holocaust (see Shavit 1994: 21). In the field of children's literature, there was a great gulf between translations of Erich Kästner in the 1930s and Peter Härtling in the 1980s.
- And not least there is the *subsidizing of translations*, including translations of children's literature, for instance by cultural funds in Belgium, the Netherlands and Israel, which promote translation from their own languages.

The imbalance of international exchange

> You will not find a single country that does not admire, even sometimes more than its own best books, books that come from the four quarters of the globe. ... Smilingly the pleasant books of childhood cross all frontiers; there is no duty to be paid on inspiration.
>
> (Hazard 1944: 147)

Hazard's high-flown concept of children's literature transcending borders may have inspired ideas of internationalism in the discourse on books for children, but it ignores the actual conditions of production and transfer. The international exchange of children's literature is not well balanced, and different countries and regions participate in it to a greatly varying extent. The direction in which borders are crossed is not determined solely by the international status of the source language and culture, but also by political and economic factors: the world of children's literature can be divided into exporting and importing countries. The countries that 'give' (export) the most also 'receive' (import) the least: they are Great Britain and the USA. At the other end of the scale are those countries that almost exclusively import children's literature and produce little or none of it themselves – for instance certain Asian and African countries. They provide a market for the global corporations. The postulated internationalism of children's literature proves to be a European and North American perspective: 'We too hastily confer the status of "international children's books" on our own [American] works that have attracted a worldwide following. ... This makes it easy to project our own assumptions about quality out into the world, never stopping to let the rest of the world speak to us' (Garrett 1996: 3).

The children's literature that is internationally distributed and read is that of the north-western region: 'The great powers of children's books are serving not only themselves but a large portion of the rest of the world' (Ørvig 1981: 232). Books from the 'North' are exported, more or less unthinkingly, to the countries of Africa, Asia and Latin America, a fact that has only recently attracted criticism. 'Beautifully packaged poison' is the way the Nigerian writer Chinua Achebe described the books from abroad that African children are given to read. 'This poison contains nothing that has to do with the environment of African children' (trans. from Schär 1994: 3). According to figures provided by the Baobab Children's Book Foundation,[19] 70 to 90 per cent of books available to reading children in non-European/American cultures – the precise percentage depends on the continent – are by European or American authors. Conversely, however, the children's literature of the so-called developing countries hardly ever reaches a European public, and 80 per cent of all books for children and young people set in non-European cultures are written not by authors from those countries themselves but by European or North American writers (see Kinderbuchfonds Baobab 2003). There is an increasing awareness that it is of no little significance whether a country or culture is written about from an insider perspective and this has been made available through translation, or whether it is authored from the outside, and the discussion of colonial and neocolonial writing has increased the awareness of issues involving what Roderick McGillis calls those 'more written about than writing, more spoken about than speaking' (1999: xxi).

A reason often given for the non-translation of certain books, or of the entire literature of a certain cultural area, is that they are too foreign for children to understand. The Brazilian writer Ana Maria Machado has indicated the unconvincing and relative nature of this argument, pointing out that the willingness to accept foreignness in literature is a very one-sided affair:

> The criteria for translations elude my understanding, but I have often encountered the attitude of translators who say: 'This is a great book, but our European children won't understand it.' I always feel very sorry for those children, since Brazilian children read European books too. After all, the children of Europe are not stupid.
>
> (trans. from Mähne and Rouvel 1994: 9)

There is similar criticism from the East, where the example of Japan shows that there is no automatic equation between economic power and the export of children's literature.[20] Since imports of literature from the West are far from being reciprocated by translations from the Japanese, Kyoto Matsuoka made the following appeal in 1996:

> I would like to put a request to Western publishers. Have more faith in your children, and don't be so anxious to preserve them from anything foreign when you translate books from the East. Today few Japanese books are translated, and I cannot help noticing how the editors of Western publishing houses avoid confronting their readers with anything foreign because they believe they are making it easier for them to understand books that way.
>
> (trans. from Matsuoka 1996: 12)

These statements clearly illustrate the different criteria for the comprehensibility of another culture and the perception of what is foreign. In this case, anything one doesn't want to become engaged with is said to be foreign, and avoidance of any exchange is founded on this foreignness.

Western classics

The development of an indigenous book trade and literature, including children's literature, is often undermined in the so-called developing countries by the dominance of imported products, particularly literature in English. Western literature in translated and revised form, especially the 'classics', which can be produced without much trouble or expense, tends to drive out domestic production: 'The traditional classics of Western literature have been translated and published over and over again [in Indonesia] by different publishers. In a developing country this is wasteful of precious capital' (Sunindyo 1980: 53). In the 1960s, according to Klaus Doderer, the Grimms' fairy tales were the most widely distributed works of children's literature in the Congo; in China it was Johanna Spyri's *Heidi* (see Doderer 1986). In a fairy-tale competition for children in Ecuador, almost 80 per cent of the entries did not qualify 'because they were only adapted versions of [European] fairy-tales or Wild West films' (trans. from Adoum 1983: 56). The influence of the tales of the Brothers Grimm is evident in the South American Indian tales of Latin America, which describe princesses as white-skinned (ibid.). European characteristics, according to Doderer (1992: 227), are attributed to anyone rich and distinguished.

A glance at a country such as Turkey will show that the constant and recurrent presence of classics on the literary market is a matter not of literary aesthetics but solely of market mechanisms. Unlike oral narrative with its traditional characters and themes, and folk and children's drama, children's literature in book form does not have a long, established tradition in Turkey. The number of genuinely new publications is correspondingly small. The market for printed children's literature is largely dominated by the so-called classics, since no royalties have to be paid for these titles, and they enjoy the bonus of prestige and familiarity independently of the character of the version concerned. On the Turkish market in 1994, for instance, there were twenty-three editions of *Tom*

Sawyer, twenty of *Pinocchio*, nineteen of *Robinson Crusoe*, nineteen of *Pollyanna*, sixteen of *Treasure Island*, thirteen of *Ali Baba and the Forty Thieves*, twelve of *Alice in Wonderland*, ten of *Five Weeks in a Balloon*, ten of *The Bremen Town Musicians*, and seven of *Uncle Tom's Cabin* (see Erdogan 1994: 576). The majority of these were 'simple – unfortunately often extremely simple – adaptations ... , badly distorted in some editions' (trans. from Schneehorst 1994: 580).

There are thus problems in assuming that children's literature as a whole and particularly its classics are truly international, since genuine cultural transfer or exchange is often equated or confused with an international book market. In addition, children's literature in translated and adapted form, as the example of that classic of children's literature *Pinocchio* will show in Chapter 6, develops a life of its own: the culture-specific educational, moral, aesthetic and literary norms of the books concerned are more or less thoroughly assimilated.

The reality of border crossing by children's literature therefore stands in glaring contrast to Hazard's ideal of world literature for children, promoting the free exchange of the best from all countries into all countries, with the aim, above and beyond that of aesthetic enrichment, of what would be described today as intercultural tolerance. This idealistic position has been criticized, and not just in the discourse of postcolonialism. As early as 1968 the librarian Anne Pellowski, who was enthusiastic in her commitment to international children's literature, expressed her doubts about the existence of a truly international dimension in the exchange of children's literature:

> There has been a tremendous increase in the number of translations and exchanges, but the greatest proportion has involved the dozen or so countries which produce three-fourths of the world's books. Exchanges among these countries are not to be disparaged, because there is as much need for understanding among them as there is anywhere else. Yet might it not be true that the commercial and governmental channels are so taken up with the volume of materials to be contended with from these dozen countries, that they have no time, patience or resources left to explore sufficiently the possibilities of exchange with their neighboring nations and with others passing through the same phases of development? Are the private and governmental publishers too concerned with the profits (both monetary and ideological) of exchange, to the detriment of quality? Is there sufficient exchange between the economically advanced and the developing countries, or is this pretty much a one-way passage? What can possibly be the results of world education which relies on so few countries for its textbooks and materials? Will it work for the common good and for mutual understanding or will it rather stifle the creative impulse to search for new and better forms? The massive programs of international aid in the production of reading and teaching materials would do well to consider these questions more carefully.
>
> (Pellowski 1968: 10f.)

4 Children's literature in translation

There is a paradox at the heart of the translation of children's literature: it is commonly held that books are translated in order to enrich the children's literature of the target language and to introduce children to foreign cultures,[1] yet at the same time that foreign element itself is often eradicated from translations which are heavily adapted to their target culture, allegedly on the grounds that young readers will not understand it. The translation of children's literature is thus a balancing act between the adaptation of foreign elements to the child reader's level of comprehension, and preservation of the differences that constitute a translated foreign text's potential for enrichment of the target culture. The actual decisions made in this zone of conflicting aims by editors and translators depend on their assessment of child readers: how, and how far, should they convey elements from the source literature that are new and (as yet) unknown, factors that are linguistically and culturally foreign?

From translation theory to translation studies

The study of translation has always been approached from the viewpoint of various different disciplines. *Philosophical* debates on translatability, such as those to be found in George Steiner's *After Babel* (1975), set out not from concrete texts so much as from a hermeneutic concept of language. In the traditional, source-oriented *literary* approach, *a priori* assumptions about fidelity and equivalence dominated. These normative, prescriptive and essentialistic theories took their guidelines from the question of 'how should/must one translate?'; they attempted to convey the principles and rules of good, 'correct' translation. Functionalist approaches centred on how information is communicated and responses produced may be found in *applied linguistics*, particularly by those who train translators of technical, commercial and official documents (see Hönig and Kussmaul 1982, Reiss and Vermeer 1984, and Snell-Hornby 1986). Although not primarily relevant to literary translation, some of these do relate to literary texts, for instance Katharina Reiss's typology of texts,[2] and, building on that, Reiss and Vermeer's *skopos* theory (1984), a reception-based model which focuses on the purpose or function of a text and its textual realization in translation.

The end of the 1970s saw the emergence of a new approach which presented itself as a way of going beyond the prevailing literary-cum-philosophical and linguistic models criticized retrospectively by Edwin Gentzler as follows:

> The two dominant modes of research in the field of translation through the seventies were those focused on primarily literary concerns, rejecting theoretical presuppositions, normative rules, and linguistic jargon, and those focused on linguistic matters, claiming a 'scientific' approach and rejecting alogical solutions and subjective speculations. Both sides limited the kinds of texts they addressed to show their methodologies to best advantage.
>
> (Gentzler 1993: 74)

It had become increasingly clear to scholars of translation that the whole subject area 'must be placed on a new basis, so that reliable information can be gained about what is actually present in existing translations' (trans. from Frank 1988: 198). The successful new approach, which saw itself as empirical and descriptive, soon became known by the name of 'translation studies'. The initial theory upon which it was based was the polysystem theory of Itamar Even-Zohar, which embraces all literary systems from the canon of 'great' literature to non-canonized forms such as popular fiction and recognizes the importance of 'the impact of translations and their role in the synchrony and diachrony of a certain literature' (Even-Zohar 1978: 15). Translation studies was promoted in particular by three linked centres, the Catholic University of Leuven, the University of Amsterdam and the University of Tel Aviv; later the Göttingen Research Group associated itself with them. This approach was really established with the publication in 1985 of *The Manipulation of Literature*, edited by Theo Hermans. Although the contributions to his volume did not add up to a distinct school, says Hermans in his introduction, they shared an aim and a basic orientation:

> A view of literature as a complex and dynamic system; a conviction that there should be a continual interplay between theoretical models and practical case studies; an approach to literary translation which is descriptive, target-oriented, functional and systemic; and an interest in the norms and constraints that govern the production and reception of translations, in the relation between translation and other types of text processing, and in the place and role of translations both within a given literature and in the interaction between literatures.
>
> (Hermans 1985b: 10f.)

The central questions of translation studies, underlining the methodological shift from source orientation to target orientation, are: WHAT has been translated WHEN, WHY and HOW, and WHY was it translated in this way? (see Kittel 1988: 160). The descriptive study of translation attempts to identify those dominant norms of the target language and literature that have influenced the translator's strategies and decisions. In addition, it aims to explain what place is occupied by translations at what time in the polysystem of the target culture, and the influence of translated works in their new environment. These new questions and guidelines meant that the field of translation analysis was opened up, for 'any and all phenomena relating to translation, in the broadest sense, become objects of study' (Hermans 1985b: 14). Thus translation studies deals with all aspects of the conditions of translation *and* reception, blurring the distinction between the modern study of translation and the older and once clearly separate areas of reception and contact studies; the history of translation becomes cultural history.

Translation studies has constantly expanded since the mid-1980s, taking up a variety of discourses in the process to become, at the beginning of the new millennium, what Lawrence Venuti calls 'an international network of scholarly communities who conduct research and debate across conceptual and disciplinary divisions' (2000: 334). Precise descriptions of translated texts and translation processes are linked to cultural and political issues such as gender, colonialism and globalization. The impact of psychoanalysis, gender studies and postcolonialism has made theorists more aware of the hierarchies and exclusions in language use, pointing to the ideological effects of translation and to the economic and political interests served by it. With the multiplication of theoretical approaches to translation, its study, in Venuti's words, 'now fragments into subspecialities within the growing discipline of translation studies' (ibid.: 333). Those working in translation studies see the relationship between their own discipline and comparative literature, which they perceive to be facing increasing problems of legitimization, as a reversal of the traditional hierarchy: 'The revised view of the translation–comparative literature position makes translation studies the principal discipline, with comparative literature as an important branch of that discipline' (Bassnett-McGuire 1991: 136). Such a debatable demarcation of special fields that would seem inevitable when such 'paradigm changes' occur is perhaps less relevant here than the question of whether the change of viewpoint gives us new insights into the translation of children's literature.

The traditional study of translation barely considered children's literature. In 1982 Katharina Reiss noticed, with surprise: 'For centuries critics have been concerned with both the theory and the practice of the complicated and complex phenomenon of translation, but scarcely anything has been said about the translation of books for children and young people' (trans. from Reiss 1982: 7). Reiss looks seriously at the subject by attempting to identify the specific problems of the translation of children's literature in the context of her typology of texts. She names three factors which justify its needing a special kind of study:

1   'the ... asymmetry of the entire translation process: ... adults are translating works written by adults for children and young people' (ibid.);
2   the agency of intermediaries who exert pressure on the translator to observe taboos or follow educational principles (ibid.: 8); and
3   'children's and young people's (still) limited knowledge of the world and experience of life' (ibid.).

In 1993 Riitta Oittinen still found that: 'As to translation of children's literature and its theoretical basis, little research has been conducted on this subject world-wide' (1993: 11). Ten years later she was the editor of a double volume of the translators' journal *META* which encompassed twenty-five contributions on translation for children by scholars from sixteen European, North and South American and African countries with backgrounds in children's literature, linguistics and translation studies. This volume indicates that the subject of translating for children is now firmly on the map.[3]

Around the time Reiss was writing, children's literature and its translation were attracting increasing attention both within and outside of children's literature studies. One of the pioneers of the subject in the first group, Göte Klingberg, coedited a first volume of contributions in 1978, a documentation of the third symposium of the IRSCL on *Children's Books in Translation* (Klingberg, Ørvig and Amor 1978). In his pragmatic study *Children's Fiction in the Hands of the Translators* (Klingberg 1986) he argues that the integrity of the original work must be touched upon as little as possible and categorizes what he regards as typical deviations from the source text. Within the context of translation studies at the semiotic school at Tel Aviv University, Gideon Toury (1980) explicitly included children's literature in his theoretical writings and case studies as a field where various translation practices can be observed in the area outside the canon, while Zohar Shavit showed how decisions made in the course of translation are determined by the position of children's books in the literary polysystem. Because of the marginal situation of texts for children, translators can be very free with them, unhesitatingly adapting them to models already present in the target system. However, Shavit says

> the translators can manipulate the texts in various other ways only as long as they adhere to guiding principles rooted in the self-image of children's literature:
>
> a)   adjusting the text in order to make it appropriate and useful to the child, in accordance with what society thinks is 'good for the child';
> b)   adjusting the plot, characterization and language to the child's level of comprehension and his reading abilities.
>
> (Shavit 1981: 172)

The first principle dominated in the children's literature of north-west Europe as long as it was regarded primarily as an educational instrument; today the second is more likely to be dominant (see ibid.).

In the early 1990s three contributions to the issue of *Poetics Today* devoted to children's literature showed how far-reaching the analysis of translated children's literature could be in the context of the polysystem theory and the extended discipline of translation studies. The essays describe the influence exerted on literary translation by the literary, social, political and educational norms of the target culture. Those norms (leaving aside the literary ones) are traced by Richard Wunderlich (1992) in his examination of the American versions of Collodi's *Pinocchio*, graphically illustrating the interaction of children's literature with norms from other systems by means of many examples, subjects and facts (for more details see Chapter 6). Nitsa Ben-Ari (1992) analysed paratexts of translations (titles, blurbs, prefaces, etc.) to elucidate what they reveal about why the text was translated, about the model in the target literature which stood sponsor to the translation, and about the position the translation was meant to occupy in the target literature, while Basmat Even-Zohar investigated the stylistic norms of Hebrew children's literature in translations of Astrid Lindgren, describing the prevailing linguistic norms as 'elevated literary language: rich, elaborate, standardized, based upon historical scripts' (Even-Zohar 1992: 232).[4]

The range of theoretical issues and corpora examined has expanded further to include such diverse areas as readability (cf. Puurtinen 1994 or Dollerup 2003), tense and translation (cf. Lathey 2003), ideological factors (cf. Thomson-Wohlgemuth 2003) and censorship in translation (cf. Craig 2001), the interaction of image and text in the translation of picture books (cf. O'Sullivan 1999 and Oittinen 2003), or how the stratification into sub-genres of differential status is linked to translating practice (Desmet 2002).

A child-centred theory of translation

In her dissertation on the translation of children's literature, the most extensive theoretical contribution to the subject yet written, Riitta Oittinen (1993 and 2000)[5] makes a point of speaking of 'translating for children', not of the 'translation of children's literature'; she concentrates exclusively on the child reader, disputing any authority for the text. She blends Bakhtin's category of dialogics and Louise Rosenblatt's transaction theory of reception aesthetics with a functionalist translation concept which says that a translation should be a 'functionally correct target text linked to an existing source text in variously specified ways, depending on the desired or required function of the target text (translation *skopos*)' (trans. from Nord 1991: 31).

In a successful translation, as Oittinen sees it, the reader of the target text, the author of the source text and the translator are engaged in a dialogue: 'if the "I" of the reader of the translation meets the "you" of the translator, the author, the illustrator, it is a good translation in that particular situation' (Oittinen 1993: 95). Oittinen frequently points out that child readers can be determined only relatively according to their period, culture and situation, but at the same time writes in general terms about the 'other' – carnivalistic – culture of childhood and 'the child' as reader. The child about whom she is writing and for whom she translates (rightly stressing the particular part played by a translator's image of childhood in the address of the translation) is a 'wise and able child with a carnivalistic culture of her/his own', 'a child to be respected, to be listened to, a child who is able to choose' (ibid.: 29). It is a construct, a Utopian idea of what children are capable of in ideal conditions.[6]

In the dialogic structure of the translation process, Oittinen believes the translator must not just project and speak, but must also listen, 'join the children and dive into their carnival, not teaching them but learning from them' (ibid.: 34). The translator owes loyalty to the author, according to Oittinen, not to the source text. She considers that the translator has been loyal to the author of the source text, if readers accept and enjoy the translation. She thus reduces the possible functions of children's literature to a single one: the target text – in whatever form – must appeal to readers.

For all her rejection of authority, Oittinen's design is ultimately prescriptive; taking her understanding of childhood and view of dialogics as her points of departure, she tells translators how to translate for children:

> Translation is in many ways a covenant. The translator of children's litera-ture *should reach out* to the children of her/his culture. The translator *should dive* into the carnivalistic children's world, reexperience it. Even if she/he cannot stop being an adult, to succeed she/he *should try* to reach into the realm of childhood, the children around her/him, the child in her/himself. This reaching into the carnivalistic world of children, this reaching out to children without the fear of relinquishing one's own authority, is dialogics. When translating for children, we *should listen* to the child, the child in the neighborhood and the child within ourselves.
>
> (ibid.: 183; emphasis added)

In the context of the discussion of children's literature, Oittinen deserves credit for indicating the role and importance of the individual translator's image of childhood, and for focusing on important aspects of children's reading – for instance, their somatic and physical relation to language – as well as on condi-tions and elements of children's reception. Her attempt to disregard the potential conflict between absolutely child-centred translation and loyalty to the author of the source text, instead seeing the one as an expression of the other, may be a bold move, but it overlooks too many aspects of the complex field of children's literature to be accepted unreservedly as a generally valid theory of its translation. Oittinen's analysis concentrates mainly on translations of books for children of pre-school age – picture books and stories for reading aloud – but she stresses that her theory can be applied to children's literature as a whole. Ultimately her approach suffers from this assumption that all children's literature is homogeneous, for not only is it addressed to a wide range of age-groups, it also encompasses different forms (such as picture books) and genres (drama, poetry, non-fiction, etc.), and, within these, sub-genres of different status (series literature, for instance) as well as a wide variety of functions and types of textual usage. Oittinen's approach, therefore, is too indiscriminate to be an all-embracing theory for children's literature and translation.

A functionalist and narratological approach

A theory of the translation of children's literature must take account of the various ways of transmitting and using children's literature discussed in Chapter 2, and assess texts and their translations according to their textual practice – whether it is in the nature of written oral transmission, popular literature or quality literature. Once such distinctions are drawn, a text with a functional character cannot be discussed and judged as if it were primarily an aesthetic text, while conversely aesthetic criteria will be prominent in the discussion of texts written by the rules of the textual practice of literature. Distinguishing between types of texts and their functions is a meaningful extension of a functionalist theory of the translation of children's literature. Seen from this angle, translators of 'literary' source texts are faithful to the texts or loyal to their authors only if the full aesthetic dimension is conveyed in translation. In such a functionalist approach, for instance, one could and indeed should distinguish between texts with aesthetic claims, texts defined by their degree of linguistic difficulty and their function of promoting literacy (for instance, children's first reading books), where, due to the limited vocabulary of target readers, ease of comprehension is the prime function, and texts in which content is more important than form, for instance information books.[7]

A productive example of such a distinction can be found in Mieke Desmet's analysis of English narrative fiction for girls translated into Dutch, in which she focuses on its internal stratification according to differential status. She discusses how novels belonging to separate text types – formula fiction series, classics and award-winning novels – perform different functions, and shows how they are translated accordingly. The translations of award-winning texts demonstrate 'a tendency to preserve as much as possible of the aesthetic quality of the ST [source text]' (Desmet 2002: 264), while the practices evident in translations of formula fiction reveal a primary 'concern for the enjoyment of the reader and his/her understanding of the text' (ibid: 265).

Another feature particularly useful in the development of a theory of translation is an extension of Bakhtin's theorem of dialogics that does not see the dialogue, as Oittinen does, solely as interaction between the persons involved in literary communication but, like Bakhtin himself, regards the presence of several voices as a feature of the narrative text. Bakhtin distinguishes between two forms of novel, the monologic and the polyphonic. In the former the author (Bakhtin's term) always has the last word, his voice remains dominant and organizing and the protagonist (or hero, as Bakhtin calls him) can only act, experience, think and perceive exclusively within the limits of his clearly defined character. The quality of the relationship between implied author or narrator and figure is entirely different in the polyphonic novel (Bakhtin credits Dostoevsky with its invention), in which the voice of the hero is allowed to stand full and unmerged in its own right (see Bakhtin 1984a).

I would like to identify this Bakhtinian concept of dialogics as a feature of translation. Every translation contains several voices – the voices of the characters in the story, the voice of the narrator of the source text, and the voice of the translator. It incorporates the presence of the implied translator, which I shall expound in terms of narratological theory in Chapter 5, a phenomenon basic to every translation which can be identified on the level of paratextual explanations as 'the translator', and on the level of the narrative text as the narrator of the translation. Dialogical translation is, accordingly, when the translator tries to allow not only the unavoidable presence of his or her own voice to be heard in the text, but also the various other voices as they were heard in the original. We have monologic translation, on the other hand, where the translator controls the source text by allowing the narrator of the translation to explain and elucidate everything down to the last detail, removing potential challenges to the reader made by the implied author of the original, even to the point of drowning out the narrator of the source text entirely.

In analysing translations of children's literature, it is extremely important to take account of the presence and weight given to the various voices of a translated text, so that what has so far often been only vaguely perceived as 'intervention' or 'change' in the translation can be defined in terms of narratological theory. I shall substantiate this point more closely in theoretical terms in Chapter 5, illustrating my thesis with examples from translations. As an introduction to the subject, however, it will be necessary to analyse the effects of linguistic and cultural norms on decisions made in the process of translating children's literature. It is in relation to these norms that the contextual conditions should be understood within which the translator's voice can be heard, to varying degrees, in the text.

The influence of cultural and linguistic norms in translation

An analysis of the values and norms conveyed in children's literature has to address both the extra-textual context of mediation and the intra-textual communication that can be directly altered through the translation process. A critique of the translation of children's literature must ask how the culture-specific norms present in the text affect decisions made in translation. Answers may be found on two levels of the narrative: the story (*what* is being told – incidents, characters, objects, locations, etc.) and its discourse (*how* it is told). Shifts may occur on both levels in translation; those on the level of the story will be analysed in the following pages, those on the level of the discourse in the next chapter.

Every text conveys norms or, as John Stephens writes, 'a narrative without an ideology is unthinkable; ideology is formulated in and by language, meanings within language are socially determined, and narratives are constructed out of language' (1992: 8). In children's literature, this is particularly clear in texts where norms and values are explicitly transmitted and the educational factor predominates – for instance in the cautionary tales and verses of the eighteenth and nineteenth centuries,[8] or more recently in what are called 'issue books' on subjects such as drug abuse. Social structures and ideas, however, are also communicated in books that have no obvious claim to be setting a moral example.

Of the types of ideology identified by Peter Hollindale, it is easiest to detect 'the explicit social, political or moral beliefs of the individual writer' (1988: 12). An example is the propagation of progressive ideas and attitudes in the 'anti-authoritarian' children's literature of Germany in the 1970s.[9] Next to these explicit beliefs stand the less easily perceived implicit and unquestioned assumptions made by authors (which Hollindale calls 'passive ideology'), those values that are taken for granted by the society in which the text was produced and read.

Until the 1990s critical studies of ideology in children's literature, such as Bob Dixon's *Catching Them Young* (1977) on 'Sex, Race and Class' and 'Political Ideas' in children's fiction, and Roy Preiswerk's *The Slant of the Pen* (1980), concentrated mainly on production aesthetics, disclosing certain elements in the texts. Little attention was paid to the area of reception, to the link between ideology and the concept of the implied reader, until, in his highly regarded study *Language and Ideology in Children's Fiction* (1992), John Stephens showed how successful reading presupposes appropriation or adoption of the ideologies implicit in the text which relate to assumptions about beliefs, politics, social structures, behaviour, etc. He argued that the relationship between a subject's activities as a reader and a work of fiction which is the object of the reading 'both replicates other forms of subject/sociality interactions and constructs a specular, or mirroring, form of those interactions' (Stephens 1992: 47), thus showing how narrative structure is an ideologically powerful component of texts.

Over and beyond the general influence of target context norms on any transference of texts across borders of time, language and culture, educational norms play a special role in the translation of children's literature. Birgit Stolt (1978) names educational intentions, which impose a taboo on unwelcome phenomena or descriptions, as the most important reason for divergence from a source text. In these cases what Göte Klingberg calls 'purification' comes into action: 'bringing the target text into correspondence with another set of values' (Klingberg 1986: 12). This leads to translation practices and strategies in which those agencies involved (translators themselves, editors, programme planners), anticipating the reaction of intermediaries (adult buyers, booksellers, teachers, etc.), delete or cleanse elements regarded as unsuitable or inappropriate in the target culture, especially accounts of supposedly unacceptable behaviour which might induce young readers to imitate it. Examples of such interventions are: changes of characterization and conduct, toning down the mention of physical functions, 'correcting' the creative use of language in translation (including deliberate misspellings), and toning down certain linguistic registers that do not conform to the stylistic norms of children's literature in the target culture, often in translation of varieties of humour.

Changes of characterization and conduct

The influence of the educational and literary norms of children's literature at various periods, in both source texts and translations, is found not just where texts cross borders between very different cultural areas, but also where works transfer between 'foreign but culturally close' cultures (see Mecklenburg 1987: 565), for instance the children's literatures of north-west Europe and the USA.

This can be observed with reference to the books of Astrid Lindgren, which signalled the beginning of a new era of children's literature in many northern European countries and are now part of the canon.

Astrid Lindgren's *Pippi Långstrump* [Pippi Longstocking], published in 1945, aroused much controversy. In Sweden the book met with a predominantly positive reception at first but, after a review in 1946 by John Landqvist in *Aftonbladet*, which criticized, among other things, the unnatural aspects of the story and the rebellious character of Pippi, the so-called *Pippifejden* [Pippi feuds] broke out. While the original text was discussed in this Swedish debate,[10] in other countries, where there was also argument about the possible harmfulness and excessive fantasy of the book, translation had already acted as a filter absorbing some aspects of the text considered unacceptable in the target culture because they celebrated disrespect for adult authority and ridiculed the rules and norms of child-rearing and civilized society. In the German version, as Surmatz (1992: 58) has shown, a significant alteration occurs in a scene where Pippi is playing with pistols in the attic with her friends Tommy and Annika. The source text, in which Pippi is talking about the presence of ghosts in the attic, runs (in a literal translation into English):

> 'Because even if there aren't any [ghosts], that's no reason for them to scare people to death, I'd say. Would you like a pistol each?'
> Tommy was enthusiastic, and Annika wanted a pistol too so long as it wasn't loaded.
> 'We can be a robber band now if we like,' said Pippi and put the telescope to her eye.
>
> (trans. from Lindgren 1945: 172f.)[11]

This becomes, in a revision of the German translation by Cäcilie Heinig (rendered here into English):

> 'Because even if there aren't any [ghosts], that's no reason for them to scare people to death. Would you like a pistol each? Or no, I think we'd better put them back in the chest. They're not for children!'
> Next Pippi put the telescope to her eye and said:
> 'We can be pirates now if we like.'
>
> (trans. from Lindgren 1965: 205)[12]

Instead of giving her friends the pistols, this German Pippi lectures both them and the reading public that children ought not to play with pistols at all, and they should now put them away.[13] This purification of the text through Pippi's instructive intervention – 'They're not for children!' – is in complete contrast to her characterization, since only just before this point Pippi was quoting such moralizing with anarchic irony as she picked up a pistol and fired it at the ceiling.[14]

In the first German version, the poisonous toadstool into which Pippi bites in the source text, with the same curiosity and enthusiasm as Lewis Carroll's Alice nibbling her own magic mushroom, becomes a harmless edible fungus in order to protect German children reading the passage from any danger of imitating her. (In the English translation it stays poisonous: 'a beautiful red toadstool' (Lindgren 1954: 87)). In general, the character of Pippi acts less subversively in the German translation, where the innovative elements of the Swedish source text are toned down for educational ends (see Surmatz 1992). This tendency is not confined to the German translation of *Pippi Långstrump*. In the French version, for instance, Fifi Brindacier[15] is not allowed to lift a horse, only a pony. When Astrid Lindgren protested, the French publisher justified the change thus: 'It might be possible to persuade good little Swedish children that someone is capable of picking up a horse, but French children, who had just been through a world war, had too much common sense to swallow such a tall tale' (trans. from Lindgren 1969: 99). Lindgren reacted to the curious argument that a girl was more likely to be able to pick up a pony than a horse by asking to see a photograph of a French child holding a pony in the air. The publisher did not provide one.

The British translation (1954), on the other hand, contains no such major deviations from the original as the German and French versions. Lindgren herself often emphasized the influence of English children's literature on her work; indeed, Pippi's affinity with figures from English fantasy, characters who act autonomously and face adult society without fear or favour, means that her characterization and conduct do not produce shock effects in English that require toning down by changes made in translation. They are received more easily in the English-speaking world than elsewhere.

Forty years after the first appearance of the German translation, *Pippi Langstrumpf*, the attitude of intermediaries involved with German-language children's books to this kind of anarchic behaviour had changed, in fact it had become a norm in children's literature, not least through the influence of Lindgren herself. As a result, many of the original adaptations were corrected in the revised translations of 1986 and 1987. This example shows how conduct regarded as unacceptable in a source text may be modified in translation, and how after a lapse of time, during which the norms have shifted, it can be brought back closer to the original text. General changes in notions of acceptability on the level of the story within 'foreign but culturally close' children's literatures are responsible for this return to the original, but so is the fact that within the realm of children's classics, to which *Pippi Långstrump* now undoubtedly belongs, translation practice has partially changed, with what has previously been a norm of translation in canonized adult literature only – respect for the integrity of the original – now being adopted in 'literary' translations of children's classics (on this subject see at greater length Chapter 6).

While the translation process acts as a filter in the transference between foreign but culturally close areas, major deviations from the norms of the target system when the cultures are both foreign and culturally distant can lead to a book not being translated at all. The Jordanian publisher Mona Henning, who is anxious to see Swedish children's literature published in the Arab countries, wrote in 1990 that Astrid Lindgren had not yet been translated[16] because children's books in those countries are expected either to teach obedience or to be in the Oriental fairy-tale tradition.[17]

Serious conflicts of values occur when extremely different forms of social and religious traditions in the source and target cultures meet. The translation of 'emancipatory' German-language children's books into Turkish, according to the translation critic Turgay Kurultay, can lead to 'difficulties and complications', since they have entirely different connotations in the target culture. He asks whether it is wise, even in the interests of children's liberation, 'to give children reading material that could make them harbour doubts and lead to open conflict with adults' (trans. from Kurultay 1994a: 194). In the translation of German books for girls which would meet with disapproval or at least be far more provocative in Turkey than in their source culture, Kurultay thinks that intercultural transference could 'not manage without textual operations' to 'defuse' it (Kurultay 1994b: 15). For instance, the acceptability of Christine Nöstlinger's *Ilse Janda, 14* (Nöstlinger 1974), a novel which uncompromisingly tackles the problems of family relationships and rebellion against parental authority, and so as a whole, according to Kurultay, would seem foreign and provocative, is achieved in the Turkish version (Nöstlinger 1993) by 'at least quantitatively reducing the provocative passages so that the reader has more time to take breath ... and concentrate on the core statement' (trans. from Kurultay 1994b: 11). In line with this idea, Ilse's 'longing' for her boyfriend Wolfgang, expressing her desire for erotic experience, is shifted to the romantic plane: she only 'misses' him. This device, says Kurultay, enables the Turkish text to retain the daring notion of defiance by hinting at a romantic relationship; the translation is equivalent here because the degree of innovation and provocation that the book had for German readers is retained thanks to, rather than in spite of, its being 'toned down'. Such an approach addresses the problem of asking too much of young readers by consistently reproducing all culture-specific factors. The reverse of this problem, when too little is asked of readers because the child's level of reception is set too low, will be examined later on in this chapter.

Physicality and prudery

One of the main sources of laughter in humorous children's literature is reference to anything to do with the body and its functions. Children take a carnivalesque pleasure in animal instincts and sensuality, the uninhibited affirmation of the natural and sensual (see Maria Lypp 1986). One of the main themes of carnivalesque literature, according to Mikhail Bakhtin, is death and revival or change and renewal, and the cyclical model of human life is reflected in the life of the grotesque body, the most important events of which are 'eating, drinking, defecation and other elimination (sweating, blowing of the nose, sneezing), as well as copulation, pregnancy, dismemberment, swallowing up by another body' (Bakhtin 1984b: 317). All these events, leaving aside copulation and pregnancy, are key preoccupations of childhood. Children who are growing and thus in a phase of

Figure 4.1 Seated goat without udder from *A Squash and a Squeeze*. © Axel Scheffler 1993

constant physical change are fascinated by all aspects of the depiction of bodily functions, by acts 'performed on the confines of the body and the outer world' (ibid.). However, it is those very depictions, and mention of parts of the body or physical actions which are considered improper, that are often cut in translation. For instance, there is strict censorship in modern American children's literature of depictions of the naked form – whether of children, adults or even animals. The final illustration in Pija Lindenbaum's picture book *Else-Marie och småpapporna* [Else-Marie and her little papas] (1990), which is about a girl with seven tiny fathers, shows the seven little men, Else-Marie and her normal-sized mother all sitting naked, playing in the bath together. In the American translation (Lindenbaum 1991) this picture was entirely cut and nothing was substituted (see Surmatz 1996: 575). When the sight of a seated goat complete with udder in the picture book *A Squash and a Squeeze* (Donaldson and Scheffler 1993) seemed obscene to the Americans, the illustrator Axel Scheffler had to amputate the udder (see Fig. 4.1). Scheffler commented on this process in a humorous drawing (see Fig. 4.2). 'Though such old-fashioned Puritanism may tempt us in this country [Germany] to smile,' says Susanne Koppe of this piece of censorship, 'our smiles fade when we recognize that the prudery of the Pilgrim Fathers is stealing into the German nursery through the back door of coproduction' (trans. from Koppe 1992: 21). For the goat has lost her udder not just in the American version, but also in the British source text and all other versions involved in the coproduction of the picture book for international editions.

Beyond the mere display of particular parts of the body is, in terms of what may be judged inappropriate, their active use. In countless children's versions of

Figure 4.2 The Scissors of International Coproduction. © Axel Scheffler 1992

Jonathan Swift's *Gulliver's Travels*, the protagonist's account of his successful attempt to extinguish the fire in the imperial palace of Lilliput is altered. In Swift's original text Gulliver puts out the fire in the burning palace by his gargantuan urination:

> The Heat I had contracted by coming very near the Flames, and by my labouring to quench them, made the Wine begin to operate by Urine; which I voided in such a Quantity, and applied so well to the proper Places, that in three Minutes the Fire was wholly extinguished.

> (Swift 1986: 42f.)

Although such a coarsely comic scene is just what child readers like, and although it is of central importance to the further development of the plot (the Empress's horror at the defiling of her palace leads to Gulliver's indictment for high treason, which in turn causes him to flee and return home), it is cut from many versions for children. In his German retelling Erich Kästner allows Gulliver to urinate, but the avuncular, playfully coy tone of the narrative is far removed from the earthy directness of the original:

> Then the solution came to me all at once! And since there was nothing else to do, I carried out my plan. Dear readers, I want to express myself as politely as possible so as not to offend your sensibilities. Well then: I did what little boys who have drunk a lot of lemonade do behind the house or in the woods. You guessed? Quite right! And the ship's doctor Gulliver, one man alone, did what not all the fire-fighting appliances of the capital's fire brigade could have done! The flames burned lower and lower. The fire went out.

> (trans. from Kästner 1961: 24f.)[18]

Conflict of linguistic norms

Misspellings, a feature of children's language, are a favourite source of humour in children's books. The comedy often arises from the sense of superiority of the readers, in the process themselves of learning to spell, towards mistakes that they no longer make, and the fact that they recognize them as mistakes at all. A classic example is the play on written language in A.A. Milne's *Winnie-the-Pooh*. Pooh says of his spelling: 'My spelling is Wobbly. It's good spelling but it Wobbles, and the letters get in the wrong places.' So he gets the scholarly Owl to write a birthday greeting. The result is: 'HIPY PAPY BTHUTHDTH THUTHDA BTHUTHDY'.[19] These passages are rectified in translations such as the first German one of 1928 (see O'Sullivan 1993), when it is apparently felt that the misspellings are inappropriate for young readers, that they should encounter correct language only. According to Basmat Even-Zohar, the stylistic norms which influenced the translation of Astrid Lindgren into Hebrew were: 'Avoid All Linguistic or Spelling "Mistakes"; Use Only "Correct" Standard Syntax' (1992: 232).

In Michael Bond's *More about Paddington* the bear writes in the source text that he is 'at a lewse end' (Bond 1959: 26), and the activity he has chosen to get over his boredom is 'DECKERATING MY NEW ROOM'. In the first German translation this is rendered in correct spelling as 'Bin ohne Beschäftigung' and 'HABE HEUTE MEIN ZIMMER NEU TAPEZIERT' (Bond 1969: 34). The author's playful use of spelling is interpreted – or rather misinterpreted – as a mistake and removed in translation, which means that the bear's childness but also his independence from authority, symbolically represented by his incorrect spelling, are brought under control. The purifying translation of wordplay which contravenes linguistic rules is primarily influenced by educational norms in the target culture, but differing degrees of comic talent and linguistic creativity among translators are also factors, as an analysis of the work of Aidan Chambers in German, by different translators, illustrates (see O'Sullivan 1998).

Stylistic elements that are particularly popular with child readers or listeners sometimes go unrecognized as such by translators, or are removed because they offend against the prevailing stylistic norms of the target literature. One such element is repetition, a typical feature of oral communication. In Milne's *Winnie-the-Pooh* Pooh hears a 'loud buzzing-noise' from the top of a tree and, after much thought, concludes that it must have something to do with bees and thus with his favourite food, honey. His slow, circular thought process is underpinned by the repetition of the identical phrase 'buzzing-noise' – five times in all:

> that buzzing-noise means something. You don't get a buzzing-noise like that, just buzzing and buzzing, without its meaning something. If there's a buzzing-noise, somebody's making a buzzing-noise, and the only reason for making a buzzing-noise that *I* know of is because you are a bee.
>
> (Milne 1965: 4)

In the first German translation of 1928, the translator runs counter to the intentions of the source text by trying to avoid repetition and find different phrases for 'buzzing'; she uses the direct translation of 'buzzing-noise', 'summendes Geräusch', only three times. The later translation by Harry Rowohlt is more faithful to this passage; Rowohlt uses the word 'Summgeräusch' six times in his version (see Milne 1987: 17f.).

Irony in the narrator's voice can also fall victim to the stylistic norms of a target literature. In the 'Foreword for Greenhorns' to his sequel *Emil und die drei Zwillinge* [Emil and the three twins], Kästner divides his readers into 'greenhorns' and 'those in the know', i.e. about *Emil and the Detectives*. According to Nitsa Ben-Ari, the phrase in which Kästner comments on this distinction humorously and with self-irony – ' "Ordnung muss sein," sagte Onkel Karl und schmiss auch noch den letzten Teller an die Wand' ['We must have order,' said Uncle Karl, smashing the last plate against the wall] (Kästner 1936a: 6) – was cut from the Hebrew translation by M.Z. Wolfowski (Kästner 1937b), since this zany behaviour ridicules a male character who would usually command respect, and the sentence was thought to represent 'an unacceptable model for children (who presumably might be moved by it to start smashing dishes against walls)' (Ben-Ari 1992: 224). The first German translations of the *Paddington* stories (Bond 1968 and 1969) are also largely free of irony, unlike the original texts. Above all, when the narrator's irony intends gentle ridicule of the head of the family in the source text, 'the translators protect [him]', says Monika Osberghaus (trans. from 1997: 95).

The educational approach to language in children's literature in the target culture is particularly obvious in the eradication of insults and bad language. Marisa Fernández López (2000) mentions the tendency that still prevails in Spanish children's literature to eliminate registers considered unacceptable for children, which among other things leads to (mild) insults in the work of Enid Blyton being exchanged for more innocuous expressions. These norms are also evident in the toning down of seemingly improper language when the target system, in gender-specific terms, requires particularly moderate language for girls. In the American translation of *Madicken* (Lindgren 1960) a whole chapter is cut because of an incident in which Madicken's little sister Lisabet sticks a pea up her nose. Soon afterwards Lisabet and Mattis, another girl, are quarrelling and the crowning insult is a humorous allusion to Mattis's nose, which is indeed snotty – Lisabet says: 'You can't stuff your nose full of peas anyway, because it's already full of snot. Snotty-nose!' (trans. from Lindgren 1960: 88).[20] Their big sisters join in, there is a scuffle and more insults, culminating in the remark by Mattis's sister Mia, 'Not to you, you little devil' (trans. from ibid.: 89),[21] which really shocks Madicken and Lisabet, because they were told that people who swear go to hell. The girls' conduct and speech in this passage presumably did not conform to the American image of young girls in the 1960s, nor, as Birgit Stolt comments, could it 'be called exactly exemplary for dear little girls (as the publishing firm no doubt imagined they should be) and thus a suitable object of identification for other little girls' (Stolt 1978: 135); hence the cutting of this chapter from the translation. In a later American translation of 1979, entitled *Mardie*, the sensitivities of mediating adults are disregarded and the passages translated appropriately.

Colloquial language as used by young people may also be omitted or adapted in translation in line with the prevalent literary norms. In 1931 British children's literature, traditionally class conscious as it was (indeed, until the late 1950s it offered few realistic depictions of any social strata below the upper middle class), could provide Margaret Goldsmith, the translator of *Emil and the Detectives*, with no slangy, colloquial equivalent of the stylized jargon used by Kästner's Berlin boys in the original. She had to resort to the kind of language for young people already established in the target literature. This was right for the age of the characters but far from right for their background, since it was the language of upper-class English public schoolboys. In the original a conversation between Gustav and Emil runs:

> 'Also, ich finde die Sache mit dem Dieb knorke. Ganz grosse Klasse. Ehrenwort! Und, Mensch, wenn du nischt dagegen hast, helfe ich dir.'
> 'Da wär ich dir kolossal dankbar!'
> 'Quatsch nicht, Krause! Das ist doch klar, dass ich hier mitmache. Ich heisse Gustav.'
> (Kästner 1984: 78)

Goldsmith's translation runs:

> 'Well, I think this thief affair is going to be tophole. First-rate. And, I say, if you don't mind, I think I'll help you.'
> 'I'd be most frightfully grateful.'
> 'That's all right; of course I'll help. My name is Gustav.'
> (Kästner 1931a: 95f.)

'Tophole' and 'first-rate' are expressions from the vocabulary of the upper classes of the time, and the exclamation 'I say' was used only by the educated elite. The British Emil is all grave formality, and when the translator came to 'Quatsch nicht, Krause!', she simply gave up. In the later, new translation of 1959, Eileen Hall was still unable to find language for the boys on an easy colloquial level: 'Morgen ihr Kanaken' becomes 'Good morning everybody', and 'und nun mach ich mich schwach' is rendered as 'I really must go'. Expressions of approval are 'super', 'smashing' and 'jolly good', and Emil's enthusiastic exclamation 'Donnerwetter noch mal ... gibt's in Berlin famose Eltern!' became 'My word, parents in Berlin are jolly decent' (64). This failure to find an equivalent social register should be put down not to the target language (English), but to the linguistic norms of children's literature in Great Britain, as becomes clear when we take a comparative look within the English-speaking countries. In the American translation which appeared a year before the first British version, the passage quoted above runs:

> 'This looks like a swell stunt to me – some class, I'll say. And, man, I'm with you, if it's all right with you.'
> 'That would be mighty good of you.'
> 'Oh, cut it out, boy. One thing's sure. I'm in on it. My name's Gustav.'
> (Kästner 1930: 106)

Here the translator, May Massee, can resort to the language of the dime novels; the petty criminal background of American detective stories provides an established linguistic model. While the British translations speak with reserve of a badly behaved 'rascal' or 'blighter', the American translator chooses the more forthright 'crook'. And when Emil is about to throw a punch because Gustav has made derogatory remarks about his Sunday suit, he says in the British translation, in gentlemanly style: 'Take that back at once, or I'll knock you down' (Kästner 1931a: 92), while in Massee's American version he threatens, much more directly: 'Take that back! Or I'll give you one that'll lay you out cold' (Kästner 1930: 105). The American translation sounds as modern, urban and knowing as the source text.[22]

Assumptions about the competence of young readers

We can broadly distinguish between changes made in translations of children's literature with the ideological aim of transmitting the 'correct' norms and values of the target culture and those made with the purpose of making a text intelligible for young readers, with many critics regarding the latter as interventions justified by the competence of the readers. This approach overlooks the fact that children's receptive abilities at any specific stage are not empirically established entities but hypothetical constructs. Comparative analysis shows that a child reader can be inscribed in a translated children's book who is not identical with the reader of the source text, and who reveals much about the child images prevalent in education and developmental psychology in the target culture at a given point in time. Studying translated children's literature therefore involves examining the assumptions made by translators and other intermediaries about the competence of child readers.

We cannot speak of '*the* child reader', any more than we can speak of 'the reader' in general. The literary competence of every child depends on his or her individual affective and cognitive development, influenced by factors of the maturing process and his or her social background, education, etc. Michael Benton saw the personifications of 'seven ghostly figures' hovering around the bent head of a child reading a book – a writer, a literary critic, a psychologist, a psychoanalyst, a psycholinguist, a philosopher and an educationalist – all of them trying to answer the question: 'What is going on in that child's head as he reads?' (1980: 14). Early in the twentieth century the psychologist Charlotte Bühler classified children's stages of development by the literary works or genres 'suitable' for each age – *Struwwelpeter* age, fairy-tale age, *Robinson Crusoe* age. This and other models of reading ages and phases derived from the idea of a quasi-natural maturing of literary practice. Later came the empirical study of emergent literacy, in which the conditions in which literary knowledge is acquired in the family are observed – for instance, the interaction of adult and child reading picture books together – and text-based research into the acquisition of literary competence, which traces the distinctions between textual structure and the child's own experience.

The reading process, according to early models, was one of decoding, beginning with the most elementary forms in the text, and passing from optical perception to the planes of vocabulary, syntax and semantics, and thus to sentences and larger textual units. The opposite of this so-called 'bottom-up' model is the 'top-down' concept, which stresses the existing knowledge of readers, the context and their attitude to and expectations of reading; according to it, the information in the text is decoded and understood on the basis of all these factors. Today the reading process is seen as a complex interaction of 'top-down' expectations and 'bottom-up' decoding. Various different terms are used for literary and non-literary referential frameworks or 'superstructures': 'repertories', 'frames', 'schemata', 'scripts', 'scenarios', 'frameworks' and 'narrative grammars'.

In discussion of children's literature in translation, particularly important factors are the young readers' 'knowledge of the world', non-literary schemata and repertories that contribute to an understanding on the content level, and their ability to deal with the aesthetic and fictional construct of literature. Some studies on the development of literary understanding in children have been undertaken, for instance on the development of an awareness of fiction, the ability to generalize and abstract, understanding of the use of indirect speech, the reconstruction of viewpoints and feelings, and the development of moral understanding. However, these studies do not enable us to say anything for certain about the precise receptive ability of children at specific stages of development. Observations of the ease with which certain age groups can understand certain texts, or literary methods and narrative conventions, can be made only on the basis of small-scale empirical investigations.

Today's 'media childhood' calls for us to test our assumptions about the literary socialization of children. Klaus Neumann and Michael Charlton ask:

> how far the mass media are already influencing the ontogenesis of the use of symbols: classic theories of development (for instance Piaget) take as their subject child development in the context of an environment consisting of material objects (building blocks, etc.). Today's small children, however, are growing up with cassette recorders and other electronic media. What significance does this symbolic environment have in the development of language and thought?
>
> (trans. from Neumann and Charlton 1988: 31)

Children's literature makes up only a small part of the cultural products available for children in the early twenty-first century; it is no more and no less than a segment of children's culture as structured by the multimedia, which is also becoming ever more closely linked with popular culture as a whole. In recent children's literature studies the question has arisen as to which of the literary competences – an awareness of fiction, an understanding of the use of indirect speech, an understanding of narrative structures, the realization of characters in a story, etc. – are really so 'reading-specific' that they cannot also be acquired by watching films and television. Hans-Heino Ewers sees the diminishing function of children's literature (because of shifts within the general use of media) as a surrender of functions to the audiovisual media, beginning with the development of a general receptive competence: 'Nursery and pre-school children in the cassette and TV age acquire a variety of receptive competences which they can later bring to the acquisition of literature, and which consequently no longer have to be first gained and practised by the consumption of literature itself' (trans. from Ewers 1995: 269).

Foreignness

Everything that children do not yet know and are experiencing for the first time is initially strange or foreign to them. 'Foreignness is not a quality that an object has for a subject looking at it; it is a relationship in which a subject stands to an object of its experience and understanding' (trans. from Krusche 1985: 13). As a relational term, the foreign, as the unknown, the unfamiliar, is the opposite of what is familiar and known; if the term is describing distinctions, differences, dissimilarities, it is the opposite of what is 'one's own'. In the context of children's literature, *foreign* usually refers to what is not yet familiar to child readers in the process of acquiring basic knowledge and experience of the world around them. This foreignness initially has nothing to do with cultural difference.

Elements in texts unknown to target readers and also those culturally foreign to them are of relevance to the discussion of the transference of children's literature. We have to ask: on what level are they found in children's literature? Which unfamiliar elements of the foreign culture are presented in translations and how are they presented? And how do intermediaries and translators deal with these elements in children's literature? Those who engaged in the early discussion of children's literature and its translation concentrated almost exclusively on a single area: the transfer of culture-bound elements.

In *Children's Fiction in the Hands of the Translators* (1986), Göte Klingberg systematically studied all the cultural and language-specific references that might occur, regarding them, in relation to the source text, as one of the main sources for 'deviations' from the original text in translation. By 'references' he meant allusions in books to various cultural phenomena that do not exist in the translator's own culture: plants and animals peculiar to a certain landscape, mentions of mythology, history and politics, consumer goods, literary allusions, quotations, etc. He discussed whether all references to elements foreign to the target public should be replaced by something familiar in its own culture (this process is now commonly referred to as 'domestication') or whether the references in the source text should be preserved (now usually called 'foreignization'), and asked: how much explanation does the reader of the target text need? What kind of explanation? Explanatory additions to the text? Metalinguistic explanations in paratexts (such as footnotes, forewords, glossaries)?

Features of a foreign culture can be intriguing or surprising, can make readers curious or inform them; in many cases they do need some kind of explanation, at least a partial one. There are elements in the texts that can be immediately recognized as foreign in a mimetic representation of a foreign cultural area (names, currency, locations, etc.), and others that are references to events, situations or conditions of a foreign culture which we may assume are not part of the general knowledge of most young readers in a given target culture at a given time. Translations of difficult culture-bound elements in children's literature are among the subjects most discussed in this field; translators themselves are happy to talk about them from the practical viewpoint. There are no major studies on the actual reception, by either children or adults, of elements obviously from foreign cultures, and thus there is no empirical basis for a translator's decision on whether to foreignize translations or to domesticate them.

Using recent theories of memory, Dietrich Krusche developed a model of the reception of foreign ('culturally distant') texts in which the two poles between which the basic tension of foreign texts occurs – the close (immediately comprehensible) and the distant (incomprehensible and requiring explanation) – can be structured in different ways. He distinguishes between *episodic* elements, based on events and perceived immediately and sensuously, and *semantic and conceptional* elements, which disclose their nature once they are understood: 'The episodic core of a literary text professes to offer us immediate identification through our *own experience*. In contrast, the semantic and conceptual elements ... point us in the direction of whatever cultural context has been activated' (trans. from Krusche 1993: 440). Identificatory reading, made possible by the episodic elements, can bridge cultural distance, while the conceptual elements continue to signal that the distance exists.

These hermeneutical reflections correspond to observations of empirical reading research, where identification with characters in a work of fiction is discussed as one of the most important aspects of the reading process, leading to gratification and contributing to the reader's motivation (see Schön 1990, an extensive survey of the reading practices of over 500 young readers). Observations made by a publisher promoting Swedish children's literature in the Arabic-speaking area indicated that children are not disturbed by an unknown or foreign setting, because their main attention is bent on the action of the plot.[23] Astrid Lindgren's translator into Arabic, Walif Saif, said of the ability of young readers to deal with foreign elements in literature:

> Provided that children's literature depicts the child's experiences, a child reader will not feel alienated as s/he encounters strange mythological or imagined creatures, forests, tools and physical features of people and environment, even if all these are not part of his/her own socio-cultural environment. After all, in the child's world of ... imagination, expectations are not constrained by cultural limits, so that a strange name or a strange place would not necessarily derive its strangeness from breaking culturally established norms.
>
> (Saif 1995: 2)

Astrid Lindgren herself attacks the assumption that children, with their limited experience, are incapable of accepting foreign places in literature or identifying with foreign people, saying she is sure that children have 'an extraordinary ability to adapt, that they are able to experience the most unusual things and situations given a good translator to help them; I am sure that their imagination takes over just when the translator runs out of breath' (trans. from Lindgren 1969: 98). She cites some Japanese children who were so fascinated by her books about Bullerby, of which she writes: 'Six little Swedes in a village in Sweden – it's Swedish, you will note, Swedish!!' (ibid.), that they wrote to the author to ask if it was a real place and whether one could go there.

The ability of child readers either to accept foreign elements or not to notice them at all in their reception of texts was also observed by Rhoda Bunbury and Reinbert Tabbert in a small-scale study of the different reception by Australian and German readers of Randolph Stow's bushranger novel *Midnite* (1967) and its German translation, *Käpt'n Mitternacht* (1972). While the former enjoyed the specifically Australian features of the book, in Germany they either went entirely unnoticed or were not considered important (Tabbert 1989: 137). The tendency 'to accept something that is familiar in its general human aspects rather than finding its culture-specific features foreign' (trans. from ibid.) is also illustrated by Tabbert's survey of the reaction of German children to a literal translation of the Australian story *The Bunyip of Berkeley's Creek* (Brooks and Wagner 1973).

The fact that something culturally alien may not really be perceived as a stumbling-block can be interpreted in various ways. Children take little notice of an author's name and do not relate to macrocontextual data. An awareness of authorship develops quite late, and the realization (not present even in many adult readers) that a translated text is in fact a translation comes even later, if at all. However, in reading – as in life – children are always being confronted by elements that they do not yet grasp and cannot understand, and so, in the process of learning to read, if it is a successful one, young readers can develop strategies that help them to cope with such things: they skip something that is incomprehensible to them or refuse to allow minor disruptions to interrupt the flow of reading. In principle, children read texts from foreign contexts in just the same way as texts from their own cultures. We can assume that the foreign contexts are assimilated in the course of reading: 'We have observed over and over again how, in the development of literary understanding, recipients adapt the sense of the text to what they understand already' (trans. from Spinner 1993: 55f.). Young readers – like many adult readers – absorb and identify with what they read, and tend to concentrate on such anthropological universals as the cycle of life, sexuality, the expression of emotion, social relationships, religious feelings, etc. (see Mecklenburg 1987: 570), that is to say on common factors rather than differences in literature.

The representational aspects of a foreign culture (time, place, natural conditions, customs, history, the cultural heritage) may be less disruptive than the norms and attitudes of a source text that do not coincide with those of the target culture. It is the conceptual elements of a foreign culture that make a text seem particularly 'foreign' and thus harder to communicate. The more 'foreign' a text is in this way, the lower are the chances that it will be translated at all. In the translation of 'emancipatory' German children's literature into Turkish, where there is a wide gulf between the source and target cultures in terms of their ideas on the behaviour of children towards parents and the conduct of girls and women, one must therefore be careful, says Turgay Kurultay (1994b), not to ask too much of young readers by presenting them with a code of conduct that conflicts with their everyday lives. Here Kurultay's subject is the problem of the boundaries of understanding in intercultural communication through children's literature, a problem which Reinbert Tabbert rightly believes should be answered with solutions based on particular cases rather than general principles (see Tabbert 1996a: 102).

Foreign mentality can also be linked to the form of presentation, to the poetic quality of a text or to unusual literary forms. An analysis of the history of Lewis Carroll's *Alice's Adventures in Wonderland* as it has been received in Germany – thirty-two unabridged translations have been issued over a period of 130 years – shows how translations deal with a literary form 'foreign' to the target children's literature.[24] After Antonie Zimmermann's auspicious but broadly unnoticed first translation of *Alice* into German in 1869, closely supervised by Carroll himself,[25] almost one hundred years were to pass before another literarily ambitious effort would be published – that of Christian Enzensberger in 1963. What character-izes almost all the translations in between is the intervention by the translators to make the book more 'acceptable' to German children, which, with its dreamlike quality, its perverted logic and its incomprehensibility, was totally unlike anything produced by German authors. *Alice* translations range from those which infan-tilize the novel to ones which offer an exclusively adult reading of it. Five main tendencies can be identified: the fairy-tale approach, the explanatory approach, the moralizing approach, the literary approach and an approach which is both literary and accessible to children.

The fairy-tale mood is frequently introduced in paratexts about the author Lewis Carroll, who, according to the translator Karl Köstlin, told the Liddell sisters the story of Alice's adventures in his room 'an den langen Winterabenden' [during the long winter evenings] (Köstlin 1949); in Franz Sester's 1949 transla-tion the point of the 'dry story' is missed entirely as it is replaced by the story of Little Red Riding Hood (see Carroll 1949). Some German translators try to turn *Alice in Wonderland* into a comprehensible book by, for instance, not only explaining what a Mock Turtle is but also supplying the reader with a recipe for Mock Turtle soup. Carroll's breadth, his fantastic, witty, playful and ominous facets, are all reined in in these nanny translations which make of *Alice in Wonderland* a jolly children's story with wordplay that is either pedantically expli-cated or muddled. It is not surprising that *Alice*, even as late as the 1960s and despite dozens of translations, was little read or appreciated in Germany.

A watershed in the history of the German reception occurred in 1963, when both *Alice* books were translated by Christian Enzensberger. Thanks to this intel-ligent and creative translation almost a hundred years after the publication of the original, German readers could finally get an inkling of the complexity and brilliance of Lewis Carroll's original. This translation of the classical text, complete with the patina lent by time and acclaim, is for adults, for intellectuals even; in contrast to the original, it pays little heed to the needs of child readers/listeners. In the wake of Enzensberger's literary translation and partly due to changes in German children's literature, which, for various reasons, was becoming more open to hitherto unknown or unaccepted forms of humour and nonsense, a small number of German translations published in the late 1980s and early 1990s began to match Carroll's wit with their own and applied the principle of Carrollian humour to linguistic and literary material. They aim to be enjoyed and understood by children but are not prepared to compromise the quality and the spirit of the original. One of the most successful of these translations is by Siv Bublitz, who, for instance, renders 'How doth the little crocodile' into German as a dynamic and cheeky parody of Goethe's famous poem 'Der Fischer' [The fisherman], which, unlike the majority of the harmless and banal ditties by her predecessors, manages to retain the threat of Carroll's smiling and murderous crocodile (see Carroll 1993).

Compared to its reception in England and in other countries, Lewis Carroll's book simply wasn't a success in Germany, for which the poor quality of many of the thirty-two translations issued in the course of 130 years is partially responsible. The translations themselves are clear indicators of how translators and publishers felt such an excitingly innovative but also puzzling book should be presented to young German readers. The reception history shows that they, unlike the modern translations, ultimately failed to bridge two seemingly incompatible worlds through their efforts.

Translators of children's literature decide, therefore, what young readers can or cannot understand; they make assumptions about elements of foreign cultures that in their view are not part of the readers' repertory. The British translator Anthea Bell, for instance, adjusts foreign elements to the age of the recipient, believing that an older reader will cope with them better than a younger child: 'The idea ... is to avoid putting young readers off by presenting them with an impenetrable-looking set of foreign names the moment they open the book. ... You must gauge the precise degree of foreignness, and how far it is acceptable and can be preserved' (Bell 1985a: 7). The acceptable 'degree of foreignness' is, of course, culturally and historically variable. British children's literature is notable for a lack of interest in translations and for publishing very few. Anthea Bell speaks of the 'inbuilt English distrust of, and resistance to, anything foreign. It seems to afflict us – from the publishing point of view – from picture-book age onward, once the words begin to assume equal importance with the illustrations' (ibid.: 3). This manifests itself in the lack of tolerance not only for 'foreign-sounding' names in texts but even for the names of foreign authors, as the publisher Klaus Flugge remarked:

> The fact that it is difficult to pronounce names like Nöstlinger and Velthuijs has made both of these international prize winners more and more difficult

to sell in this country [Britain], and an outstanding creator of picture books like Philippe Dupasquier is still considered too foreign in style and name.

(Flugge 1994: 212)

By way of contrast, contemporary children's literature in the Netherlands and Scandinavia is more tolerant, supported by such factors as early foreign-language learning in schools as well as by the general practice of showing TV programmes and films in the original language with subtitles, which contributes to an easier and early acceptance of foreign-sounding names and elements in literature.

But the degree of cultural adaptation depends not only on the target culture but also on the time in which a text is translated; domesticating translation strategies can have different functions in a given source literature at a given time. Irma Hagfors shows how the domestication of children's literature in translation in Finland in the immediate post-war period was to offer an escape from 'the materially and emotionally strained circumstances in a country recovering from the war' (2003: 119). To this end, to help the readers identify with a story, culture-bound elements such as proper names and food items were often domesticated (see ibid.).

Decisions on cutting or adapting foreign elements also depend on the status of the text. The first German and Spanish translations of Enid Blyton, for instance, were almost entirely domesticated.[26] This way of dealing with culture-specific elements in popular or series children's books tends to be the general norm in translating non-canonical texts,[27] indicating that the lower the status of a text, the more freely is it treated. This is illustrated in detail by Mieke Desmet (2002) in her analysis of a significant corpus of narrative fiction for girls translated from English into Dutch, and further confirmed by a study of the children's literature translated from German into Turkish: 'While in translations of popular or instructive children's literature foreign elements were frequently eliminated and defused, in translations of more highly regarded children's literature the foreign elements were retained almost "untouched" ' (trans. from Kurultay 1994a: 195).

Adaptation of references

Different methods can be observed in the translation of texts with foreign features: foreignizing translations record and try to preserve the foreignness; neutralizing translations attempt to tone down concrete foreign aspects; and domesticating translations adapt culture-specific foreign elements to make them those of the target culture. Many translations contain a combination of the various strategies. An unusual example of a consistently foreignizing version of a children's book is the American translation by May Massee of Kästner's *Emil und die Detektive* [Emil and the detectives], published in 1930. In this version – despite a good deal of linguistic clumsiness as the result of her leaning towards literal translation – the translator took great pains to emphasize the German nature of the original text, leaving the German names and other culture-specific features as they were, so that Emil's mother, for instance, is called 'Frau Friseuse Tischbein' and the currency is German. Massee makes cultural distance and its preservation a theme of her translation, adding explanations and a simple aid to pronunciation in her introduction; this is one of the reasons why her version is said to have 'a rather German flavor' (Stahl 1985: 32). In contrast, the British translation by Margaret Goldsmith, published one year later, is less consistent, partly foreignizing, partly domesticating. Most German names and styles of address are given in German (for instance 'Herr Grundeis'), but in the account of the Berlin bank branch we read: 'Sometimes messengers come to the bank to change a ten-shilling or a pound note into silver or coppers ... . People who have dollars or Swiss francs or Italian lire can change this money into English money' (Kästner 1931a: 159).

When tea is offered in an English translation of a Swedish source instead of the afternoon coffee drunk in the original (see Klingberg 1986: 42), when 'ginger beer' in an English source text becomes 'cranberry juice' in a Swedish target text (see ibid.: 42) or when, in several German versions of *Alice in Wonderland*, the Mad Hatter serves coffee instead of tea (see O'Sullivan 2000: 304ff.), we have a domesticating translation. Such adaptations would seem hardly necessary today, with the cultural distance between European countries decreasing: the cranberry is indeed Sweden's most important berry, but, at the time of Göte Klingberg's publication, it was known little or not at all in the environment described in the English original, the coast of Norfolk. Klingberg takes these examples from two books where the context as a whole is not domesticated, and where the scene is therefore clearly set in Sweden and England respectively, but certain details have been adapted, and the result is a confusing conglomeration of inconsistent cultural elements.

Such discrepancies can be most evident in illustrated books or picture books in translation, when domesticating translations are paired with the original pictures. Features of the pictures reveal that they are still of the source culture, while the text gives other signals associating it with the target culture. In the French picture book by Philippe Dumas, *Laura sur la route* [Laura on the road] (1978), translated into German as *Laura unterwegs* (1981), a story about a Newfoundland dog who acts as a children's nanny, the dog travels from Dieppe to the capital city, Paris. In the localized German text she goes from Feldafing to Munich. However, we see the Eiffel Tower in the background of one picture and a Parisian *flic* in the foreground of another (cf. Tabbert 1991a: 139), sights that one would hardly expect in Munich.

Pictures with typographical elements – labels, street signs, advertisements, newspapers, magazines, books, shop names, etc. – are a particular problem in translation. Foreign written material that forms part of a picture is usually translated and placed over the original, sometimes spoiling the artistic impression, since it may be in print instead of the illustrator's original script. Alternatively, pictures containing writing may be used untranslated to save money and trouble; inconsistent mixtures may include some writing that is translated and some that is not. In the German translation of Jean de Brunhoff's *L'Histoire de Babar, le petit éléphant, Die Geschichte von Babar* (1946), for instance, there is a mixture of French and German: the French term 'occasions' [special offers] is visible in the right-hand display window of the big store with the words 'Grand magasin' [department store] over it, but the shop window opposite offers, in German, 'Spiele' [games]. On the whole, wording taken over from the French predominates. In this case the variety of languages spoken in Switzerland may have influenced the decision to expect readers to understand the French inscriptions (the German translation was published by Diogenes Verlag of Zürich).

On the other hand, elements of the foreign source language may be included in illustrations for translated texts in order to evoke the source culture and provide local colour. The French edition of *Emil und die Detektive, Émile et les détectives* (Kästner 1980), with illustrations by Daniel Maja, uses German signs to indicate the German setting. In these pictures Émile carries a case with a sticker saying 'Neustadt' on it, and there are German notices bearing the words 'Bahnsteig 2' [platform 2] and 'Berliner Zeitung' [the *Berlin Times*]. We see 'Wurst' [sausages] over a snack bar and 'Blumen' [flowers] above a florist's. However, although the text in the pictures is mostly German, the drawings do include some French wording as

Figure 4.3 Illustration with inconsistent bilingual text. © Daniel Maja; *Émile et les détectives*, Livre de Poche Jeunesse

well: the 'Commerz und Privatbank' of Walter Trier's original illustrations becomes the 'Banque du Commerce et', with a French notice in the window ('Votre argent nous interesse'), although Deutschmark notes are to be seen in the foreground. While one could interpret this in the illustrator's favour by suggesting that he is envisaging a united Europe with a bilingual branch of the French bank in Berlin, so that perhaps the illustration is not inconsistent after all, the drawing reproduced here as Figure 4.3 clearly is. Despite the German environment, complete with German script, in the scene where Émile and Gustave are hiding behind the advertising column (which bears the words, among others, 'täglich Tanz' [daily dancing]), keeping watch on Grundeis as he sits outside the Café Josty, Gustave is onomatopoeically hooting '*Pouet pouet*' in French.

Levelling out cultural differences in international coproductions

Such problems of cultural discrepancy in illustrated translations and picture books could soon be a thing of the past. The ever-rising costs of production, storage, advertising and distribution make the publishing of ambitious picture books, lavishly illustrated story books and extensively illustrated non-fiction books almost impossible without international cooperation, which means shared costs and amalgamated markets.[28] Parts of books with coloured illustrations are produced for several countries at once, with the running text printed on a separate black plate. Every change in the pictures means additional expense, so they are devised with an eye to international exploitation from the first. As a result, culture-specific features and the diversity that they entail disappear. Publishers prefer something non-provocative, unlikely to offend, and adaptable in streamlined form to the requirements of the international market, and have to bear in mind any different ideas their business partners may have of 'unacceptable' subjects and methods of presentation. This can lead to pre-censorship on the part of publishing houses economically dependent on international partners. For the sake of successful negotiations, 'the British "weed out" everything that could give offence in the USA at the earliest stage of production: a baby's bare bottom can lose a licensing agreement as easily as a clear affirmation of the theory of evolution' (trans. from Koppe 1992: 21).

The need for licences results in international insipidity: culture-specific subjects or artistic trends are avoided for reasons of cost, while buildings, clothing and everyday objects are pictured non-specifically so as to strike no one as foreign. In an article on international coproductions, Horst Künnemann tells of an unsigned document which has been going the rounds of German publishing houses. Under the significant heading 'Avoiding Mistakes in Illustrations for International Productions' (trans. from Künnemann 1994: 3), illustrators are given instructions for making their work internationally publishable:

Unless these items are the actual subject

- No pictures showing local customs, costumes, typical clothing, typical modes of behaviour, etc.
- No pictures showing mailboxes, telephone kiosks, taxis, buses, police cars and policemen, uniforms of any kind, trams, ambulances, fire engines, traffic signs of any kind (except those that are internationally familiar, such as STOP, right of way signs, etc.)
- No pictures containing typography, for instance labels, notices, advertising posters, newspapers, magazines, books, shop names, car registration plates, etc. However, internationally used and easily understood words such as 'Hotel' are permissible. If typography is absolutely necessary in pictures, make sure it is only in black on a small separate section.

(ibid.)

A relatively new trend in international publishing, packaging, is found in lavishly illustrated non-fiction books, where a packager buys the work of illustrators and producers of text and makes a master copy, which is then sold to publishing firms in as many countries as possible. Here again the requirements of simultaneous coproduction can have a very odd effect, even in those countries that are culturally close. For instance, the German *Mein erstes Wörterbuch* [My first dictionary] (Wilkes and Schindler 1992), which is intended to help children acquire their first verbal understanding of their environment, was taken from the omnipresent Dorling Kindersley. The German children at the pre-literate age of keen observation, for whom this edition is meant, must surely be surprised to see that all cars have their steering wheels on the right, or that, instead of the equipment for sports popular in Germany such as handball, tobogganing and cross-country skiing, the section on sport prominently features such items as a baseball, a rugby ball and a cricket bat. One might expect that in an area such as the first verbal identification of the environment, that environment should coincide with the child's own. The notion of a presentation allegedly free of any specific single culture can only be a fiction; what it frequently means is no culture other than the dominant Anglo-American one is presented.

In all packaged editions the illustrations remain the same; the text is translated or adapted for the separate language areas. The arrangement of text on the pictorial pages is fixed in advance, so that the translator or, in those cases where familiar fairy tales are retold, the adapter, is obliged to fill a predetermined amount of space on the page with text, in the same way as in translations of strip cartoons. When Anthea Bell was providing the English text for Japanese-illustrated editions of Andersen's *Little Mermaid* and the Grimms' *Snow White*, she was surprised to see how much space the beginning of the Grimms' tale occupied in its Japanese version:

> The ... book begins with no less than four double spreads covering the queen's wishing for a child white as snow, red as blood, black as ebony, the

birth of the baby herself and no more. I haven't a word of Japanese myself, but there are plenty of Japanese words on each double spread – what do they say, I wonder? For it's quite difficult to share out my translation of the original German between the four double spreads so that each contains some wording.

(Bell 1985b: 141)

The opposite was the case with the *Little Mermaid*, where there was too little room available for the entire text. An entirely different placing is often impossible, even if it might be desirable because of, say, a different sentence structure in the target language.

Instead of multiculturality based on knowledge and acceptance of the differences between cultures, we have here an (alleged) cultural neutrality, resulting in non-specific, levelled-out, international products. The mere fact that children's literature is being translated or coproduced thus has no particular cultural value in itself. I shall return to the apparently international nature of children's literature in Chapter 6 and ask to what degree it is just a new variant of the cultural hegemony of traditionally dominant (children's) cultures.

5 The implied translator and the implied reader in translated children's literature

When scholars or critics identify 'changes', 'adaptations' or 'manipulations' in translations of children's literature, they often describe and analyse them in terms of the differing social, educational or literary norms prevailing in the source and the target languages, cultures and literatures at that given time, as examples in the previous chapter have shown. The point of focus of this chapter will not be so much the manipulations themselves; instead I want to concentrate on the agency of such changes, the translator, in order to identify his or her presence in the translated text.

The translator's visibility has been a much discussed issue in translation studies since Lawrence Venuti used the term 'invisibility' to describe both the illusionistic effect of the translator's discourse and the practice by publishers, reviewers and readers in contemporary Anglo-American culture of judging translations as acceptable when they read fluently. His 'call to action' to translators has been for visibility by use of nonfluent, nonstandard and heterogeneous language, by producing foreignized rather than domesticated texts. He rightly insists on talking about translators as real people in geopolitical situations and about the politics of translation and ethical criteria (see Venuti 1995). But the translator's discursive presence can, I submit, also be identified in texts which aren't nonfluent, nonstandard and foreignized; it can be located on a theoretical level in a model of narrative communication, as shown by Giuliana Schiavi in 1996,[1] and on the level of the text, where the translator's presence is evident in the strategies chosen and in the way a translator positions himself or herself in relation to the translated narrative. The guiding questions here are: what kind of translator can be perceived in the text? Where can the translator be located in the act of communication which is the narrative text? How does the implied reader of the target text differ from that of the source text? To address these questions, I will present a theoretical and analytical tool, a communicative model of translation which links the theoretical fields of narratology and translation studies.

Agencies of communication in translated narratives

The basic difference manifesting itself in the narrative communication act between a source text narrative and a translation, on the level of the implied reader and the agencies generating him or her, has so far received remarkably little attention in narratological research: 'Narratological models routinely ignore the translator's discursive presence' (Hermans 1996: 26). The models proposed by Wayne Booth, Seymour Chatman, Gérard Genette and others relate to narrative texts in general and fail to distinguish between original texts and translations. The illusion that a translation is equivalent to the source text, 'the illusion of transparency and coincidence', which Theo Hermans calls the 'ideology of translation' (ibid.: 27), has hitherto prevented the discursive presence of the translator in a translated text from being closely studied from the narratological viewpoint. The observation made by Chatman that 'the narrator, and she or he alone, is the only subject, the only "voice" of narrative discourse' (1990: 87) is, as we shall see, simply not true of translated texts.

The translation of texts can be depicted, as in Figure 5.1, as a sequence of two consecutive processes of the narrative communication act discussed in Chapter 2. There, in Figure 2.1 (p. 15), the model applies to an original (non-translated) text and its readers. The implied reader of that text is modelled by the choice of a specific linguistic code, through a certain literary style and through specialized references, that is, through the 'encyclopaedia' (see Eco 1979). The implied reader of a text is thus a time-specific and culture-specific entity. In translation, the translator acts in the first instance as the real reader of the source text. As someone familiar with the source language and culture, the translator is in a position to assume the role of the implied reader of the source text and, above and beyond that, to try to identify the natures of the implied author and the implied reader(s).

Parallel to the source text is the target text (the translation). As the creator of the translation, the translator acts, in the second half of the process shown on the right-hand side of Figure 5.1, as a counterpart to the real author of the source text; the translator is the one who creates the target text in such a way that it can be understood by readers in the target culture whose language, conventions, codes and references differ from those in the source culture. However, the translator does not produce a completely new message, but rather, as Giuliana Schiavi who identified the translator's presence in narratological terms writes, 'intercepts the communication and transmits it – re-processed – to the new reader who will receive the message' (1996: 15). By interpreting the original text, by following certain norms, and by adopting specific strategies and methods, the translator, according to Schiavi, 'builds up a new ... relationship between what we must call a "translated text" and a new group of readers' (ibid.: 7) and in doing so also creates a different implied reader from the one in the source text: *the implied reader of the translation* (ibid.). This implied reader can be equated with the implied reader of the source text to varying degrees, but they are not identical. The implied reader of the translation will always be a different entity from the implied reader of the source text. This statement applies to all translated fictional texts.

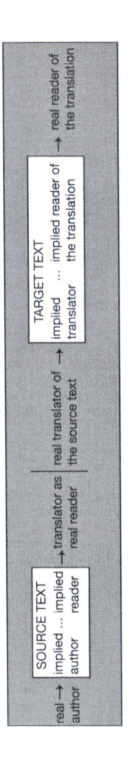

Figure 5.1 Translation in narrative communication, incorporating the implied translator and the implied reader of the translation ('…' notes narrator and narratee).

If the implied reader of the translation differs from his or her counterpart in the source text, then the question has to be asked: what is the agency which creates the difference? The implied reader of the source text, the reader inscribed in the text, is generated by the implied author. By the same token the implied reader of the target text is generated by a similar agency: *the implied translator* (ibid.: 15). By setting out the points of communication between the narrator, the narratee and the implied reader of the source text, Schiavi showed the area in which 'a translator negotiates all the patterns in the text. From that point of "negotiation" he intercepts the communication and transmits it – re-processed – to the new reader' (ibid.). (In her scheme, Schiavi situates the real translator within the framework of the narrative text itself, next to the immanent agencies of narrator, narratee and implied reader. However, just like the real author and real reader, this real translator does not belong on the level of the text but is an external agency with the two functions that he or she exercises – reception and production –clearly separated from each other, as shown in Figure 5.2.) All involved in a translation – translators, editors, programme planners – can be found in the agency of the implied translator; the 'translator's consciousness' is not necessarily or exclusively that of the real translator. This can be shown, for instance, through a comparison of differing editions of the same translation, such as the French translation of Erich Kästner's *Pünktchen und Anton* (Kästner 1931b), *Petit Point et ses amis* (Kästner 1936b and 1982), in which the 'Nackdenkereien' [reflections], metafictional commentaries after each chapter, were simply omitted from the later paperback edition, significantly altering the whole effect of the novel, which is in part based on the interaction between these two contrasting elements of chapter and reflection (see O'Sullivan 2002b).

Based on these deliberations, Figure 5.2 presents a final scheme of the translated narrative text – in amendment of Schiavi (1996: 14) – incorporating all the agencies and processes mentioned above. It can be described as follows: the communication between the *real author of the source text* and the *real reader of the translation* is enabled by the *real translator*, who here (in contrast to Schiavi's model) is positioned outside the text. His or her first act is that of a receptive agent, who then, still in an extratextual position, transmits the source text via the intratextual agency of the *implied translator*. The *narrator, narratee* and *implied reader* of the target text, all generated by the implied translator, can be roughly equivalent to their counterparts in the source text, but they can also deviate significantly, as analysis will show. In translated texts, therefore, a discursive presence is to be found above and beyond that of the narrator of the source text, namely that of the (implied) translator. We could say that two voices are present in the narrative discourse of the translated text: the voice of the narrator of the source text and the voice of the translator. Schiavi's theoretical outline dispenses with actual textual illustrations of the discursive presence of the translator, but in his 'companion piece' to Schiavi's, with concrete examples, Theo Hermans identifies this specific voice in situations where the translator is forced 'to come out of the shadows and

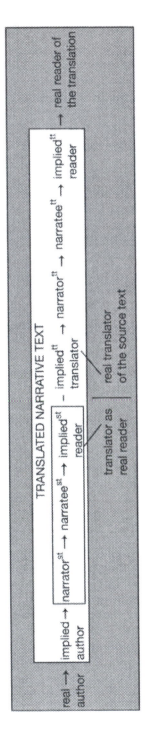

TRANSLATED NARRATIVE TEXT

real → implied → narrator^st → narratee^st → implied^st
author   author   reader

  – implied^tt → narrator^tt → narratee^tt → implied^tt → real reader of
    translator   reader   the translation

translator as   real translator
real reader   of the source text

Figure 5.2 Scheme of the translated narrative text and all its agencies (st= source text, tt = target text).

directly intervene in a text which the reader had been led to believe spoke only with one voice' (Hermans 1996: 27).

In my view there are two levels on which the discursive presence of the translator can be identified in the narrative text. The first is that of the implied translator as the originator of such paratexts as forewords and metalinguistic explanations like footnotes, as identified by Hermans. These are primarily moments of paratextual intervention by the translator where explanations are crucial, where (the source) language itself is the theme and 'when "contextual over-determination" leaves no other option' (ibid.: 23). The voice of Hermans' translator is thus almost exclusively metalinguistic; in principle it is 'wholly assimilated into the Narrator's voice'. I would argue that the translator's voice can also be identified on another discursive level, on the level of the narration itself as a voice dislocated from the voice of the narrator of the source text, which it usually mimics. This specific voice, hitherto unrecognized by translation studies or narratology, is what I call the *voice of the narrator of the translation* (see O'Sullivan 2000: 246). It is not heard only where some need for explanation exists or language itself is a theme; it is present in all translated narrative texts on the level of the narrative itself.

The relationship between the voice of the narrator of the translation and that of the narrator of the source text can vary widely, depending on the translation practices observed in a given context. The voice of the narrator of the translation can slip in behind that of the narrator of the source text, that is to say mimic it entirely or (to use a musical metaphor) sing in unison with it. Translations in which the address of the text in translation does not differ significantly from that of the source text, and in which all the voices in the source text are fully heard in their own right in the translation, could be called dialogic (see Chapter 4). However, the voice of the narrator of the translation can also dislocate from that of the narrator of the source text or sing in a slightly different register. This can result in a translation in which the implied translator tries to control the source text with a voice which always remains dominant and organizing and always has the last word, ultimately changing the address. This type of translation could, accordingly, be called monologic.

The voice of the translator and the voice of the narrator of the translation

It is no coincidence that, while Schiavi and Hermans recognize the narratological significance of the implied translator, they give no concrete examples (Schiavi) or cite instances of the translator's voice only on the metalinguistic level of expression (Hermans) for, in canonical adult literature, on which their analyses concentrate, the translation norm of mimicry or both narrators 'singing in unison' generally prevails. The implied translator is a part of every translated text, but in the field of the modern canon of *belles lettres*, apart from offering rare but necessary explanations of historical, literary or other such references, does not usually initiate any crucial change: 'As a rule ... translations, and certainly modern translations of canonical literary fiction, stop short of reorienting the discourse so radically that the orientation of the original Implied Reader disappears altogether' (Hermans 1996: 29).

The particular voice of the narrator of the translation would seem to be more evident in children's literature than in other areas due to the specific, asymmetrical communication structure which characterizes texts written and published by adults for children. In these texts, contemporary and culture-specific notions of childhood play some part in determining the construction of the implied reader. What do 'children' want to read? What are their cognitive and linguistic capabilities? How far can/should they be stretched? What is suitable for them? What do they enjoy? These are only some of the questions implicitly answered by the assumptions evident behind the 'child' in children's literature and behind the child in any specific children's book. The answers provided by a translator in a given time and culture can lead to the implied reader in a translated text differing substantially from the implied reader in the original. The influence of the implied translator, and the presence of the translator's voice and that of the narrator of the translation, are hence disclosed more easily, obviously and extensively in children's literature.

The four individual analyses that follow in this chapter will illustrate how the voice of the narrator of the translation can entirely drown out the voice of the narrator of the source text, producing a new constitution of the implied reader. First, however, I will briefly discuss paratexts as locations where the explanatory voice of the translator as 'translator' is heard. In these paratexts the way is paved for a certain kind of reception of the narrative text, for instance by indicating the fact that it is a translation, but there is not necessarily any reorientation of the narrative text itself. In addition, I will discuss different methods applied by narrators of the translation – amplifying narrative, reductive narrative, and the reduction of multiple address – which lead to shifts in translated texts and their address.

The voice of the translator in paratexts

The voice of the implied translator can be heard in paratexts such as footnotes, glossaries, forewords, etc. These are new messages to the reader of the target text and originate entirely with the translator. Since, if they appear in a literary context, they are a pragmatic addition to a nonpragmatic text, inevitably modifying the character of the communication,[2] the (prescriptive) question of whether paratextual elements in children's literature or indeed in adult literature are desirable is controversially discussed:

> The comments external to the text catapult the reader out of the 'internal situation' and create a metatextual or metacommunicatory situation in which he reflects on the text and his own distance from it. The contrast between the function of the text and the function of the comments not only

changes the effect of the text to a crucial degree, but also associates the text as a whole with a different kind of text.

(trans. from Nord 1993: 413)

The explanatory element, understood as supplementing knowledge about the facts on which the narrative is based, plays a relatively small part in adult literature, where it tends to be avoided as 'non-literary' and alien to the narrative. Not so in children's literature, where the 'explanation of facts, in their most elementary form, has an existence that is taken for granted' (ibid.). In footnotes, for instance, explanations are provided of what may be assumed to be unknown to the reader of the target text. When the translator tells the reader of the German version of Barbara Park's *My Mother Got Married (and Other Disasters)* in a footnote that Thanksgiving Day 'in America is a harvest festival celebrated on the fourth Thursday in November' (trans. from Park 1991: 115), it is clearly not the translation of an explanation to be found in the source text (American readers hardly need to be told what Thanksgiving Day is), but new information composed for readers of the target text, proffered in the translator's own voice.

Paratexts with the greatest possible distance from the narrative text can take the form of forewords or afterwords, which are in the nature of non-fiction. Information about the author of a book and the circumstances in which it was written,[3] or about the historical, political or cultural background of a story, are among the most frequent additions to the text. The implied reader of an afterword, that is to say of a pragmatic text, does not coincide with the implied reader of the fictional text, as is the case in the German translation of Joan Lingard's novel *The Guilty Party* (Lingard 1989), about a girl anti-nuclear campaigner, which includes a fourteen-page afterword on the legal background added by the translator Cornelia Krutz-Arnold. While in this case the distance is great between the narrative text and the paratext, in others an attempt may be made to decrease it. An unusual example of an afterword with an integrated glossary in which the style of presentation tries to close the gap as far as possible between this kind of text and the narrative itself, and between the implied reader of the afterword and the implied reader of the novel, occurs in the German translation by Mirjam Pressler of a children's story by Ruth Almog set in the early days of the state of Israel, *Die Silberkugel* [The silver ball]. An explanation of the background to the plot is given by the translator in the form of a story, and the terms to be explained (printed in italics) occur both in the explanatory narrative text and set separately in the margin:

> The story of the silver ball takes place in a time when the present state of Israel did not exist. Once the country was called *Palestine* and until the First *Palestine* World War it belonged to the Ottoman Empire. Jews had always lived there, *Jews* together with the Arabs.

(trans. from Almog 1993: 116)

In this paratext we hear the voice of an implied translator mimicking the voice of the narrator of the source text.

While these translators are speaking in order to offer the reader additional factual information about a story, others give information about the source text or their own translation. The American translator of Erich Kästner, May Massee, precedes the author's own two forewords to *Emil und die Detektive* with a third, entitled 'This Explains About Some of the Names', in which she directly addresses her readers speaking as the translator (and using the royal 'we'): 'There is no need to tell you that we like this story and believe you will like it too or we would not have translated it for you. But there is need for a word about the German names' (Massee 1930: ix). She explains that 'Mr Kästner' enjoyed finding names for his characters, and that some of the names had a 'special meaning', while others did not, but they all had 'a good German sound', so she wanted to keep them. She not only tells readers what they mean but offers help with pronunciation: 'You must remember that *e* is often pronounced like long *a* and the *i* is often pronounced like long *e* so that *Emil* is pronounced as if it began with a long *a*' (ibid.: x).

There are other types of paratextual explanations that are written by the translator and in which 'the translator' is as much of a fictional figure as the narrator of the novel. Harry Rowohlt took this approach in his foreword to the German translation of Shel Silverstein's *Uncle Shelby's Story of Lafcadio, the Lion Who Shot Back* (1963), published twenty-four years after the American original. The story of a lion who is 'lionized' in society is told by Uncle Shelby, a narrator who makes laconic authorial comments and directly addresses his readers. Uncle Shelby likes to occupy centre stage himself and enjoys playing with the conventions of narrative:

> And now, children, your Uncle Shelby is going to tell you a story about a very strange lion – in fact, the strangest lion I have ever met. Now, where shall I start this lion tail? I mean this lion *tale*. I suppose that I should begin at the moment I first met this lion. Let's see … […] No, I suppose I should start this story long before that. I suppose I should tell you about the lion when he was very young. All right.
>
> (Silverstein 1963: unpaginated)

The lion Lafcadio has a passion for marshmallows, and even has a marshmallow suit made for himself. He eats:

> a boiled marshmallow and a scrambled marshmallow and a poached marshmallow and a marshmalloup (which is a marshmallow soup) and marshmallops (which are marshmallow chops) and marshmallew (which is marshmallow stew) and a marshmomlette (which is a marshmallow omelette) and marshmeverything!
>
> (ibid.)

What is a translator to do when marshmallows are unfamiliar in his culture? Harry Rowohlt adopts the elaborate course of writing a comical 'Translator's Foreword' in a narrative voice which imitates Uncle Shelby's playfully ironic tone, in order to explain the nature of marshmallows to his German readers. Rendered into English, it runs:

> A bit later in this story you will find marshmallows, and if you don't know what marshmallows are then none of the story will make much sense (at least not in the places about marshmallows). Marshmallows ... are round, about the size of a two-mark coin, as fat as a good book, and pretty yukkily sweet and sticky. They rot your teeth. If you have a camp fire you can skewer them on a stick and hold them in the fire until they are all black and nasty, but still as sweet as ever, and even stickier, and now they are only the size of a two-pfennig coin and still as thick as a good book, and they still rot your teeth and probably give you cancer too. Marshmallows come in white and pink; the pink ones taste just like the white ones only much better. So now we all know what marshmallows are. Those of you who already knew know even more about them now, and those of you who have only just found out now know as much about them as the others.
>
> (trans. from Silverstein 1987)[4]

Rowohlt's wordplay is not confined to producing a mock explanation in this narrative voice, he also plays with the formal nature of such forewords, adding an 'Afterword to the Foreword'.

In these examples of explanatory paratexts, the voice of the translator intervenes to say what no other discursive presence in the text could have done. As we have seen, this voice can be of very different kinds – it may speak in a factual, explanatory or didactic tone, it may be muted or take centre stage or it may try to simulate the narrative tone of the source text. Because paratexts are separate from the narrative text, while they might slightly change the character of the translated work compared to the original, they do not actually affect the tone of the narrative text itself; the voice of the narrator remains untouched by these additions. Only an examination of the translated narrative text will show whether the implied translator has constructed a new implied reader by using narrative strategies which differ from those of the narrator of the source text.

The narrator of the translation

The presence of the narrator of the translation is perceptible where the translation is narrated differently from the source text. Among the forms of divergent narration are amplifying and reductive narration, and approaches that, out of concern for the supposed ability of readers and in line with the prevalent norms in the target literature, completely change the address of the text, creating an implied reader of the translation who differs significantly from that of the source text.

Amplifying narration

Explanatory additions to a text can provide an alternative to paratextual explanations. These can confine themselves to a minimum of factual information – for instance, in a Spanish translation of the specifically British terms 'Norfolk suit' and 'Eton collar' the relevant information is added: ' "Traje Norfolk con chaqueta suelta" o "cuello duro de Eton" ' (Beuchat and Valdiviseo 1992: 12). Extensive additions to the text, however, can amplify it to the extent that the explanatory voice of the translator as narrator of the translation is so different in nature from that of the narrator of the source text that it drowns out the original narrative voice. We then have a new constitution of the implied reader. This can be well illustrated from the German translation of Roald Dahl's *The Vicar of Nibbleswicke* (Dahl 1991), *Der Pastor von Nibbleswick* (Dahl 1992).

The clergyman of the title, who has overcome his childhood dyslexia, is suddenly attacked by a condition linked to his former disability.[5] Its symptom is speaking back to front, and Dahl, an expert practitioner of wordplay, is very good at making comic capital out of it. The German text, like the source text, begins by introducing the Reverend Robert Lee's problem. The translation goes on, not exactly making the most of the comic potential: 'To explain this by a couple of German examples, if you read "Leben" (life) backwards it becomes "Nebel" (mist, fog), and the remark "Ich lese" (I read) suddenly becomes "Ich Esel" (I [am an] ass)].' (trans. from Dahl 1992: 9). But when we come to the heart of the humour in the story, the way in which religious terminology or the names of ladies in the vicar's congregation are twisted into sacrilegious or insulting terms, the German version rather surprisingly reads:

> Doch Hochwürden Lee sprach Englisch. Aber auch im Englischen wird beim Rückwärtslesen manchmal aus einem Wort ein anderes. So wird zum Beispiel God zu dog, und God heisst Gott, und dog meint Hund.
> [But the Reverend Mr Lee spoke English. However, sometimes a word read backwards turns into another word in English too. For instance, God becomes dog, and God means 'Gott', and dog means 'Hund'.]
>
> (ibid.: 9)

The explanatory didactic tone of the voice speaking here – clearly that of the narrator of the translation and not the narrator of the source text – turns Dahl's humour into an indigestible language lesson. When the vicar visits a member of his congregation, the dignified Miss Prewt (an English-speaking reader is already smiling in anticipation of the back-to-front version of her name), the original runs: ' "I am Eel, Miss Twerp!" cried the vicar extending his hand. "I am the new rotsap, the new raciv of Nibbleswicke! Dog help me!" ' (Dahl 1991: 23). In the German version we get this passage from the source text in triplicate:

'Meine lieber Miss Twerp!' rief Hochwürden Lee aus. 'Ich bin der neue Rotsap! Mein Name ist Eel. Robert Eel.' Wenn man das im Deutschen hört, klingen die verdrehten Wörter ziemlich harmlos. Aber im Englischen ist twerp ein Ekel, rotsap ein Faulsaft und eel ein Aal. Also sagte Hochwürden Lee zur Begrüssung in Wirklichkeit: 'Meine liebe Miss Ekel! Ich bin der neue Faulsaft. Mein Name ist Aal. Robert Aal.'

['My dear Miss Twerp!' cried the Reverend Mr Lee. 'I am the new rotsap! My name is Eel. Robert Eel.' If you hear that in German, the back-to-front words sound quite harmless. But in English twerp means an objectionable person, rotsap means rotten juice, and an eel in English is an *Aal* in German. So the Reverend Mr Lee was really saying: 'My dear Miss Pain in the neck! I am the new rotten juice. My name is Eel. Robert Eel.']

(Dahl 1992: 11f.)

The elucidation of a joke that explains the meaning of the original and its distortion in order to demonstrate *why* it is a joke can hardly be funny itself; here we have metalinguistic descriptions of comic phenomena rather than their generation in the text. The translation functions only as an explanation of why an English original was funny; instead of appropriate transference of the word-play into German, it has become a language lesson, and the definitions of the 'meanings' in English as a foreign language inhibit any motivation to read on. Here the voice of the narrator of the translation is that of a pedantic language teacher, ultimately destroying the humour and presupposing an implied reader who is happy to absorb information about the comic potential of dyslexia in English.

Reductive narration

While the last example showed the narrator of the translation adding components not present in the source text, the following passage will analyse changes in the constitution of the implied reader of the translation made by the implied translator omitting features, cutting sections of text, or reducing several readers' roles inscribed in the source text to only a few in the target text.

The narrative voice of Erich Kästner, which is theatrical in its self-production, ironic and inclined to metatextual wordplay, seems particularly prone to having certain aspects suppressed in translation. The foreword to *Emil und die Detektive* (Kästner 1929), warning that 'the story isn't beginning yet' and taking as its subject the creation of the book, the writing process, and Kästner's thoughts on children's literature in general, is omitted from many translations,[6] and so are the notes accompanying Walter Trier's 'Ten pictures' that 'have their say' as a preview to the story, the 'building blocks' of characters and settings which the readers are invited to combine to make up a version themselves before reading the novel. They playfully offer metanarrative elements and ideas that children might adopt in making up stories for themselves. They are 'used, like the stills from a film in the cinema showcase, to activate certain expectations

and attitudes by offering characters with whom to identify, scenes of
"suspense", and exciting "action" ' (trans. from Karrenbrock 1995: 187). It is
no coincidence that most translators either leave out this extremely modern
use of elements taken from the new medium of film or integrate it with the
work in some other way. In some versions, the 'ten pictures' of the introduction
are found in the main text as full-page illustrations together with the texts that
went with them in the German 'preview'. The Irish translation is one of those
to offer this rather confusing mixture. Here, for instance, the following text
with the picture of Emil's grandmother, a lady whose acquaintance the reader
has already made at length, is out of place where it appears just before the end
of the story:

> Sí an tseanbhean is gleoite dár casadh araimh liom í, i n-aindeoin a bhafaca
> rí de bhuairt agus de thruibhlóid. Tá daoine ann a bhíor gleoite i ngan fhios
> dóibh fein. Tá daoine eile ann agus is deachair dóibh a bheith gleoite, mar
> ní mhaith leo an ghleoteacht. Bhíodh Máthair Mhór Emil ina cómhnaidhe i
> n-aon teact le n-a mhuinntir i Neustadt ...
> [She is the best-humoured grandmother I know, but she has had nothing
> but trouble and worries all her life. Some people don't have any bother at all
> to keep cheerful. For others it's a strenuous, serious business. Emil's grand-
> mother used to live with his parents in Neustadt ...]
> (Kästner 1937a: 137)

Reduction can make texts intended for both adults and children appear to have
been written for children alone. For instance, the fairy tales of Hans Christian
Andersen have long been considered solely children's stories in the English-
speaking world because of their translations into English (see Pedersen 1990),
and James Fenimore Cooper's *Leatherstocking* tales were regarded as works for
young people in Germany because they had been translated especially for a
young readership; in both cases this was a reduction of multiple address. The
first German translation of A. A. Milne's *Winnie-the-Pooh* shows how a text with
double or multiple address in the original can become a text with single address
in translation. *Winnie-the-Pooh* is one of the most quoted children's books in
British culture, and it has enjoyed almost cult status amongst young adults in
America. The first German translation by Edith Lotte Schiffer, *Pu der Bär*, which
appeared in 1928, two years after the original, was never more than a moder-
ately successful children's book. Although factors external to the text can also be
held responsible for the popularity, or lack of it, of any translation, it seems
reasonable to claim that the comparative lack of status of this translation is a
consequence of the way in which aspects which appeal and are addressed to
adult readers were translated into German.

The 'adult' reading of the elements of Golden Age and the lost paradise of
childhood which infuse Milne's work is a nostalgic one. Indeed, nostalgia informs
the book as a whole and communicates itself to the adult reader in the way
childhood itself is presented. But beyond this general level of appeal for adult

readers, there are specific elements in the text addressed only to them which reveal Milne's ironic view of the adult world. The toys, cleverly personalized in *Winnie-the-Pooh*, are discernible social types – Owl the old pedant, Rabbit the officious civil servant, Eeyore the eternal pessimist, Piglet the coward, Kanga the over-protective mother and so on. The way the animals converse with one another conforms to the social conventions observed by members of polite society at the time in which the book was written:

> they began to talk in a friendly way about this and that, and Piglet said, 'If you see what I mean, Pooh,' and Pooh said, 'It's just what I think myself, Piglet,' and Piglet said, 'But, on the other hand, Pooh, we must remember,' and Pooh said, 'Quite true, Piglet, although I had forgotten it for the moment.' And then, just as they came to the Six Pine Trees, Pooh looked round to see that nobody else was listening, and said in a very solemn voice: 'Piglet, I have decided something.'
>
> (Milne 1965: 52)

Here a conversation is presented in which both parties use polite and ritualized turns of phrase to signal the expression of an opinion or of agreement. However, no opinion is expressed and there is, therefore, nothing to agree or disagree with. The comic effect of this passage for the adult reader lies in the fact that these phrases are spoken for their own sakes only and also in the fact that they are removed from their usual social context. Highly conventionalized small talk is reproduced here by two toy animals who are stumping through the wood. That they are speaking in this manner because they think someone could overhear them augments the comic effect. Nothing is actually said in this conversation. The translator Schiffer took this *nothing* as the synopsis of the conversation instead of reproducing it as a process of communication. Rather than showing how the animals 'say nothing' in German, she lets them literally say nothing – the conversation is not presented in her translation. In the short passage we read: 'they began to talk in a friendly way about this and that. And just as they came to the six pine trees, Pooh looked round to see that nobody else was listening, and said in a very solemn voice: "Piglet, I have decided something." ' (trans. from Milne 1947: 75f.).[7]

In describing Owl's residence, Milne makes fun of the linguistic conventions of English estate agents while at the same time exposing Owl's pretensions and Pooh's easy impressionability: 'Owl lived at The Chestnuts, an old-world residence of great charm, which was grander than anybody else's, or seemed so to Bear, because it had both a knocker *and* a bell-pull' (Milne 1965: 43). The name of the dwelling, 'The Chestnuts', plays on the fact that Owl lives in a chestnut tree; it is also a not uncommon name for an English country house. The phrase 'old-world residence of great charm' has come straight off the pages of an estate agent's advertisement. Schiffer, in her translation, strips the passage of the markers which signal to the adult reader that what is being described is not to be taken at face value. She fails to realize the cultural references of both the name of the house and the estate agent's jargon, and has her Owl living in a strange mixture of a tree and a palace. Even the distance marker 'or so it seemed to Bear' is disposed of, as is the emphasis of the italics, in a statement which claims that it *was* so, hence ridding the German translation of the fun poked at Owl and Pooh: 'Owl lived in the chestnuts in an old, beautiful palace which was grander than anything else the Bear had ever seen, because on the door was a knocker and a bell-pull' (trans. from Milne 1947: 65).[8] These examples of the translation of small talk and parody show how Schiffer dispenses with elements which constitute the multiple address of *Winnie-the-Pooh*, rendering the translation less attractive to adult readers,[9] a factor which surely contributed to its relative lack of success in Germany. This assumption is partly confirmed by the contemporary success enjoyed by the second translation of Milne's book, published in 1987. The renowned translator Harry Rowohlt had introduced 'Pooh' to an adult German audience some time before this through his column 'Pooh's Corner' in the weekly newspaper *Die Zeit*, in which he adopted the seemingly naive persona of a bear of little brain to comment on political, cultural or social matters. Rowohlt, a master of parody, irony and understatement, has righted the shortcomings of the first translation. His version, like Milne's original, is enjoyed by adults and children alike.

Drowning out the narrator of the source text

Shifts in the narrative style of the translation provide evidence of the preferences of translators and their assumptions about their readers, and also of the norms and conventions dominating the translation of children's literature. Even more clearly than in the examples of amplifying and reductive narration above, this is evident when the voice of the narrator of the translation differs significantly from that of the narrator of the source text, drowning out the latter. Various factors may induce a translator to adopt this strategy: the translator may wish to tell the story differently from the narrator of the source text; may have difficulty in mimicking that particular voice; may think that children should be addressed in a way other than that adopted by the source text; or may be guided by narrative methods of children's literature more familiar to the target culture. What follows now are four examples that illustrate how the voice of the narrator of the source text can be drowned out in this way by the narrator of the translation.

The translation by Josef Guggenmos of Edward Lear's The Story of the Four Little Children Who Went Round the World

The first German translation of Edward Lear's nonsense story of the 1860s *The Story of the Four Little Children Who Went Round the World*, published under the title of *Phantastische Reise* [Fantastic journey] (Lear 1973), was by Josef Guggenmos, described in the blurb as 'the most English of German writers of nonsense verse'.

The story of the four children, always calm, composed and anxious to be polite while they have curious and alarming adventures on their strange journey through a world with its own topography and flora and populated by nonsense creatures, is told by Lear's narrator in elevated language, adopting a sober, factual tone. He likes to use so-called 'difficult' words for the sake of their sound, particularly in semantically absurd passages, and uses great detail, generally making essential elements sound incidental and preserving a formal distance without directly addressing the reader or trying to arouse sympathy. The comedy of the story depends on this sense of distance:

> Once upon a time, a long while ago, there were four little people whose names were Violet, Slingsby, Guy and Lionel; and they all thought they should like to see the world. So they bought a large boat to sail quite round the world by sea, and then they were to come back on the other side by land. The boat was painted blue with green spots, and the sail was yellow with red stripes; and when they set off, they only took a small Cat to steer and look after the boat, besides an elderly Quangle-Wangle, who had to cook the dinner and make the tea; for which purposes they took a large kettle.
>
> (Lear 1949: 91)

The narrator of the Guggenmos translation does not want to preserve Lear's distance between himself and the readers he is addressing:

> Once upon a time, it's a long time ago now, there were four children – Susi, Schlawuzi, Max and Milian – who took it into their heads to go and see the world. So they bought a proper boat in which they were going to sail around the world; they planned to come back the other way round by the land route. The boat was painted blue with green spots, and the sail was yellow with red stripes. When they set off they took nothing with them except a small cat, who had to steer and look after the boat, and an elderly Quengelbengel who was to cook the food and make tea, for which purpose they took a fine tea-kettle on board with them.
>
> (trans. from Lear 1973: 5f.)[10]

In translation, Lear's 'large boat' and 'large kettle' become 'ein ordentliches [proper] Boot' and 'ein stattlicher [fine] Teekessel' – adjectives implying evaluation with positive affective connotations, instead of the mere neutral reference to size. The mysterious and inexplicable nonsense figure of the Quangle-Wangle, shown by Lear in his illustrations as a grotesque shadow creature like a match-stick man with long, skeletal, black arms and gigantic fingers, usually hidden behind something, is called by Guggenmos a 'Quengelbengel', suggesting a 'whining' [quengelig] human 'Bengel' [boy]. In the illustrations to the German version he is shown in the same human form as the children, looking like a kindly old sailor. The narrative attitude tends to evaluate and categorize, is less distant. It is suggested to the reader that the journey will go well; the strange and alienating elements are brought back to a predictable world.

Guggenmos's translation is creative. Parts of it are very lyrical; he makes clever use of alliteration, assonance and internal rhyme, and he plays with variations and repetitions (for instance: 'Ihre Aussprache hatte etwas Surriburrendes' and 'friedlich-zwieblich-abgeschieden'), but in using these methods he is practising a kind of verbal humour different from Lear's. It is closer to the silly joke and has more of a cheerful kindergarten tone, appealing to readers younger than Lear's original addressees. In Lear's story, the language, whose logic is partly eroded, is a means of producing worlds of limitless fantasy in itself. Guggenmos smoothes out many contradictions and usually dispenses with the confusion created by Lear's use of opposing adjectives. 'Perfect and abject Happiness' becomes simply 'glückselige Eintracht' [blessed harmony]; 'joy tempered with contempt' becomes a more easily understood 'Mischung aus Staunen und Entsetzen' [mixture of amazement and horror]. Many small explanations and judgemental decisions add up to an altered narrative style, as comparison of the following passage and its translation will show:

> After sailing on calmly for several more days, they came to another country, where they were much pleased and surprised to see a countless multitude of white Mice with red eyes, all sitting in a great circle, slowly eating Custard Pudding with the most satisfactory and polite demeanour. And as the four Travellers were rather hungry, ... they held a council as to the propriety of asking the Mice for some of their Pudding ... . It was agreed therefore that Guy should go and ask the Mice, which he immediately did; and the result was that they gave a Walnut-shell only half full of Custard diluted with water. Now this displeased Guy, who said, 'Out of such a lot of Pudding as you have got, I must say you might have spared a somewhat larger quantity.'
> (Lear 1949: 97f.)

> After sailing peacefully on for several days they reached another country, where they found something wonderfully pretty. For countless white mice with red eyes were sitting round in a big circle there, eating vanilla pudding with quiet satisfaction and in a very well-behaved way. The four travellers ... were extremely hungry. So they held a council to discuss the best way of begging some pudding from the mice. ... Max was to go and ask them. He did so at once. But what was the result? A walnut shell only half full of pudding, and diluted with water too! Well, Max was furious! 'With all the pudding you have there,' he shouted, 'you could have given us a bit more!'
> (trans. from Lear 1973: 33ff.)[11]

The trivialization of the scene presented to the children as 'etwas Wunderhübsches' [something wonderfully pretty], the reduction of 'a countless multitude' to simply 'unzählige' [countless], the rendering of 'the most satisfactory ... demeanour' as an emotional 'stillvergnügt' [quietly contented], the outright and emphatic 'Riesenappetit' [extremely hungry] for the reserved 'rather hungry', the rhetorical question to the reader 'Was aber war das Ergebnis?' [But what was the result?], the strong description of an emotional outburst presented by the narrator with an initial 'Na' [Well] and an exclamation mark, 'Na, da wurde Max aber wütend! ... so schrie er' [Well, Max was furious! ... he shouted'], instead of the cool, 'Now this displeased Guy, who said' – all these shifts produced by the narrator of the translation show that the German version was written for a reader whom the translator does not think capable of dealing with the paradoxes and inconsistencies, the peculiar intellectual play and humorous language, and above all the distanced narrative that are characteristic of Lear's text. Guggenmos makes Lear's extremely artificial prose into a text that 'his' reader will find easier to understand, by adding emotional and trivializing features, smoothing out contradictions and introducing measures intended to appeal to readers. He thus decreases the distance between the implied reader of the translation and Lear's own narrative.

Demands made on the reader by the implied author of the source text can be cancelled out in this way by the implied translator through the agency of the narrator of the translation. This kind of translation practice is monologic; by adopting it, the implied translator tries to drown out the voice of the narrator of the source text through that of the narrator of the translation; this voice is dominant and organizing, it has the final word.

This translation was quickly forgotten, and almost twenty years later the same publisher, Beltz & Gelberg, could bring out a new translation by Volker Pohl with illustrations 'in the manner of Lear' by Axel Scheffler, which was treated as if it were the first German translation. One reason for the lack of success of Guggenmos's version was certainly the illustrations by Anne Bous, which were unsuitable for this story and often downright kitschy. They show children portrayed in a naturalistic manner intended to arouse the reader's sympathy and facilitate identification, and are thus not at all in the spirit of Lear's story. However, a further reason lies in the fact that, in Germany at the beginning of the 1970s, a nonsense story of this nature was not deemed to have a place in children's literature, despite all Guggenmos's efforts to make it more comprehensible. Almost twenty years later, at least a part of the audience for children's books felt differently, so that the new translation by Pohl (Lear 1991) met with an almost entirely positive response – for instance, it was on the shortlist for the *Deutscher Jugendliteraturpreis* [German state prize for children's literature]. However, this new translation, which preserved the sense of distance in the original, also aroused 'old' reservations: 'Beltz & Gelberg have published a wonderful children's book – unfortunately it is not suitable for children' (trans. from Ladenthin 1991: 22), said Volker Ladenthin's review, adding: 'The book is undoubtedly very important and worth reading, but I hardly think it will enrich the world of childhood experience. A child's imagination does not work like Lear's' (ibid.).

The translation by Margo Lundell of Michel Gay's Papa Vroum

In contemporary picture books, words and pictures interact in many different ways to construct meanings; they no longer simply reproduce each other. A famous early example of productive tension between the verbal and the visual is *Rosie's Walk* by Pat Hutchins (1968), a tale of the happy, carefree hen Rosie who goes for a walk round the farmyard, which is told in both text and pictures. The text, which mentions the stages of Rosie's walk on every other double spread – 'around the pond', 'past the mill', 'through the fence' – adopts Rosie's own innocent perspective. But on the pages bearing this text a fox can be seen lying in wait, ready to pounce; the same pages show the oblivious Rosie not only unwittingly escaping him but also setting a trap for him every time. The threatening tale of a creature being hunted, caught and even eaten, and the foiling of that threat, is told only in the pictures, thus lending the verbal narrative its comic effect.

In the translation of picture books neither element – words or pictures – can be isolated, nor are they isolated when the translator translates. In this genre combining words and pictures, an ideal translation reflects an awareness not only of the significance of the original text but also of the interaction between the visual and the verbal, what the pictures do in relation to the words; it does not verbalize the interaction but leaves gaps that make the interplay possible and exciting. The implied reader of the translation should have to do the same work as the implied reader of the original to resolve the complex connections between text and pictures. If a translator is moved by an image in the source text to verbalize elements understood in the original from the picture alone, the special irony of such a picture book is lost and the creative reception of the child looking at the book is restricted. We then have a new constitution of the implied reader arising from the amplifying narration of the translation. The American version of a French picture book by Michel Gay, whose brief texts often leave unsaid exactly what the pictures tell us, is an example of the way in which the verbalization of pictorial information by the narrator of the translation can substantially alter the character of a picture book in which image and text originally complemented each other.[12]

The night-time adventure in *Papa Vroum* (Gay 1986) starts when Gabriel and his father, stuck in traffic, decide to spend the night in their van. While the father is asleep in the back, the van is towed away and Gabriel, who is joined by various animals, is left 'driving' it. The narrative, though in the third person, is focused on Gabriel's point of view and thus relates directly what Gabriel is seeing, thinking and feeling. He thinks that he is driving the van and the reader is not told anything to the contrary. The pictures reveal that Gabriel is not the agent of the action, however, and the point of the story is that this is not made explicit, so Gabriel's trepidation and surprise are conveyed directly without commentary.

A lorry which Gabriel hasn't noticed reverses close to the van and hits the front bumper. Gabriel thinks the noise is someone knocking at the door. In Figure 5.3 he tells the kittens not to wake his sleeping father, which implies that he believes they have made the noise. The text runs: 'He opened the door and looked. "Be quiet, kittens. Papa is asleep." // "Is that your car? Can we get in?" the kittens asked. "Miau, there's a delicious smell of sausage" ' (trans. from Gay 1986).[13] In the picture we see a monkey, again unnoticed by Gabriel, jumping

Il ouvre la portière et regarde.
«Moins de bruit, les petits chats,
Papa dort!»

«C'est ta voiture? On peut monter?»
demandent les petits chats. «Miam!
la bonne odeur de saucisson!»

Figure 5.3 The truck picks up Gabriel's van in *Papa Vroum*. © l'école des loisirs, 1986

onto the van. The text is narrated in the present tense with liberal use of direct speech, making action and words immediate for the reader/viewer.

The American text accompanying the same picture describes what can be seen and interprets it, thus causing a shift in the relationship between picture and text. It runs:

> He opened the door and looked out. There were three kittens all by themselves in the parking lot. They were too little to have made that sound. Gabriel decided to let the kittens into the van. He did not see the monkey that quickly, silently, climbed down to see what was going on.
>
> (Gay 1987)

The narrator of the translation unnecessarily explains what we can see in the picture: that there are kittens in the parking lot and that they are alone. Whereas in the original the narrative is frequently constructed as a dialogue, Gabriel is made into the main actor in the translation; the narrative is now about him. What he perceives and how he reacts are described rather than indicated in his own words. Immediacy is reduced by the elimination of direct speech and the substitution of past tense for present tense. Explaining that the kittens couldn't have made the noise because they are too small and that Gabriel didn't notice the monkey violates a central device of Gay's picture book: the variance between what is shown and what is said. When the van begins to move – the monkey has just been shown playing with the steering wheel – the French text exclaims 'Oh là là! Ça démarre!', but the American text spells it out ('Suddenly the van jerked forward. They were moving! It wasn't the monkey's fault. The trailer was pulling out of the parking lot – and dragging the van behind'), thus ruining the surprise of the later picture showing the van being towed by the lorry. The narrative of the American translation also differs from the original in the stated reassurance that Gabriel is in control and that he is not afraid. Constant verbal reminders of the father's presence in the van – in the pictures he is visible only as a sleeping shape until the final pages – further reassure the reader that there is no cause for alarm.

In the original the pictures tell a different story from the words, the text doesn't divulge more than Gabriel knows, but readers can experience the thrill of noticing more in the pictures than the words have told and draw their own conclusions. They can savour Gabriel's fear, excitement and surprise from the perspective of a knowing reader. The American translation eliminates the tension and, instead of playful irony, we have a nanny text which removes challenge and unexpectedness. Even the cover blurb tells all: 'And when the van jerks forward – hooked by accident to the huge trailer parked in front of them – Gabriel bravely stays at the wheel as they roll faster and faster through the night.' The narrative voice of the translation, explaining everything, is contrary to that of the original, which, brief and succinct, confines itself mainly to direct speech between the characters, thus leaving many gaps for the reader to fill. The narrator of the American translation is unwilling to trust its readers to put the verbal and pictorial elements together, telling them in good time what has happened. The pictorial information given in advance of verbal information in the original, encouraging readers to look and make connections, and constantly producing surprise effects, is transformed in translation into feeble simultaneity (see Tabbert 1991a: 133).

The translation by James Krüss of Leo Lionni's Swimmy

Particularly striking are transformations of the reader's role resulting from the adaptation of translations to certain narrative traditions in the target literature: in Germany, for instance, adaptation to the 'pronouncedly emotional German picture book style' (trans. from Krüger 1968: 41). A good example is the German translation by James Krüss of Leo Lionni's *Swimmy*, which in 1965 was the first foreign picture book to win the *Deutscher Jugendbuchpreis* [German state prize for children's literature]. A kind of fable which does not formulate the moral, it shows the survival of small creatures (here fish) threatened by a tyrant, but saved by their creative ideas and by sticking together in a group. The source text, in the tradition of the fable, does not describe the protagonist's thoughts. In Krüss's translation, which is about twice as long as the original, the main character Swimmy is anthropomorphized to a much greater extent than in the source text – the reader learns much in the translation about Swimmy's feelings and ideas. The narrator of the translation intervenes as an authorial presence, commenting, interpreting, and showing sympathy with the protagonist. The sentence 'But the sea was full of wonderful creatures, and as he swam from marvel to marvel Swimmy was happy again. He saw a medusa made of rainbow jelly' (Lionni 1963) becomes in translation:

But the sea is full of wonderful creatures that Swimmy had never seen at
home in his own corner of the sea. When the great ocean showed him
marvel after marvel, he was soon as happy once again as a fish in the water
(and after all, he was a fish in the water, if only a little one).
First Swimmy saw the medusa, the jellyfish.
He thought it was wonderful. It looked as if it were made of glass, and it
shimmered with every colour of the rainbow.

(trans. from Lionni 1964)[14]

Krüss tells the story in a tone of intimacy and interprets the pictures, unlike the
source text which simply accompanies them. Besides the expansions and the
addition of descriptions of the character's state of mind, which change the
narrative voice to one pronouncedly emotional in style, there is a shift in the
statement of the translation. In the source text a character with the features of
an outsider (i.e. of another colour) discovers that he and his species are in
danger of being eaten by a predator until they find a common solution: they
swim close together in a formation that makes them look like one gigantic fish.
Krüss, on the other hand, concerns himself with the psychology of Swimmy,
profiling him as a distinctive main character (see Meckling 1975: 47). The
common search for a solution – 'We must think of something' (Lionni 1963) –
becomes Swimmy acting as leader – ' "Da muss man sich etwas ausdenken!"
dachte er. Und er dachte nach.' ['Someone must think of something!' he
thought. And he did think.] (Lionni 1964). Thus the German translation of
Swimmy shows how the change of narrative approach 'adapts liberal ideas of
childhood and society in imported modern classics to the more conservative
norms of West German children's literature of the post-war period' (trans.
from Tabbert 1996a: 104).

Such tendencies in translations into German of the 1960s and 1970s can be
observed in other translated books of that period.[15] According to the leading
contemporary theorists concerned with 'das gute Jugendbuch' [good children's
books], German children's literature of the time had to be strictly tailored to
various stages of childhood, and its business was to approach child readers on
the assumed level of their ability to deal with the text, to remove any difficulties
of understanding, and above all to make the reader want to read good children's
books. These ideas became the norms of children's literature and are especially
evident in translations, because these allow comparison with source texts which
embody other concepts of children's literature. Through the shifts in emphasis in
translations we can clearly see what was considered appropriate and good in the
target culture at that given time.

Since the changes of form and function in German children's literature after the
1970s, which resulted in the emancipation of certain areas of children's literature
from explicitly child-related concerns, allowing them to stake purely aesthetic claims,
different norms have also prevailed in the translation of children's literature. In
quality children's literature, within the last three decades we can observe an increase
in translation practices which try to reflect the agencies and narrative tone of the

source text, so that a translation is not adapted in line with ideas of 'suitability for children', but mirrors, as closely as possible, the source text. This is particularly obvious in new translations of texts that had already been translated in the 1960s and 1970s – for instance, the new translation of Lear's *Story of the Four Little Children Who Went Round the World* by Volker Pohl mentioned above, with illustrations by Axel Scheffler (Lear 1991), and the *Paddington* stories translated by Monika Osberghaus (Bond 1995a and 1995b). The practice of translation has thus become more of a dialogue; the implied translator allows the voices of the source text to be heard in translation, and not drowned out by the voice of the narrator of the translation.

The translation by Irina Korschunow of John Burningham's Granpa

A book translated into German in the 1980s in line with the norms of the 1960s and 1970s was so severely criticized that another translation, observing more recent conventions, followed four years later. These translations were of John Burningham's ambitious and much-discussed picture book *Granpa* (Burningham 1984a).[16] *Granpa* is a collection of episodes about a girl and her grandfather, presented as scenes in the greenhouse, on the beach or sitting at home. In most of the double spreads a full-colour picture in a distinctly naive style, showing a situation experienced by the pair, faces a faint sepia picture depicting the old man's memories, the child's imaginings, or some form of association which illuminates or elaborates what is shown in its partner image. The links between the pictures are generally as open as those between the pictures and the fragmentary text, which consists of snippets of dialogue between the old man and the girl. Different typefaces indicate the two speakers; they are shown in word and picture to have two distinct but equal subject positions. The same attention is given to their differing modes of perception, types of fantasies and means of communicating. There is no narrator, no explicit commentary and, other than roughly following the pattern of the seasons, no apparent sequence of events until the final pictures portraying the grandfather's illness and death. The text is distinctly undercoded and there are substantial gaps between the text and the pictures. What does a translator make of it all?

The title of the German translation by Irina Korschunow, an author of children's books in her own right, is *Mein Opa und ich* [My grandfather and me] (Burningham 1984b). The girl is now clearly the focus of the story; it has become the story of her relationship to her grandfather. The dialogue of the original is replaced by a first-person narrative in the past tense. The soundtrack is no longer immediate, what is being told happened some time ago. Where the first picture in the original text shows the girl running into the arms of her grandfather, accompanied by the direct speech of the man 'And how's my little girl?', the German text runs: 'Mein Opa und ich, das war schön. "Hast du deinen alten Opa noch lieb, mein kleines Mädchen?" "Du bist überhaupt nicht alt, Opa." ' ['Me and my granpa, that was nice. "Do you still love your old granpa, my little girl?" "You aren't old at all, granpa." ']. The tense ('that was nice') tells us that their relationship is a thing of the past, pre-empting the old man's death in the final pages. The mode is sentimental, the grandfather wants to be assured of his granddaughter's love while she is at pains to tell him that he isn't old, and the pattern of communication – the simultaneity of the two discourses – has changed. The grandfather has become the object of the girl's concern and no longer features as an autonomous subject in the text. The translator's reading of the text has begun with its ending, the grandfather's death. A popular topic in German children's literature in the 1980s, she elevates it to the central theme of her translation, with consequences for the characterization of the girl. Gone is the unburdened child perspective of the original. Korschunow's girl is defined solely in terms of what she thinks about and feels for her grandfather; she is fixated on him in an over-protective, anxious way.

The picture in Figure 5.4 shows the grandfather, taken ill in the previous scene, and the girl indoors watching television together. Her plans and hopes for their continuing adventures are expressed, in the English original, in her question 'Tomorrow shall we go to Africa, and you can be the captain?', which remains unanswered by the grandfather. There is no other text on this opening in the original. A ship sailing away under gloriously billowing clouds can be seen in the sepia picture. We can't see whether two of them are on board, as the girl probably imagines, or whether the old man, in what is more likely to be his association, is embarking alone on his last trip. The openness of picture and text allows a multitude of possible interpretations.

The text of the German translation in Figure 5.4 crowds this simple scene and closes most of the gaps. The indeterminate ship has become one which the girl in the translation claims to have painted herself. The narrator of the translation takes the scene as a cue for a lengthy discussion about the impending death of the grandfather and about how the granddaughter will cope. Exclamations of mutual affection verbalize in an almost unbearably sentimental manner the closeness so eloquently expressed by the body language of the two people in the pictures. The German text translates as:

Figure 5.4 Discussing death in *Mein Opa und ich.* © John Burningham and Jonathan Cape, 1984

I painted a ship and we sailed to America.
'Do you want to be captain, Granpa?'
'Yes please, if I may.'
'I love you, Granpa.'
'I love you too, my little girl.'
'Mama said that soon you'll be going away for ever, Granpa.'
'Maybe. I am so old now. But when I'm no longer here, all you have to do is
close your eyes and think of me. Then you'll be able to see me.'
'Is that true, Granpa?'
'Have I ever lied to you, my little girl?'

(trans. from Burningham 1984b)[17]

In the final double spread of the original the symbolic force of an empty chair is
strengthened by the visual expression of silence on the textless page. The grandfather's chair is empty on the right-hand opening, while the girl, on the opposite
page, is left alone staring at it. There can be no words because words, in this
book, have only ever been part of a dialogue. Once the grandfather is gone,
dialogue is no longer possible. The almost deafening and certainly very moving
silence on this page is a fitting expression of loss. It also leaves the reader space
to grasp and to respond to the death of the grandfather. There is room for
sorrow. Not so in the German translation (Fig. 5.5). The translator obviously
believes that the antidote to the final silence of death is garrulousness. On this
page the narrator tries to undo the grandfather's death or, at the very least, not
to leave the readers of the translation alone to digest what has happened; the
vacuum is filled with words and the man is brought back to life by having him
talk in the familiar manner with the girl. The tone is one of hope for the future,
the girl has coped quickly with bereavement. The picture is no longer a self-
sufficient expression of loss but an incidental illustration to go with what the
narrator of the German translation wants to tell us about death and how to deal
with it. The German text translates as: 'And then my Granpa really wasn't there
any more. First of all I was sad, but after a while I wasn't. My Granpa hadn't lied
to me. Whenever I close my eyes and think of him, he is with me again. "My little

Figure 5.5 The empty chair and the full page in *Mein Opa und ich*. © John Burningham and
Jonathan Cape, 1984

girl!" "I'm not that small any more, Granpa. Soon I'll be as big as you'" (trans. from Burningham 1984b).[18]

Rather than translating the words of *Granpa*, Korschunow uses Burningham's pictures to tell a different story – a story about old age, death and mourning – in a different way. The implied reader of Burningham's original is trusted to be capable of reading between the lines and the pictures, but the translator clearly considered that text far too open and thus not suitable for young readers who couldn't or shouldn't be expected to understand the complex narrative interaction between the pictures and fragmentary text. The translation fills all the possible gaps with elements of continuity, with a narrative focus and with numerous explanations, thus delivering an infinitely less interesting and less skilfully told story than Burningham's for implied readers who may not be left alone with pictures conveying strong statements. Here, as in the translation of *Papa Vroum*, the translator obviously felt unable or unwilling to reproduce a text in translation which trusts children to be able to resolve the sophisticated connections between the verbal and the visual elements of the books. The preferred solution was to create an implied translator who resolved these in a re-narration of the stories.

However, this kind of translation, allegedly made suitable for young readers, was no longer *de rigueur* in Germany in the 1980s and had unusual repercussions. *Mein Opa und ich* is one of the rare examples of a translation from which the licence was withdrawn by the original publisher. Four years later a new 'authorized' translation was published under the simple title *Grosspapa* (Burningham 1988). Translated by Rolf Inhauser, who has served not only Burningham but many other excellent picture-book artists and authors well with his translations into German, it is true to the spirit of the source text. In this version the voice of the narrator of the source text is no longer drowned out.

In amplifying and reductive narration, in the reduction of multiple address in *Winnie-the-Pooh* that excludes adult readers, and especially in the four cases where the voice of the narrator of the translation drowns out the voice of the narrator of the source text, forcing it into the background and leading, in picture books, to a shift of the relationship between words and images, we are dealing with translation practices that would have been severely criticized by literary pundits as bad translations in the realm of adult literature, with its aesthetics of autonomy. The more children's literature associates itself with the prevailing literary norms of the adult system, the more strongly do that system's criteria begin to take hold in children's literature too, as witness the example of the rapid retranslation of *Granpa*.

Unlike mainstream comparative literature, comparative children's literature must bear in mind that its object of study belongs to both the educational and the literary systems, with a more or less strongly marked tendency towards one or other of those systems at different times and in different cultures. The influence of non-literary standards of transmission and evaluation means that to this day translation practices other than those of adult literature can still predominate in children's literature. Consequently, it is in considering translations of children's literature that the concept of the voice of the narrator of the translation, set out here and illustrated by textual analysis, becomes particularly evident.

6 World literature and children's classics

In the course of my argument so far I have shown, especially in Chapter 3, that 'international' children's literature is predominantly the literature of one part of the world for children all over the world, and that works of fiction flooding the international market are, in the levelling process of globalism, increasingly losing their culture-specific nature. In the following chapter these findings will be studied in the context of the discussion of 'world literature' and children's classics.

Weltliteratur and the canon

In comparative literary studies, *Weltliteratur* or world literature – in the international discussion the term is often left in German because it originated with Goethe – was for a long time the objectification of a Utopian idea of timeless, universally valid aesthetic norms which transcend linguistic and cultural boundaries, and anthropological universals of humankind. While Goethe still meant the term to express literary cosmopolitanism,[1] after the middle of the nineteenth century *Weltliteratur* came to be linked with the idea of a (normative) canon of major works, known as 'great books'. In the 1960s there were calls in comparative literature for a revision of the concept of *Weltliteratur*, supposedly universal but in practice purely Eurocentric, and of the corpus of works associated with it; and since then the idea of *Weltliteratur* has been controversially discussed. While in some quarters there are suggestions to expand rather than abandon the older canon (see Bernheimer *et al.* 1995), others criticize not only the body of works selected but more particularly the criteria that gave rise to it; merely opening up the canon of *Weltliteratur* to let in the previously excluded literatures of Asia, Africa, South America, etc. would not, in this view, constitute a far-reaching revision. Consequently, it is claimed that a consistent decoupling of *Weltliteratur* and canon formation should be the fundamental principle of a new approach in postcolonial discussion, since, in the canon-oriented approach to *Weltliteratur* to date, it had been not the 'difference but the identity of (national) cultures that was decisive' (trans. from Bachmann-Medick 1994: 588). In recent discussion *Weltliteratur* is also related to the new concept of 'world fiction' or 'global literature' by authors like Michael Ondaatje and Salman Rushdie who move between cultures, a concept which can no longer be traced back to nationally specific traditions of reading and writing.[2]

Parallel to the misgivings towards the whole concept of *Weltliteratur* in comparative literature, we find a fundamental questioning in individual literature disciplines of the idea of the canon and its formation, above all in the teaching of literature. Among the objections to a canon are its principles of selectivity, its elitist nature, its claim to be generally valid, coherent and exemplary, its rigid and prescriptive nature, its ethnocentricity, the way in which it relates solely to the values of a cultural upper class, and its status as a collection of works supposed to be above criticism (see, for instance, von Heydebrandt 1993: 10). After two decades of consensus on the negative aspects of canon formation, a counter-tendency emerged in the 1990s, a call for a socially sanctioned canon of literary works as the basis of literary education. George Steiner supports this revision and sees the canon as the result of a historic filtering process that 'sifts and winnows so as to direct our time and resources of sensibility towards certified, plainly-lit excellence' (1989: 90). Anyone who rejects it is 'a waster of our limited receptive means' (ibid.: 91). Renate von Heydebrandt distinguishes between a ' "material" canon of authors and works' (trans. from 1993: 5) and a normative 'canon of the criteria and interpretation' behind the material canon. She pleads for a merely material canon as suitable for a pluralistic society, since it allows 'many people to talk to each other about the same subjects, bringing their different values into play' (ibid.). This material canon should also encompass genres and areas previously excluded from the literary canon, such as children's literature, women's writing, crime novels, and so on. Von Heydebrandt's proposition envisages canon formation 'from below' within different areas of literature; at the same time, she suggests, each area should be represented by its leading contenders in an extended, pluralistic and comprehensive canon.

Since schools and universities, with their need to impart exemplary values, have been and still are the main agencies in canon formation, one can understand why, although some individual works of children's literature have been acknowledged as classics, there is no canon of children's literature based on the authority of carefully cultivated tradition. As it was not regarded as part of great literature, it was not taught as an academic subject and received hardly any attention in universities. But the need for a canon is now also becoming evident in children's literature studies, for the purposes of writing the history of the literature and for university teaching. This canon is established by means of consecrating and preserving the most important texts, by the endeavours to make the subject academically respectable – for its status as a subject for teaching and research is still relatively new – and by teaching requirements at tertiary-level institutions. In 1980 the board of the Children's Literature Association appointed a 'Canon Committee' because, as Perry Nodelman writes in his introduction to *Touchstones* (the product of that committee's work), without a list of works everybody agreed were the important ones,

> there was no agreement about what children's literature could safely be
> assumed to consist of, and above all, about what especially mattered in it –

what most needed to be discussed and studied and understood. ...
Children's literature studies would remain chaotic until such a shared
concept could be developed.

(Nodelman 1985: 6)

J.D. Stahl argues for a university canon of children's books 'that unites a historical survey with examination of the psychological and social contradictions – or,
at the least, tensions – inherent in literature written by adults for children' (1992:
12). Consequently, he includes such texts of relevance to literary history as
Aelfric's *Colloquy* (*c.* 1000) and James Janeway's *A Token for Children* (1672) in his
proffered canon. Only recently, therefore, has academic teaching and criticism
provided the criteria for canonization, the interpretation and analysis of the
appropriate texts and critical editions of (historical) texts that are necessary to
support the process of canon formation.

Texts in the canon of literary criticism are primarily of relevance to literary
history; their reading must be motivated by an interest in the history of children's literature or childhood, which does not make them suitable or attractive
reading for contemporary children. The interests at work in that canon formation, and the criteria of selection used, are not the same as those of a canon of
children's literature for schools, which must accommodate the interests of pupils,
the curriculum and the academic institution (see Rosebrock 1998: 96f.); it must
be based on educational norms and values, and unlike the canon of literary criticism will have, as one of its prime concerns, the ease with which the texts can be
mediated and received.

At present, then, we can speak of endeavours to form a canon (or rather
canons) in the field of children's literature. On the other hand, however, we have
texts and publications that are described as classics of children's literature and
can be associated, although only conditionally, with the idea of a canon. These
classics of children's literature are not what society, academia and educational
authorities have selected as 'the best'; they are often no more (and no less) than a
market phenomenon.

Children's classics

Classics of children's literature comprise works from three distinct sources:

*   adaptations of works from adult literature (*Robinson Crusoe, Gulliver's Travels,
    Don Quixote*, etc.);
*   adaptations from traditional narratives often originating in oral stories
    (sagas, fairy tales, legends); and
*   works of literature written specifically for children (*Struwwelpeter, Alice's
    Adventures in Wonderland, Pinocchio*, etc.), the predominant form since around
    the middle of the nineteenth century.

Some 30 to 50 texts are regarded by the general public and the book trade as
children's classics, from one of the oldest, *Don Quixote*, written over 400 years ago,

to *Pippi Långstrump*, one of the most recent. In between lie such titles as *Robinson Crusoe*, *Gulliver's Travels*, the *Fairy Tales* of Grimm and Andersen, *Struwwelpeter*, *Alice in Wonderland*, *Tom Sawyer*, *Heidi*, *Pinocchio*, *Treasure Island*, *The Jungle Book*, *Peter Pan*, *Emil und die Detektive* and *L'Histoire de Barbar, le Petit Éléphant*. Most international classics come from Europe, mainly north-west Europe, and America. Of all originating languages, English is by far the most prevalent. The function of publishing firms as agencies of selection or at least of transmission, keeping the group of classic children's books on the market, should not be underestimated. Classics are a safe bet for publishers: they sell well, copyright has usually run out so that no royalties are payable and, as they have no immediate topical relevance, their shelf-life is not limited.

Children's acquaintance with classic figures who originally appeared in books is today based more often on their appearance in the media (films, CDs, cassettes, etc.), as toys, domestic accoutrements or advertising items, with commercial as well as technological changes affecting the ways in which children engage with them (see Mackey 1998: xiii). Today the classic nature of these once literary characters and subjects is evident in the fact that, as Bettina Hurrelmann observes, we take them entirely for granted as part of our symbolic environment

> without knowing exactly what stories are really linked to them. Their classic nature is manifested in the diversity and dynamics of their transformations, actualizations and modes of use, which almost always involve processes of de-historicization, standardization, and functionalization according to market laws. Everything stands side by side, as if projected on a flat surface.
>
> (trans. from Hurrelmann 1996: 19)

Classics of children's literature have produced subjects and characters that, like those of the old myths and fairy tales, encourage liberal treatment. That is to say, they are both unique and universal. They can be culturally and historically changed, transplanted to other language areas and other times and media with the appropriate alterations, without entirely losing their identity. In what does their potential for survival lie? What is the source of their individual dynamics which enables them to retain their place on the market in all sorts of different versions and goes on inspiring new adaptations?

There is no single generally valid definition of children's literary classics. This is because of the different contexts found in children's literature: on the one hand, we have the concept of the classic in children's literature research, on the other we have a body of allegedly international classic children's books, of 'popular' classics, present in actual fact (on the market and in the public awareness), which have been handed down over a long period. The concept of the children's classic has been a subject of literary discussion since around the end of the 1960s. In 1969 Klaus Doderer ushered in the beginning of a lively critical and ideological debate about children's classics in Germany. The classics and canon discussion in children's literature in the USA unfolded in the context of the rapid development of children's literature as a subject for university courses in the 1970s.

The origins of the books nominated as classics in critical studies emerging from these ongoing debates vary depending on the compiler's or author's focus of attention and nationality. In Charles Frey and John Griffith's *The Literary Heritage of Childhood: An Appraisal of Children's Classics in the Western Tradition* (1987), for instance, there are discussions of 29 texts, 9 of them not originally written in English; in her *Classics for Children and Young People* (1986), Margery Fisher cites 90 titles, 12 of which were not initially in English; of the 63 titles listed in Perry Nodelman's *Touchstones* (1985–9), only 8 are translations into English, and just over half of Bettina Hurrelmann's 27 classics in *Klassiker der Kinder- und Jugendliteratur* [Classics of children's literature] (1995a) deal with works by non-German authors. A truly international volume is Bettina Kümmerling-Meibauer's *Klassiker der Kinder- und Jugendliteratur* [Classics of children's literature] (1999) with 534 books from 65 countries, although the distinction of 'classic' has been awarded to many by Kümmerling-Meibauer alone rather than having been acquired by traditional means.

In the critical discussion, the potential of a text to be a classic is (ideally) determined by analysis of the source text in its original historical and cultural context, but forms of transmission give rise to products that bear scant similarity to that original, as John Goldthwaite (1997: 67) wrote with reference to Collodi's *Pinocchio*: 'What critics have in mind when they discuss a book and what parents actually bring home to read to their children are more often than not two different species altogether.' It is always possible to rebut critical theories of children's classics by citing contrary evidence from the corpus as it actually exists; such theories cannot explain the selection, evaluation and lasting popularity of works from different epochs and cultures, if they do not also take into account the body of popular classics on the market and how it came into being.

Of the traditional trio of criteria accepted by critics as defining classics in adult literature – quality, evaluation and reception – the last is most frequently emphasized in the children's field. Christian Emmrich writes, of the term 'classics for children':

> It comprises books that have been successful with young readers of different classes and nationalities over several generations, and thus have become favourite books, sometimes described as 'long sellers' or 'evergreens'. In the public mind, they are therefore regarded as models and norms.
>
> (trans from Emmrich 1988: 59f.)

The mention of the exemplary and normative features of a classic in this quotation are adopted from the discussion of classics in general. Emmrich obviously did not realize that it robs his definition of consistency: if a book can become a model because of its enduring popularity, should not the books of Enid Blyton be seen as exemplary models because they have been read with pleasure by several generations in many cultures? More are still bought than many of the titles regarded as undisputed classics. Blyton's *Famous Five* books are included in Bettina Hurrelmann's *Klassiker der Kinder- und Jugendliteratur* [Classics of children's literature] in line with her descriptive definition of classics as "'favourite books" and "long-sellers" ... which have achieved high cultural significance through "persistent" transmission, enduring esteem ... and much media exploitation' (trans. from Hurrelmann 1995b: 20). However, what is consistent for her is not for Emmrich when he tries to adopt the criteria of normativity, for the much-bought Blyton is 'frequently disliked by adults' (Rudd 2000: 204) and not regarded as an example of a children's writer to be emulated.

The criterion of aesthetic quality as a feature defining a classic will not take us far in the discussion of children's classics. In view of the inclusion of works of dubious literary merit in many lists, it is impossible to equate books which have become classics with works of literary quality. Consequently, the attempt made by Bettina Kümmerling-Meibauer to emphasize 'their importance for the development of the history of children's literature and their quality as a criterion' (trans. from Kümmerling-Meibauer 1997: 5) for distinguishing classic children's books from best-sellers is not without its problems. Her prescriptive concept, which informs the selection of titles for her international 'Great Books' of children's literature, ignores aspects of reception, sees the classics of children's literature as 'supreme achievements that have introduced new themes, materials, forms and genres into children's literature' (ibid.), books which 'have played an outstanding part in the children's literature of a country or language area, and are notable for particular innovations or for being representative of their epochs' (ibid.: 6). With this last part of her definition, however, she removes the exclusive link with 'supreme achievement'; in many cases the 'representative' texts also allowed to be classics by that inclusive 'or' are the same books, works of little importance for the development of children's literature, which she previously distinguished from true classics as mere best-sellers.

The yardstick of innovation as a defining feature is itself not undisputed: the criteria for writing a history of literature are not the same as those of its effect and reception. Not all epoch-making books are among those generally regarded as classics. For instance, E.T.A. Hoffmann's *Nussknacker und Mausekönig* [Nutcracker and mouse king], now considered a particularly important and innovative contribution to the fantasy genre in children's literature, was not received at the time as a great (international) success: the subject has become better known through Tchaikovsky's ballet than Hoffmann's fairy tale; doubt has often been cast on its character as a work of children's literature; and it is not necessarily numbered among the titles internationally regarded as children's classics. Norman Lindsay's nonsense novel *The Magic Pudding* (1918), an innovative and important work in the history of Australian children's literature, was not particularly successful internationally or indeed within the English-speaking area outside Australia itself.

Texts classed as innovative in terms of literary history, therefore, often fail to meet the criterion of making a broad impact that is the crucial factor determining the children's classics actually on the market. One can describe them as classics 'that have not yet received the attention they deserve'

(Kümmerling-Meibauer 1997: 5) only from a prescriptive perspective that grants relevance to the quality criterion alone and cannot be applied to all 'actual' classics of international children's literature. But in this case it would surely be more sensible to work with a concept that does justice to these works independently of the effect of their particular historical and aesthetic achievement. In Perry Nodelman's *Touchstones*, which sees itself as a canon but goes to great lengths to avoid calling the titles selected 'classics', the selection was clearly also value-led, but ultimately the books had to combine 'distinctiveness with popularity', eliminating books which 'were undeniably worthwhile, but widely unread', as well as those which were 'widely popular but not particularly worthwhile' (Nodelman 1985: 7).

Selection and reception of children's classics

Reasons to account for the selection and reception of classics of children's literature have been proffered in terms of reader response, of literary history, of the history of ideas and of childhood, or of factors immanent in the text. In terms of reader response, critics try to explain the source of the lasting appeal that allows them to be widely received as classics. One such approach by Gisela Wilkending identifies, as a central element, the 'contradiction between transgressing boundaries and educational function' (trans. from Wilkending 1984: 58). The layer of the work acceptable for educational purposes, we are told, is generally on the surface and immediately perceptible; the contradictory part tending in the other direction goes 'into the unconscious' (ibid.). Similarly, in their interpretations of various classics of children's literature, Charles Frey and John Griffith come to the conclusion that they contain 'disruptive energy, rapid and shocking experience, and persistent revelations of contradictions and strangeness at the core of personal, family and social life' (1987: ix). A good example is *Struwwelpeter*, a book in the tradition of the old cautionary tales, with an educational model which puts all we know of black pedagogics from the eighteenth century in the shade. At the same time, all the stories have in them unfettered drives depicted at length, and the defiance of children who reject all the educational rules and are prepared to suffer the consequences, even the ultimate one of death. For readers, the pleasure lies in the fact that they can follow the hero in a way other than simply that of the linear didacticism of the surface story.[3]

But even a classic like Johanna Spyri's *Heidi* (1880), which from the educational perspective may seem to be a plea for pious delight in renunciation, and a sentimental defence of childhood and nature against the sickness-inducing civilization of big cities, has unsettling elements in it and can be cited as evidence for Wilkending's 'contradiction' theory. Through her sleepwalking in Frankfurt, which is caused by mental turmoil, Heidi achieves no less than permission to regress: she is allowed to go back home. She will not and cannot master the challenge of growing up far away – and this too is a subversive act. She succeeds in fulfilling her regressive childish desire to live in the Alpine meadows with her grandfather (see Hurrelmann 1995c). Those contradictions seen as an element defining a classic of children's literature are linked to the subject of childhood, one of the major themes of the literature of modern times. Childhood as a personal and social theme is expressed by children's classics constructing images of childhood which appeal to both adult and young readers. Fundamental subjects addressing the readers' experience occur in these texts: the challenges of growing up that are either faced or not faced, family ties that are loosened or not loosened.[4] Above all, they offer constructs of childhood underpinned by social myths and autobiographically tinged longings, which are permeated by ambiguities and contradictions.[5]

The idea that childhood is something separate which can be scrutinized and assessed is, as Jacqueline Rose tells us, the other side of the illusion which makes of childhood something which we have simply ceased to be part of. The most crucial aspect of psychoanalysis for discussing children's fiction is 'its insistence that childhood is something in which we continue to be implicated and which is never simply left behind' (Rose 1994: 12). It is a subject which constantly inspires new versions and is differently configured all the time. The depictions of childhood consequently reveal time-specific and culture-specific social and individual images of the child, and ideas of the relation of children to adults, as well as the social and individual needs and projections at the heart of such images and ideas.

Classics of children's literature, then, are also always a field for discourse about childhood. When re-read, they mediate between the former child and the present adult:

> adults often re-read them, once again reading a meaning out of or into the children and childhoods addressed by the works. The works ... thus speak to and mediate between our child and grown-up states. They both define and measure our sense of maturation. They provide one crucial reading of where we have come from and of what paths we are traveling.
>
> (Frey and Griffith 1987: vi)

The different appeal of the text to adults and children derives from its thematic concern with childhood. The 'double-layering of adult and child perspectives' (ibid. 1987: viii) produces an ironic narrative situation that is one of the structural features of multiple address. It means that the adult recipient is 'sometimes offered a second, personal level of understanding on which the typically childish or youthful side of the attitudes depicted is seen ironically in retrospect' (trans. from Hurrelmann 1995b: 17). Many famous English children's books, for instance, are

> read by adults for their own pleasure, not just at the demand of little tyrants. ... A book like Kenneth Grahame's *The Wind in the Willows*, for instance, reveals its whole range of significance only to the adult reader (or re-reader). Reading children's books and reading them aloud thus becomes a continuous Möbius strip in the English-speaking world.

(trans. from Appleton 1991: 30)

This is a quality which leads to a work of children's literature being allotted higher value and status in its country of origin than elsewhere, as it is linked to the source text and can only too easily disappear in translation. This is clearly illustrated by an analysis of Lewis Carroll's *Alice's Adventures in Wonderland* and its thirty-two (unabridged) German translations published since 1869. Although constantly retranslated, it was not until over one hundred years after the publication of Carroll's novel that a translation appeared which gave adult readers an inkling of the complexity and brilliance of the original (see O'Sullivan 2001).

Because of their peculiar forms of transmission, certain titles now regarded as classics have undergone a variety of retellings and adaptations in textual form and in the media, and explanations of why a particular story is a classic, worked out on the basis of the original text, often do not apply to those adaptations; the versions current in other cultures at a later point in time usually deviate a great deal from the original texts. While the more ambitious literary types of translations accept the challenge of the strange, disruptive and contradictory elements that seem to be peculiar to these now classic depictions of childhood written by adults, and try to preserve them, adaptations intervening more radically and rewriting the story tend to tame anything provocatively alien, making the unacceptable more acceptable or entertaining, and removing disturbing ambiguities. This can be illustrated by examples of the transmission of that children's classic *Pinocchio*, features of which also apply to the transmission of a number of other classics.

The transmission of classics: *Pinocchio*

Over 120 years ago the journalist Carlo Lorenzini, using the pseudonym of Collodi, wrote *Pinocchio*. It first appeared in 1881–3 as a serial entitled *La storia d'un burattino* in the newly founded children's magazine *Giornale per i bambini*,[6] and since then has been translated, adapted, abridged and reworked in various media in many different ways. In the print media, besides more or less complete translations (over 220 into at least eighty-seven different languages) and abridged editions in book form, there are picture-book, pop-up book and comic-strip versions. *Pinocchio* films with 'animatronic' puppets or live actors, the most recent one directed by and starring Roberto Benigni, assorted animated films, video versions and countless TV series rub shoulders with the more recent audiovisual media of Super Nintendo games and CD-ROMs as well as traditional audio recordings on cassette and disk. In addition, Pinocchio features as a toy, a motif on wallpaper and bedlinen, and advertising various products (for instance Benetton), in the names of restaurants, particularly pizzerias, and shops. Pinocchio is thus totally integrated into the media system. In contrast to this international reception is the mythologizing of Pinocchio as a 'hero of national identity' (D. Richter 1996: 146), and the high cultural esteem and intellectual attention paid to the work in its land of origin: 'Almost all postwar Italian writers have paid serious attention to *Pinocchio* at some time ... . The academic world of Italy also devotes itself whole-heartedly to the *burattino*' (trans. from D. Richter 1996: 140f.).

I shall take two regions, the German-speaking countries and the USA, to show how differently the story and the character of Pinocchio are transmitted there, and what difficulties for the concept of a children's classic arise from the fact that all the versions bearing the name of the 'classic' are associated with it in the public mind.

Pinocchio *in the German-speaking countries*

In 1905, twenty-two years after the publication of the original, *Pinocchio* was twice translated into German. Dieter Richter sees the reasons for the late reception of the work in the fact that *Pinocchio*, with the rebellious characteristics of its child-hero,

> did not fit well into the climate of German children's literature of the late 19th century, marked as it was by pedagogy, patriotism and religiosity. The author's ironic style and the presentation of his characters as caricatures were ... also alien to children's culture of the German-speaking area.
>
> (trans. from D. Richter 1996: 126)[7]

The translation by P.A. Eugen Andrae, *Hippeltitsch's Abenteuer. Geschichte eines Holzbuben* [The adventures of Hippeltitsch. The story of a wooden boy] (Collodi 1905), which has received hardly any critical attention to date, is a complete version which does its best to be faithful and to reflect the comic, ironic and satirical dimensions of the source text. The translator does not appear to have any programme of his own in mind.[8] Only the names are Germanicized, rather unfortunately in the case of Gepetto, in this version known as 'Schlampel' [suggesting ideas of 'slovenliness'].[9] We have here a remarkable parallel in the translation history of the two children's books that have been more often rendered into German than any others, *Alice in Wonderland* and *Pinocchio*. The first translation of *Alice in Wonderland*, by Antonie Zimmermann (1869), which was also neglected for a long time, is an almost complete version, careful, modestly creative, foreignizing (that is to say, it retains the English features of the story) and endeavouring to be faithful. However, it was not successful and established no tradition, unlike the subsequent, reductive translation by Helene Scheu-Riesz (1912), which was adapted to the norms of the system of German children's literature. The transference of *Pinocchio* follows a similar course. Andrae's translation of the book, keeping close to the original, did not prove as popular as the far better-known and more influential version of *Pinocchio* that also appeared in 1905, *Zäpfel Kerns Abenteuer* [Little pine-cone's adventures], translated by Otto-Julius Bierbaum and issued under his name, or the next translation by Anton Grumann published in 1913, a moralizing version drawing to some extent on Bierbaum and addressed exclusively to children.

Bierbaum, who was well known as a journalist and poet, wrote that he could not give a direct rendering of the Italian original because the clearly national character of the book made straight translation impossible. His interest in *Pinocchio* stemmed first and foremost from the challenge of adapting it to German tradition (see Koppen 1980). The side-swipes at the law, medicine, etc. in Collodi's source text are replaced by new, separately constructed episodes that correspond to nothing in the source text,[10] satirizing the German monarchy, the army, academic life and the jingoistic patriotism of his time (Bierbaum even invents a national anthem for 'The Land of Eternal Games', parodying the real German national anthem). He is criticizing the Germany of Kaiser Wilhelm II under cover of a so-called 'Kasperle' story, Kasperle being the German equivalent of Punch in the puppet show.

Cultural adaptations occur on various levels. Food is made more German, and so are 'foreign' creatures (the cricket becomes a maybug, indeed a Professor Maybug). Especially striking is the difference in setting. Collodi had successfully shown that fairy tales can be located in the bright Mediterranean climate and need not rely on dark forests and castles with many towers (see Santucci 1958: 112). Bierbaum brings *Pinocchio* back to the German fairy-tale forest,[11] at the same time placing him in the tradition of the German Kasperle puppet play and giving him a neo-Romantic German ending: instead of turning into a 'real child', an ordinary human being, Zäpfel Kern prefers to remain a child of nature and an artefact. Bierbaum retains Collodi's satirical dimension, while Germanicizing the text on the planes of both action and interpretation in such a way that only adults can see the meaning behind his free version attacking the era of Kaiser Wilhelm II. This is first and foremost a cultural adaptation of the work for adult readers.

There are some interesting similarities between Bierbaum's adaptation and the Russian adaptation of 1936, *Zolotoy Klyuchik* [The golden key], by Alexei Tolstoy, which also employed contemporary satirical elements. Here the existential theme of becoming human in Collodi's source text, which is also one about acquiring individuality, is replaced by the idea of becoming a useful member of society, so there is no reason for the character of Pinocchio, now living in a puppets' collective, to be transformed into anything else.

Adaptations made with an eye to the taste and traditions of the target culture also permeate the most successful of all German translations, published in 1913, by the teacher Anton Grumann, *Die Geschichte vom hölzernen Bengele – lustig und lehrreich für kleine und grosse Kinder* [The story of the wooden boy – amusing and instructive for children large and small]. It contains additions which refer to popular children's books such as Busch's *Max und Moritz* and Defoe's *Robinson Crusoe*, and has stylistic echoes of the Grimms' *Fairy Tales*. The fairy with turquoise hair becomes blond here, like the boy into whom Pinocchio changes at the end. The dramatic speed of the monologues and dialogues which dominate the original story gives way to a slower and more emotional narrative flow. Instead of the graphic vigour of the original, we find sentimentality reinforcing the moral attitude. The narrator of Grumann's translation clearly takes sides with the father figure ('Tears glittered in the good old man's eyes' (trans. from Collodi 1913: 23)), condemning the wooden boy's pranks – a position counter to that in Collodi's source text. Collodi's narrator allows other characters like the talking cricket or the blackbird to do the moralizing (and instead of being praised or rewarded for doing so, they are significantly beaten or eaten), and makes Pinocchio criticize himself, but he almost never adopts the position of criticizing his protagonist.[12] The ambivalence of the original is replaced in Grumann's translation by clear, condemnatory comments. The end of the story, going even further than that of the original, is a betrayal of the egotistic, life-loving puppet child Pinocchio in favour of the *ragazzo perbene* (good boy). Grumann's Pinocchio, or rather the 'hölzerne Hampelmann' [wooden jumping-jack], explicitly utters the moral in this adaptation: 'How stupid of me to be a jumping-jack so long! I will be a good boy now, and I advise all naughty children not to be fidgety jumping-jacks!' (ibid.: 257). This version with its extra dose of didacticism is the first German adaptation to be solely addressed to children, and it began a tradition of similar translations and adaptations (see Marx 1987).

An educational adaptation made in an entirely different vein appeared in 1988. The protagonist of Christine Nöstlinger's *Der neue Pinocchio* is very much a modern character in his behaviour, language and thinking. *Pinocchio* is given an explicitly psychological dimension that turns the basic educational idea on its head: children, who are small and weak, must make sure they get what they need, must achieve independence, for they can expect only exploitation and lack of understanding from adults. This is how Pinocchio explains his wish to be transformed:

> Pinocchio sat up in his little bed. 'Then I shall stay a child for ever,' he cried in horror. 'I don't want that! Children get a raw deal! People shout at them and order them about, preach them long sermons. And if they're unlucky they get beaten, and they can't defend themselves. Now that I don't even have a father any more, surely I've a right to be grown up.'
>
> (trans. from Nöstlinger 1988: 131)[13]

He knows exactly what his rights are, and what he can demand of the adult world. This retelling of *Pinocchio* discloses, as any particular retelling always will, 'some aspect of the attitudes and ideologies pertaining at the cultural moment in which that retelling is produced' (McCallum and Stephens 1998: ix), in this case a late twentieth-century Western European and American view of children which draws on recent research into the history and conditions of childhood. The version of the story by Christine Nöstlinger, which has been translated into Italian, is as independent of the original as Bierbaum's version and as didactic as Grumann's, although taking the opposite educational attitude. Nöstlinger's adaptation is not particularly attractive to adult readers and can be classified as one of the long series of versions addressed exclusively to children. But in parallel with such versions is another series of translations into German which try to ensure that the appeal of the source text to adults is not lost in translation.

An Italianizing translation addressed to adults as well as children, by Heinz Riedt, was first published by the East Berlin publishing house of Aufbau in 1954 (Collodi 1954) and has been in print in various editions ever since. Other ambitious translations with double address include Paula Goldschmidt's (Collodi 1966), also published in East Germany, the careful bilingual edition by Helga Legers (Collodi 1967), and the version by Brigitte Eichhorn (Collodi 1972). That is to say, a new kind of *Pinocchio* translation began as early as the 1950s in the German Democratic Republic, where its reception as a novel of social criticism undoubtedly encouraged its translation for adults, and in West Germany around the middle of the 1960s, reaching its zenith with the creative translations of Hubert Bausch (Collodi 1986a) and Joachim Meinert (Collodi 1988). With this change of direction since the 1950s and 1960s we can also trace a gradual adjustment towards the Tuscan original (see D. Richter 1996: 132). A long road leads from such entirely Germanicized versions as Grumann's of 1913 to the increasing Italianization of the German-language translations of *Pinocchio* up to Meinert's, which not only preserves Italian proper names and the names of the *commedia dell'arte* characters, but gives the whole text an Italian flavour by using Italian terms that are generally familiar today (*mamma mia, carabiniere, signora*, etc.) and borrowing many expressions from the Italian language. Pinocchio, in this version, is referred to not as a puppet or jumping-jack, but in Italian as a *burattino*.

The history of the reception of *Pinocchio* in Germany is structurally parallel to that of *Alice in Wonderland*, which began with a first complete translation that kept close to the original but was ignored since it did not suit the norms of German children's literature of its time. The reception history of *Alice* was one of 'child-friendly' versions addressed exclusively to children and showing little creativity, gradually coming back closer to the source text again with 'literary' translations in the 1960s, at first addressing only an adult readership but more recently intended for children as well as adults (see O'Sullivan 2001). *Pinocchio* too began with a faithful translation which did not attract much notice, was followed over a long period by translations solely for children, which were adapted to German traditions and above all moralizing in tone, leading on to a more recent tradition of literary translation.

Over and beyond both traditions – translation solely for children, with a strong educational focus, and translation which also bears adult readers in mind and allows the original cultural references to make their mark – there is a third tradition, the strongest and culturally the most influential: the international mass-marketing of the character of Pinocchio for children. I shall turn to that tradition after briefly describing the history of the reception of *Pinocchio* in the USA.

Pinocchio *in the USA*

In his study of various American versions of *Pinocchio*, the sociologist Richard Wunderlich shows how an original text can be adapted to the cultural and social norms of the target culture in order to make it more acceptable.[14] These versions introduced 'deliberate changes in the story, its basic theme, and the very personalities Collodi had fashioned' (Wunderlich 1992: 198) with the result that the popular image in the United States 'of what Pinocchio is all about bears little or no relation to Collodi's original' (ibid.) (see also Wunderlich and Morrissey 2002). The first American translation,[15] by Walter S. Cramp in 1904, is adapted to the new social order and to moral attitudes resulting from the industrialization of America towards the end of the nineteenth century. Self-discipline, industry, obedience to authority and self-denial were the new catchwords. In this cultural context all scenes of violence, social criticism and the criticism of adults, particularly when children are ridiculing grown-ups, are systematically cut from *Pinocchio*. In this first version, and those later American translations defined by Wunderlich as the products of 'industrial moralism', children are a nuisance.

Such versions were superseded in the 1930s by a more appealing Pinocchio, whose image gradually became the standard one still widespread in American mass culture. The character in Walt Disney's *Pinocchio* of 1939 is 'docile, loving and innocent, incapable of provoking anger and more lovable precisely because of his "pranks", which have now become innocuous and cute' (Wunderlich 1992: 207). The outright recalcitrance and childish obstinacy, the personification of suppressed and tabooed drives and desires of adults, are turned into Disney's affectionate, 'sweet' Pinocchio, who raises only a smile; there is nothing wild or alien in him any more – no secrets, no mysteries, no threat to order. In this domesticated Pinocchio rebelliousness becomes attractive impudence. His transformation into a real human child at the end no longer relates to his wish to be grown up, for the American child-Pinocchio does not want to grow up; he wants to be a good boy, an integrated part of a harmonious, loving family unit.

Wunderlich situates this version in the context of the Great Depression and the approaching world war,[16] at a time when the family seemed to be the only secure world and it was better for children not to grow up. With this innocent child, the political message altered too. While Collodi's Pinocchio must learn not simply to obey – it is no coincidence that the state authorities are satirized in the source text – but must assume responsibility for himself and his actions as a prerequisite of growing up, it is incumbent on his obedient American counterpart in the restless 1930s, a time of heightened political awareness and social movement in the States, to promote family harmony and the family hierarchy: 'just as the child should be in harmony with the family, so should the citizen be in harmony with the state – for that is the natural order' (ibid.: 215).

Pinocchio *in mass culture*

From 1922 onwards, according to Ann Lawson Lucas, the Pinocchio industry became a phenomenon of mass production, 'unabated, even in wartime' (1996: viii). Pinocchio became a figure of mass culture who has little to do with Collodi's original text. He now looks the same in Germany as in France, America and many other countries – even Italy itself. Disney's version can still be understood in relation to the norms and projections of American society at the time when the film was made. The fifty-two-part Japanese animated cartoon series for television, made in 1977, goes a step further, even outdoing Disney in simplifying and standardizing the permanently entertaining character of Pinocchio, and in its international media marketing. This Pinocchio is not a 'Japanese', 'Italian' or any other specific kind of child, but is a silhouette which can be identified as a 'child' all over the world (see D. Richter 1996: 135). Its influence on the international reception of *Pinocchio* in the mass media and through licensed products cannot be overestimated. Its Pinocchio is a true jumping-jack, an adventure machine who has lost his individual character; at best the original plot is perceptible only as a rough outline. Pinocchio's wish to become human is no longer the subject, and his random adventures can be repeated at will (for instance with supporting characters such as pirates or zebras, making the distance from the story's Tuscan roots very clear). *Pinocchio* has become a source of material for endless stories, a figure without character or culture.

The range of transmission of Pinocchio

Because the source text has the structure of a serial story, and is a conglomerate of fairy tale, fable, moral tale, fantasy and popular puppet theatre, is both a comedy and a satire, with adventure and moments of gravity, and a book for both children and adults, most adaptors and rewriters (translators included) fail to reflect the complex diversity of Collodi's work in their versions, emphasizing only the dimension of the text that suits them best. In extreme cases, Collodi's *Pinocchio* becomes a kind of quarry from which scenes can be hewn. Leaving aside intertextual references to Pinocchio in connection with the motif of automatons such as the android Lt. Commander Data from *Star Trek*, or the super-robot Number 5 in the film *Short Circuit*, whose deepest wish is to become human (and whose favourite book is *Pinocchio*), the main forms of transmission in the reception of *Pinocchio* can be classified as:

a) literary translations attempting to do justice to the complexity of the source text – in Germany, for instance, those by Heinz Riedt (Collodi 1954), Hubert Bausch (Collodi 1986a) and Joachim Meinert (Collodi 1988), in the USA the one by Nicolas Perella (Collodi 1986b), in Great Britain the one by Ann Lawson Lucas (Collodi 1996);

b) cultural adaptations mainly for an adult readership (for instance Bierbaum 1905 or Tolstoy 1936);

c) adaptations of a more didactic and moralizing nature for an exclusively child readership, usually domesticated, in which rebellion against the compulsion to be a useful member of society is far from being at the centre (for instance in Cramp's (Collodi 1904) and Grumann's (Collodi 1913) versions); and

d) adaptations for the mass-market culture which project a universally acceptable image of childhood, not specific to any culture and eradicating the rebellious, refractory, egotistical, cruel and alien facets of Pinocchio's character in favour of the lovable, cheerful, amusing, ultimately domesticated child who at worst plays harmless, entertaining pranks.

Commercial, literary, didactic internationalizing and Tuscanizing approaches stand side by side with each other in the transference of *Pinocchio*. Mass-produced goods have the strongest cultural influence:

> The problem with Pinocchio is not so much an absence of good editions, for there have been a few of them over the years, but rather their survival in a marketplace that is everywhere driven by Gresham's law, with an unending flood of bad editions inexorably driving the few good ones either out of circulation or else so far into a corner that readers will never find them.
>
> (Goldthwaite 1997: 67)

So what is really left of Collodi's *Pinocchio* in all these translations, adaptations, instrumentalizations and trivializations? According to John Cech, a mythical nucleus remains: it is a 'tale about one of the most basic and universal of transformations: the process of growing up, of moving towards conscience and consciousness' (1986: 176). But this applies neither to the Disney version nor to other products of the *Pinocchio* industry in mass-market culture. If we exclude those versions with episodes that can go on endlessly, we perceive, as the permanent core of the fantastic story, a boy puppet who leaves home to go out into the world, has a series of dangerous adventures which he survives, comes home again, and there turns into a real human boy. The character of Pinocchio, his motivation and the moral of the story are variable: 'The world has distilled the story's meaning into a blunt moral thesis and a couple of weird physical images, the growing nose and the odd-colored hair' (Frey and Griffith 1987: 106). Even if we accept Cech's postulate of a mythical nucleus, we must acknowledge that each presentation and evaluation of the theme of growing up bears the stamp of its specific culture and time. This is very clearly illustrated by the degree of autonomy allowed to children and adolescents. If we had to look for the common denominator in all stories based on *Pinocchio* in all media, we would probably be left with no more than a long-nosed wooden puppet.[17]

The transmission of classics of children's literature

Analysis of the transference of *Pinocchio* across linguistic and cultural borders shows that a subject taken from a now classic work of children's literature can have a dynamic of its own, and that it is therefore essential to look at the time-specific and culture-specific features of translations and adaptations, as well as the mode of transmission. Classics of children's literature are distinguished from adult classics chiefly by different forms of transmission which arise from the necessity of making (old) texts accessible to young readers who, unlike adults, cannot read them 'historically'. This justification for changes and interventions on the grounds of reception entails the risk that arbitrary alterations will be made, with translators and adaptors going on changing texts until they find them 'suitable'. What is more, in versions adapted purely with an eye to

the market, any change that makes a text not just accessible but more entertaining is regarded as legitimate. The transmission of classics of children's
literature thus does not usually correspond to that of adult classics, where the
first commandment is the inviolability of the original wording. Instead,
different modes of transmission in the field of children's literature can be
placed on a scale with its poles defined as 'literary translation' and 'written oral
transmission'.

Literary translation is most compatible with what conventional translation
theory regards as a good translation. This mode applies only to one of the three
sources of classics of children's literature cited above: books written specifically
for children. Literary translation tries to achieve a complete reflection of an original text in all its aesthetic complexity. For instance, Christian Enzensberger's
translation of *Alice in Wonderland* (Carroll 1963), which finally enabled adult
German readers to see why Carroll has won so much critical praise and attention, falls into this category. So do the translations of *Pinocchio* by Riedt, Bausch
and Meinert mentioned above. With this kind of translation it is possible for
adult readers, critics and students of children's literature to read a book in the
target language from a perspective of literary criticism, but it will often be
beyond the receptive abilities and requirements of child readers. An example of
a literary translation than can be easily read by modern children, at the same
time reflecting the subtleties of an original from the past, is Harry Rowohlt's
translation of *Winnie-the-Pooh* (Milne 1987).

The opposite pole to 'literary translation' can best be described by the term
'written folklore' or 'written oral transmission' (see the discussion of the term in
Chapter 2). Written oral transmission replaces the inviolability of the wording
with variability and changes stories to suit the circumstances of time and audience. Instead of coherent and complete works we find compilations. A Turkish
publisher explained his method of dealing with the translation of children's classics thus: 'Why should I bother? The same title has already been published by
many firms. I sit down at my desk in front of the typewriter. Then I take all the
versions already published and write a new one based on them' (trans. from
Erdogan 1994: 576). In written oral transmission, the dominant but not the only
mode of transmission of classics of children's literature, a focus on the function
of a text replaces the notion of the autonomous status of the work in literary
translation. Characters, plots and settings are taken from books and, in the
synergy of cross-medialization and cross-promoting merchandise, are integrated
into other books and products of the media system (audiovisual media, computer
games, toys, the hyperreality of theme parks, etc.), which often relate only
marginally to the original text and context. The Andersen expert Bredsdorff
describes a particularly flagrant case of the rewriting of a plot and, with it, a
whole narrative:

> In 1944 an edition of 'The Little Matchgirl' was published in New York
> with the following note printed on the dust-jacket: 'Children will read with
> delight this new version of the famous old Hans Christian Andersen tale.

For in it the little matchgirl on that long ago Christmas Eve does not perish from the bitter cold, but finds warmth and cheer and a lovely home where she lives happily ever after.'

(Bredsdorff 1993: 337)

No educational dimension can be discerned in either purely literary translations or extremely commercialized products. In the cases in between, which make up the majority of purely textual versions, the translations bear the mark of the dominant educational values and concepts of their specific time and culture, including assumptions about children's receptive capabilities. This educational dimension of the texts is not a distinct point on the scale between the poles of 'literary translation' and 'written oral transmission'; with the exception of the texts at those extremes, it influences all translations and adaptations of classics of children's literature, thus ensuring a form of transmission that is specific to children's literature and distinguishes it from the adult literary system.

Discussion of the concept of classics of children's literature in critical discourse and the analysis of an exemplary transmission have shown how questionable the whole idea of a canon of children's classics is. In practice, we have a number of disparate texts for which there is not, and cannot be, any single explanation of the (canonical) processes of selection, evaluation, preservation and safe transmission. Editions of titles trading under the rubric of 'classics' proliferate, and as a rule their forms of transmission cannot be compared to those of works from the adult literary canon. They are a market rather than a literary phenomenon.

In the discussion of children's literature up to this point, two problems have emerged where 'classics' written in other cultural contexts have been treated in translation as if they were no different from texts written in the source language area.[18] Failure to discriminate between translations and original texts is inappropriate because of the influence, described above, of social, linguistic, educational and cultural values and norms on the transference of children's literature across barriers of language, culture and time,[19] and because of changes brought about in the practice of translation, some of them radically affecting the narrative structure. When people in France, Kenya or Japan speak of *Gulliver's Travels*, *Robinson Crusoe*, *Alice in Wonderland* or *Pinocchio*, it is often not clear which translation or adaptation they are referring to. With such an approach to the discussion of children's literature, one must always doubt how far the statements made can really apply to the original text. In a comparative study, however, the original text must be examined as it is rooted in its original linguistic and cultural context, and the translations and adaptations analysed in the context of their transference.

The second, related problem, shown here in the case of *Pinocchio*, is that interpretations of the original text that try to name the elements which made it a classic do not apply to every translation and adaptation of it, and certainly not to every media adaptation. In children's literature, the ambivalences and contradictions that have been discussed as a possible feature defining a classic can be identified with absolute certainty only in the original text. In every individual case there must be comparative examination of what happens to classics of children's literature in their various translations, retellings, media adaptations, etc. For instance, the first German translation of *The Wind in the Willows* (Grahame 1908), by Else Seup in 1929, which appeared under the title of *Christoph, Grossmaul und Cornelius. Die Abenteuer einer fidelen Gesellschaft am Fluss, im Wald und anderswo* [Christoph, Bigmouth and Cornelius. The adventures of a jolly group by the river, in the woods, and elsewhere] (Grahame 1929), gives no idea of the whole spectrum of meaning that reveals itself only to the adult reader (or re-reader), as it leaves out such passages as the pantheistic, mystical experiences of Ratty (here Christoph Braunröckchen [Christopher Little Brown Coat]) and Mole (here Cornelius Grabfuss [Cornelius Digging Foot]). Only after the publication of the first complete translation in 1996 by Anne Löhr-Gössling – which was actually the sixth German translation of the book – a careful, respectful and indeed reverent version that deliberately reflects the book's classic patina and encourages a nostalgic reading, were German-speaking readers able to receive Grahame's text in this way.

A sober, critical study of classics of children's literature shatters many illusions. Comparative analysis of the texts regarded as classics has shown that the corpus of so-called classics of international children's literature, actually present on the market and the subject of long transmission, cannot be equated with a canon of children's literature. With such titles – books that have sold over a long period rather than being a selection of authors and works regarded as exemplary by a community – the primary agencies of selection and certainly of transmission are the publishing houses. Their classics are not, in the main, original texts or literary translations, but are more likely to be arbitrarily adapted editions of 'well-known' works.

The actual stocks of classics of children's literature, and a possible canon or canons of children's books, the need for which has already been expressed in children's literature studies and teaching, are clearly separate entities. Comparative children's literature could shoulder the task of promoting an objectively legitimate canon. Such a canon, bearing in mind the receptive limitations of children when it comes to historical texts, for example, would have to be a canon for experts; it would not need to resemble an international literary canon in the traditional sense, but could be decentralized. One could envisage, for instance, a canon of north-west European children's literatures that were similar in their development and mutually influenced each other, or one of Asian or African children's literature, or one devoted to modern and aesthetically complex children's literature which would at the same time encourage its gradual rise to literary recognition. Another possibility would be canons relating to certain genres or kinds of texts, for instance a picture-book canon. Taking up von Heydebrandt's concept of a 'pluralistic' canon involving canon formation in partial areas, with 'leading representatives' being placed in an extended canon, one could then do equal justice to the different genres and traditions within the geographical regions of children's literature by honouring whatever is outstanding in its field. This canon of children's literature could thus be genuinely international. Over and beyond participation in the establishment of a canon of children's literature, comparative children's literature would also have to consider which works should be accepted into an extended general canon of the kind proposed by von Heydebrandt.

Children's literature and comparative children's literature in the age of globalization

While up to and during the nineteenth century, colonization by European powers led to the establishment, spread and consolidation of specific hegemonies, the much-cited internationalization and globalization of the late twentieth century, accompanied by what appears to be an ever stronger similarity of lifestyles, is a global interlinking of states and local sovereignties in a system of coordinates which entails economic and political dependency (see Bachmann-Medick 1994: 588). Spatial limitations disappear with the internationalization of culture in what is sometimes called the 'world society', with its omnipresent mass communication and information technologies. We see 'Coca-Colonization' at work, particularly in youth culture:

> MTV, Microsoft, McDonald's – fast music, fast computer and fast food –
> have reduced the aspirational world of most young people on all continents
> to a uniform Magic Kingdom controlled by America. A gigantic network of
> channels of communication and entertainment has come into being, a
> network that floods all markets with US-produced films, TV productions
> and music clips, in order to make more profits. After the aircraft and
> aerospace industry, the entertainment industry is America's second biggest
> successful export, and the tendency is rising.
>
> (trans. from 'Baden wir in unserem Ruhm' 1997: 163)

In the view of most contemporary observers, the oligopoly of rival colonial powers has now been superseded by an American cultural monopoly. The most striking changes in children's culture in the Western countries over the last few decades have been its commercialization and internationalization. Since the end of the phase of reconstruction following the Second World War, and with the general rise in prosperity, Western European and American childhood, as a result of the great rise in children's purchasing power, has increasingly become a consumer childhood. Besides the commercialization and deregulation of children's television, there is a close connection between the media markets and mass-produced goods for children, a field where merchandising is coordinated by licensing agencies. A few examples of the range of goods available in what Margaret Mackey calls 'the commercial multiplication of children's literature' (1998: 188) include cassettes and CDs, plastic models and fruit gums, stickers, colouring books, ice-creams, comics, soft toys, sticker albums, puppets, felt pen sets, bath-foam figures, bedlinen, car cushion embroidery patterns, card games, stencils, dance instructions and cookery ideas for use in nursery schools, and designs for wallpaper and children's potties.[20] The conditions of literature for children have changed, the children's book industry in the leading market of the USA is increasingly dominated by a handful of large media conglomerates for whom publishing is a small section of their entertainment business. This leads to backlists being mined for highly recognizable characters and stories that offer strong merchandising possibilities. As Daniel Hade observes (2002: 511), 'the mass marketplace selects which books will survive, and thus the children's book becomes less a cultural and intellectual object and more an entertainment looking for mass appeal'. With the globalization of (children's) culture, the international influence of these multimedia giants is immense.

The enormous capital expenditure on new international concepts means that only global players can finance them. In commercial television small suppliers must take ready-made programmes instead of producing their own, which means that certain children's programmes are distributed worldwide, or at least throughout the Western hemisphere. The multinational media and companies manufacturing mass-produced goods for children coordinate their strategies beyond the borders of individual countries, further changing and globalizing what were once regionally contained children's cultures. Children's reading matter in Poland in 1995 can illustrate the case: a survey showed that in the younger age groups the book versions of the Disney films of *Beauty and the Beast*, *Robin Hood* and *Cinderella* were easily the most popular, followed by those of Astrid Lindgren. The novels of Frances Hodgson Burnett became very popular after the screening of the film *The Secret Garden*. The biggest sellers among girls of 14 and 15 were the books of the TV series *Beverley Hills 90210* (see Swierczynska-Jelonek 1995–6).

Multinational media conglomerates are perceived to encourage cultural levelling out, plundering mass culture as a whole and taking what they want from various genres, cultural circles and periods. This, it is said, has led both to an internationalization of children's culture and to the technologically equipped childhood world of the 1990s, an event-led society of heavily marketed merriment and instant consumption. However, as Preuss-Lausitz (1995) stresses, not only must we register the risks of a changed kind of childhood, we should also acknowledge the opportunities that come with it, and the same is true of the new media.

For comparative children's literature, the multimedia and mass cultural dimension of its subject present a new challenge. The interaction of print and audiovisual media becomes a focus of analysis, as does the appearance of characters originating in children's literature as companions or electronic playmates in theme parks. Over and above this, comparative children's literature faces a special task in studying the intermediality of children's literature when it analyses the proximity of oral narrative cultures to the new media, the direct connection between (non-European) oral and audiovisual forms of conveying information, both of which dispense with having to decipher written language. As Anna Katharina Ulrich observes:

Traces of living oral traditions are to be found everywhere in books from the cultures where they occur, often in the form of special dialogic and pluri-logic procedures, in some cases as decidedly modern literary processes showing familiarity with the new oral culture of films and the electronic media. These forms are not necessarily, but could be, of particular interest in children's literature.

(trans. from Ulrich 1998b: 121)

On the relation between children's literature and the oral tradition, called 'orature' by Anne Pellowski, in the so-called developing countries, we must ask such questions as:

Do they [theories of orality] distinguish separate types of orature for children, or is all orature for general audiences of all ages? Is there a special language used with and/or by children? Does one find, in the literature and orature for children commonly found in developing countries today, a mixture of the oral and the visual? ... What constraints on children's literature occur in cultures where the language exists in written form but in several different orthographies? What happens in those cultures where written language is very far removed from the spoken language of ordinary people?

(Pellowski 1996: 667)[21]

We have here an interesting volte-face where internationalism in the field of children's literature is concerned. In the 1950s, in Western Europe and the USA, the idea of internationalism deriving from Hazard's ideas was promoted, and children's literature was idealistically declared to be international, although no one knew precisely how truly international it really was. In the contemporary mass-media society internationalization, dominated by American culture, is a fact. The concept of an idealistic *Weltliteratur* for children has been replaced by a real international world market for children's literature, media and other products; the Utopian idea of a world republic of childhood has become the worldwide children's market. In principle, the task of comparative children's literature studies remains the same: just as we must look beyond the Utopian ideal of international understanding between peoples through children's literature to give a precise description of what is genuinely international, just as we must analyse what kinds of transference have taken place when and how, with the dominant factors that have been involved, so we must also, in the world of the new media-led internationalism, accompany the transference of children's literature and culture – different in nature now because of the electronic conquest of space – across the boundaries of cultures, languages and media, describing and interpreting it.

Notes

1 Comparative literature and children's literature

1 Internationalism in children's literature did not begin with Hazard, who had already published several articles on children's books before 1932, but in him the subject found its most widely received exponent. One of the first institutions to concern itself with international children's literature was the Bureau International d'Education in Geneva, which, after the First World War, 'took advantage of the general longing for peace and cooperation and … produced the first surveys of children's literature which were international in scope and intent' (Pellowski 1968: 9).

2 An overview of Jella Lepman's legacy and the 'International Children's Literature Movement' can be found in Tomlinson 1998.

3 See the bibliographies up to the year 1890 (Klingberg 1967b and Klingberg and Bratt 1988). The bibliography from 1890 to 1899, compiled by Ingar Bratt, appeared in 1996.

4 In 1986 Zohar Shavit applied Itamar Even-Zohar's polysystem theory (see 1979 and 1990) to the field of children's literature. According to this theory, literature is to be seen as a differentiated and dynamic conglomerate of systems which exist in a hierarchical relation to each other. Its typical features are internal opposition – for instance between the centre of the system and its periphery – and constant change. The term 'polysystem' was intended to denote the variety and diversity of literal, cultural and social systems that are constantly interacting.

2 Constituent areas of comparative children's literature

1 Translation studies, in the opinion of those working in that field, has developed from what used to be one subject area in comparative literature to a discipline taking a systematic view of all the different forms of contact between cultures: 'We should look upon translation studies as the principal discipline from now on, with comparative literature as a valued but subsidiary subject area' (Bassnett 1993: 161).

2 In this section I am confining my analysis of communication in children's literature to narrative texts only. A model for drama or poetry would call for appropriate modifications.

3 Oswald is a particularly tantalizing narrator because he plays with the conventions of the first-person narrative. Although speaking as 'I', he doesn't identify himself outright and lets the reader guess which of the six Bastable children is narrating: 'It is one of us that tells this story – but I shall not tell you which' (Nesbit 1899: 4).

4 See, in contrast, the remarks of the novelist Michel Tournier, famous as a 'cross-writer', who has rewritten for children several of his novels originally intended for a

general public: 'Sometimes I apply myself so well and have so much talent that what I write can also be read by children. When my pen is less lucky, what it writes is only good enough for adults' (quoted in Beckett 1995: 11f.). His artistic ideal is that of brevity. Consequently, he sees his adaptations for children as a distillation 'resulting in a more concentrated mythic quality' (ibid.: 30).

5 Since the 1950s English/American and Scandinavian literature in particular have had a dominant influence on young adults' books in Germany. In the field of children's books, Dutch/Flemish children's literature has played a leading part since the late 1980s.

6 In its early years, immediately after the war, the IYL positively bombarded publishers with ideas for translations: 'We became as zealous as missionaries in a savage land. No sooner did a first-rate foreign book fall into our hands, than we argued about which German publisher should have it' (Lepman 2002: 117f.). See the annual catalogue of recommendations published by the IYL, *White Ravens* (www.ijb.de).

7 Richard Bamberger and Mary Ørvig, the founding leaders of the Austrian and Swedish institutes, were active mediators, with their work involving them with children's book publishing in their respective countries. This, in James Fraser's assessment, made them forces for translation encouragement: 'Both Bamberger and Ørvig worked directly as unofficial consultants to publishers. Both read widely in English and other languages and traveled widely' (DeLuca and Natov 1986: 145). In American children's literature a small number of women – usually librarians – were influential, such as Margaret McElderry and Ann Beneduce, who were 'widely traveled, widely read, and had a missionary attitude about the importance of children's book translation' (ibid.: 145), or Mildred L. Batchelder, whose name has been given to an important American prize for children's literature in translation.

8 By his own account of it, Guggenmos began writing for children himself after working on the translation of the children's poetry of Robert Louis Stevenson (see Dierks and Nottebohm 1975: 509).

9 For instance, after what in terms of his life as a whole was a relatively short but extremely successful period as a writer of children's books, A.A. Milne took very little notice of children's literature. 'Milne tried to keep his distance from writing for children in general', writes his biographer Ann Thwaite (1991: 411). However, he did make one exception when he introduced Jean de Brunhoff's *Babar* stories into England. He read *L'Histoire de Babar, le petit éléphant* a year after it first appeared in 1932 and urged his publisher to bring out an English version, for which he even wrote a foreword (see de Brunhoff 1934). It is easy to see the elements in *Babar* that might have appealed to Milne: the light satire on French colonial life, the mixture of realism and fantasy and above all the central theme of civilization and civilized behaviour.

10 See the 'readability' studies by Tiina Puurtinen (1989 and 1994) and Cay Dollerup (2003) on translating for reading aloud.

11 See Klingberg (1964 and 1967b), Klingberg and Bratt (1988) and Bratt (1996). See, for documentation of individual areas, such works as Tähtiin (1993), a bibliography of Russian children's literature in Finnish translation, and van Uffelen (1993), a bibliography of Dutch literature for children and young people in German translation for the period 1830 to 1990. Children's books published in German from 1830 to 1990 have been recorded in Klotz (1990ff.). Since this bibliography also consistently lists translations, it represents the first survey of translated children's literature in German.

12 Scherf mentions a collection of 300 old children's books owned by the family of a Prussian general: one-third of them were in German, one-third in French and one-third in English. Until the First World War it was not unusual for middle-class German families to have a private library with this linguistic spread (Scherf 1981: 255). And the first German discussion of Carroll's *Alice's Adventures in Wonderland* as a 'truly classic and typically English children's book', in the journal *Die literarische Welt* in the 1920s (Simons 1926), was based on the original and not the German translation for children. This tradition of reading in the original language is carried on today by

those readers who are not prepared to wait for the translations of the latest *Harry Potter* novel.

13 For instance, the literary fairy tales of Oscar Wilde (1888 and 1891) were used widely in foreign-language teaching, and there are many editions of Erich Kästner's children's books intended specifically for teaching German as a foreign language.

14 The forerunner of the woman teacher in Germany, where teacher training was institutionalized after the middle of the nineteenth century, was the *gouvernante* or French governess, one of whose tasks was to teach the daughters of the house to speak French and instruct them in the 'elegant manners' of France. To have 'foreign employees for teaching in the home, a French "Mademoiselle" or an English "Miss", was considered especially distinguished, and was reserved for the more prosperous middle classes, which thus came closer to the life-style of the aristocracy' (trans. from Becher 1992: 188).

15 Zohar Shavit's monograph *Poetics of Children's Literature* (1986) is, despite its title, more concerned with systems theory than with poetological questions.

16 See, as a further poetological study by the same author, *The Rhetoric of Character in Children's Literature* (2002).

17 See, for instance, Lewis Carroll's parodies of poems and songs in the *Alice* books. One of the most inventive practitioners of metafiction and intertextuality in the late nineteenth century was Edith Nesbit, who often draws our attention to the narrative act and the structure of the story. See, for example, *The Story of the Treasure Seekers* (1899).

18 Death as salvation, in the religious sense, is a widespread theme of children's literature. See the Spanish story *Marcelino pan y vino* [Marcelino bread and wine] (Sánchez-Silva 1953).

19 See, in anticipation of Section 4, the comic intertextual handling of famous death scenes in Lois Lowry's *Anastasia at Your Service* (Lowry 1982), where Anastasia, lying on the living-room floor feeling bored at the beginning of the novel, 'had been acting out all the deathbed scenes she could think of. Beth, in *Little Women*. (A few small coughs, and then, weakly, "Farewell, my dear sisters.") Juliet. (A gulp of poison, a horrible face because poison probably tasted terrible, and then, sadly, "Sorry things didn't work out, Romeo." Charlotte in *Charlotte's Web*. (No final words, because spiders couldn't talk ... .)' (ibid.: 1).

20 See, on the links between children's stories and play, Fox (1993), whose analysis of narrative calls the language of children 'the language ... of pretend play, story, role-play, poetry and song' (ibid.: x). She shows how children intentionally narrate intertextually by building elements or stylistic features (such as a fairy-tale tone) into their own narratives.

21 At the beginning of *The Wouldbegoods* (Nesbit 1901), the heavily referential description of an aunt shows that she is not an enlightened woman: 'No one but that kind of black beady tight lady would say "little boys". She is like Miss Murdstone in *David Copperfield*. I should like to tell her so; but she would not understand. I don't suppose she has ever read anything but Markham's *History* and Mangnall's *Questions* – improving books like that.' Such passages suggest to readers that 'as surely as "you are what you eat", so you are what you read' (Reynolds 1990: 153).

22 Engl. translation *Jamie and His Friends* (Hein 1988).

23 It has to be said that they also went unnoticed in the Federal Republic, where Hein's novel was also issued in 1984. On the back cover of the West German edition a review is cited in which Hein is placed in the literary tradition of the masters of fantasy – the Grimms and Hans-Christian Andersen.

24 The picture book *Les Jeux de la poupée* [The doll's games] (1806) made 'the way girls play with their dolls the central theme of a book for the first time in French children's literature' (trans. from Barth 1998: 31).

25 An exception is Flemish children's literature of the late nineteenth century: 'There were almost no girls' books or adventure stories, although both genres were popular

in other countries' (Bouckaert-Ghesquière 1992: 91). Even today the majority of girls' books in Belgium are translations rather than home-produced (see Desmet 2002).

26 An attempt to write a history of European children's literature was made in *La littéra-ture d'enfance et de jeunesse en Europe. Panorama historique* [Literature for children and young people in Europe. A historical panorama] (Escarpit 1981). However, it was judged 'a crazy undertaking to try discussing so comprehensive a subject in a mere 127 pages' (trans. from Nières 1994: 217).

27 See, for instance, Bekkering and Heimeriks (1989), Noaves (1991), Sønsthagen and Eilstrup (1992) and Birkeland and Storaas (1993).

28 As far as English departments in German universities are concerned, children's litera-ture is, in Dieter Petzold's words, 'a *quantité négligeable*' (1997: 75). Among the few seriously studying children's literature in a foreign language are the German English scholars Dieter Petzold and Reinbert Tabbert, the English Italianist Anne Lawson Lucas and the Irish Italianist Lindsay Myers. In France, children's literature studies gained considerable impetus from the Anglophile tendencies of some of its main representatives. Denise Escarpit, Isabelle Nières and Jean Perrot, who were later active in the comparative field, originally came to it through the study of English literature. Jack Zipes, an American Germanist, has frequently pointed out the influ-ence of German social theory on his work.

29 While in Germany in the 1990s there were 'two well-developed and finely staffed academic institutes devoted solely to children's literature (Cologne and Frankfurt) as well as several influential professorships', in Great Britain, according to Bottigheimer (1993: 91), there was only one 'academic slot for English children's literature'. To my knowledge, only German children's literature studies has made a comprehensive crit-ical reconstruction of its own history (cf. the essays in Dolle-Weinkauff and Ewers 1996).

3 The development, culture-specific status and international exchange of children's literatures

1 'Because of the ideological relations between the Jewish and German Enlightenment movements, German children's literature was not only a natural frame of reference, but also an ideal to be imitated, albeit a century later' (Shavit 1986: 149).

2 The development of the children's literature of North America ran parallel to and was influenced by that of north-west Europe, similarities in society and culture meaning that 'patterns of change in the experience of childhood in Europe and North America ... were broadly similar' (Cunningham 1995: 2).

3 As Osazee Fayose tells us, 'African children have often been accused, whether rightly or wrongly, of not reading outside of the classroom. The fault is not entirely that of the children. Many social and economic factors are responsible for this. There are no cultural or social rewards for reading. ... Children who read are often viewed as lazy, idle children who pretend to read so that they can escape from housework or being sent on errands. Parents and other adults rarely read, so children do not have adult role models to imitate' (Fayose 1991: 76).

4 This situation is not confined to Africa. Manorama Jafa says of Sri Lanka: 'Like other developing countries, the text books have remained in the main focus in the field of children's books. ... In the field of non-text books the market is flooded with books from other countries' (1991: 133).

5 See also the criticism by Riitta Kuivasmäki (1995: 99): 'Zohar Shavit has claimed that literature for children and young people cannot [be] created without the existence of an institutionalized literature for adults. ... This was not the case in Finland. The literature for adults and that for children were developed side by side in the nine-teenth century.'

6 Sheila Ray describes how some Asian countries have been swamped by British and American children's books, and have had to struggle against this flood of imports to produce indigenous children's literature: 'This is particularly true of Malaysia and Singapore where the influence of writers such as Enid Blyton is apparent. ... Singapore imports so many English and American children's books, with no need for translation, that local publishers see little point in trying to compete' (Ray 1996: 823).

7 Although there is an Irish tradition of children's writing encompassing some three hundred years, an authoritative history of the subject – which will be, according to Robert Dunbar, 'a very lengthy and wide-ranging work' (Dunbar 1997: 309) – still remains to be compiled. This is mainly due to the 'strange, complex and fascinating' (ibid.) world of Irish children's literature, which encompasses books in English and Irish, published in Ireland, Britain or elsewhere, by authors born in the United Kingdom of Great Britain and Ireland before Irish independence in 1922 or, after that, in the Republic of Ireland or Northern Ireland, or in one of the many Irish emigrant diasporas, or by writers born elsewhere but now living in Ireland.

8 See for a detailed account of this development O'Sullivan (1996), on which the following passage is based.

9 Since then two of these have ceased to operate and the output of three others has fallen considerably (see Coghlan in press).

10 The *Children's Literature Association of Ireland* and the *Irish Children's Book Trust* later merged to form a single national book organization, *Children's Books Ireland* (CBI).

11 See Rutschmann (1994) for a comprehensive analysis of the special part played in civic education in Switzerland by historical narratives addressed to young people.

12 In 1964 by H.C. Artmann (Lear 1964), a year later by Grete Fischer (Lear 1965). Not until 1977 did Hans Magnus Enzensberger venture on the complete works of Lear and 'smuggle' *Edward Lears kompletter Nonsens* into German (Lear 1977). The first trans- lations of Lear's limericks specifically for children appeared in James Krüss's anthology *Seifenblasen zu verkaufen* [Soap bubbles for sale] (Krüss 1972).

13 They include William Faulkner, James Joyce, Sylvia Plath and, most recently, Madonna. See the bibliography *They Wrote for Children Too* (Apseloff 1989) and Allsobrook (1996).

14 From a study of the titles entered between 1968 and 1977 for the Mildred L. Batchelder Award for children's literature in translation, Joan Stidham Nist concluded: 'In the publication of children's books translated from other languages, the United States is a member of a western European cultural constellation, special bonds being with Germanic language countries' (Nist 1980: 137). In an investigation of 550 translations qualifying for entry at the end of the 1980s, translations from the Germanic languages and French made up over 61 per cent of the total (see White 1990).

15 http://databases.unesco.org/xtrans/stat/xTransStat.html (information retrieved 10 February 2004).

16 http://databases.unesco.org/xtrans/stat/xTransStat.html (information retrieved 10 February 2004).

17 There are no separate statistics for translated works in the USA; the figures for books imported from abroad include English-language titles from other countries (Britain, Australia etc.).

18 It is to be hoped that the biennial 'Marsh Award for Children's Literature in Translation', whose inception in the UK in the mid-1990s was aimed at bringing translated children's literature to public attention, encouraging publishers and promoting a cross-cultural dimension in children's literature in the UK, will help to raise the profile of translated children's books in Britain.

19 The Baobab Children's Book Foundation (http://www.evb.ch/index.cfm?page_id=461) funds the publication of literature for children and young people by authors from Africa,

Asia and Latin America. It produces three or four Baobab books (in German translation) every year and also provides reading lists of children's literature on the subjects of the developing world and ethnic minorities (see Kinderbuchfonds Baobab 2003).
20 Leaving aside Mangas, the international influence of Japanese (para)culture is on a different plane, particularly in the area of leisure electronics, which have become part of global pop culture.

4 Children's literature in translation

1 As Chapter 2 showed, the vast majority of texts are translated from English, so the range of 'foreign' cultures to which children are introduced is actually limited. In addition, not all translations can be classified as literature of a quality which genuinely enriches the target literature; popular fiction series, for instance, make up an ever increasing proportion of translations. Therefore the 'often quoted but seldom substantiated claim that translation brings the "best" of children's literature from many cultures to young readers in other countries ... is undermined by the closer analysis of importation patterns' (Desmet 2002: 263).
2 The typology of texts was developed as an instrument for the assessment and criticism of translations. According to Katharina Reiss, the aim of every translation must be 'to preserve in translation the essentials that determine the type of a text' (trans. from Reiss 1971: 31). In analogy to the three functions of the linguistic sign described in Bühler's *Sprachtheorie* (1965) – depiction, expression and appeal – Reiss identifies three text types, each dominated by a certain function: text in which the content is emphasized ('informative type'), text in which the form is emphasized ('expressive type'), and text in which the element of appeal is emphasized ('operative type') (cf. Reiss 2000: 163). She also accepts a 'mixed form', the 'multi-medial type' (ibid: 164).
3 See the comprehensive review of critical studies on the translation of children's literature since 1960 in Tabbert (2002).
4 Some years later Rachel Weissbrod (1999) showed how this stylistic elevation produced a mock-epic tone in the Hebrew translation of *Winnie-the-Pooh* of 1943, which made it amusing in a different way from the source text but which changed the address, leaving Hebrew-speaking children puzzled rather than amused.
5 Oittinen's dissertation *I Am Me – I Am Other: On the Dialogics of Translating for Children* was published in 1993; her *Translating for Children* (2000), a bibliographically slightly updated version of the earlier work, is enlarged by a chapter on three Finnish translations of *Alice's Adventures in Wonderland*. Oittinen, a lecturer in translation studies, is herself a translator and illustrator of books for children.
6 Her ideas of childhood derive, amongst others, from Alice Miller (1990) and Hans-Ludwig Freese (1989). The damaged, abused, crippled child of whom Miller also writes is not mentioned by Oittinen. But as the author Paul Maar points out in his autobiographical sketch *Meine beiden Biographien* [My two biographies] (Maar 1994), it is this child who often acts as the motive force in the adult who writes or translates for children.
7 These distinctions within a functionalist approach will not be pursued any further in the chapters that follow, as they concentrate on texts from the field of 'literary' children's literature in the widest sense.
8 For instance, Elizabeth Newbery's *Vice in its Proper Shape. Containing Prose accounts of the wonderful and melancholy transformation of several naughty masters and misses into those contemptible animals which they most resemble in disposition* (1774) or, in the German-speaking countries, Johann Baptist Strobl's *Unglücksgeschichten zur Warnung für die unerfahrene Jugend* [Tales of misfortune as a warning to inexperienced youth] (1788). The last great example of the cautionary-tale genre is Heinrich Hoffmann's

Struwwelpeter (1845), which transcends the tradition with its grotesque comedy. After Hoffmann, this form of drastic didactic verse is to be found only in parodies such as Hilaire Belloc's *Cautionary Tales for Children* (1907).

9 See, for instance, *Wie eine Meinung in einem Kopf entsteht. Über das Herstellen von Untertanen* [How an opinion forms in the mind. On creating subject people] (Rauter 1971), and *Als die Kinder die Macht ergriffen* [When the children seized power] (Gormander 1970), books which are concerned to 'denounce imperialism and exploitation in the workplace, and make readers aware of the necessity for a fundamental change in society' (trans. from Kaminski 1990: 4).

10 It should be briefly mentioned that there was a first version of *Pippi Långstrump*, described by Ulla Lundqvist in 1974 as the *Ur-Pippi* and in many respects more 'outrageous', which was rejected by the publishing house of Bonnier. It was the heavily revised version that then won first prize in the literary competition held by Rabén & Sjögren, and was subsquently published. The revisions affected about 40 per cent of the text: 'There is a great deal of nonsense, not least nonsense rhymes, in the original text, which is bizarre and crazy with Pippi making travesties of folk songs and popular hits' (Edström 1995: 3). Edström shows how the sense of humour in *Ur-Pippi* is tougher and more challenging and the character of Pippi is not nearly as social as in the printed version and sums up: 'The *Pippi Longstocking* that revolutionized our children's literature appears as a well-groomed version of an originally more nonsense-oriented Pippi who was not at all good' (ibid.: 4).

11 ' "För att även om dom inte finns, sa behöver dom väl inte skrämma folk från vettet för det, skulle jag tro. Vill ni ha var sin pistol förresten", frågage hon. Tommy blev hänförd, och Annika ville också gärna ha en pistol, bara den inte var laddad. "Nun kan vi bilda ett röverband, om vi vill", sa Pippi och satte kikaren för ögenen' (Lindgren 1945: 172f.).

12 ' "Denn selbst wenn es keine gibt, brauchen sie doch deswegen nicht die Leute zu Tode zu ängstigen. Wollt ihr übrigens jeder eine Pistole haben? Aber nein, ich glaube, wir legen sie lieber wieder in die Kiste. Das ist nichts für Kinder!" Nun nahm Pippi das Fernrohr vor die Augen und sagte: "Wenn wir wollen, können wir jetzt Seeräuber werden" ' (Lindgren 1965: 205).

13 The pistol scene in the first edition of the German translation of 1949 differs from later editions in following the original. Rendered into English it reads: ' "Would you like a pistol each?" Thomas was enthusiastic, and Annike wanted a pistol too so long as it wasn't loaded. – "We can be a robber band now if we like" ' (trans. from Lindgren 1949: 205). A revision of the first translation, never described as such in the publishing details, 'seems to have crept in and ... slowly deviated from the original text' (trans. from Osberghaus 1996: 27).

14 ' "Låt aldrig barn handskas med skjutvapen", sa Pippi och tog en pistol i vardera handen.' (Lindgren 1945: 27) ['Children should never be given guns,' said Pippi, taking a pistol in each hand].

15 Pippi's name was changed in the French translation to avoid echoing the childish phrase for urinating, doing *pipi*. Although the same word exists in German, the German translation was apparently ready to take the risk.

16 Since then a translation by Henning herself of the picture-book version *Känner du Pippi Långstrump?* has appeared in Arabic; a translation of *Pippi Långstrump* by Walid Saif is in preparation.

17 A statement confirmed in the study of children's literature in Morocco by Christine Beirnaert, according to which those responsible in the few Moroccan publishing houses that produce children's literature regard it as a means of conveying educational trends, intended to teach the moral values of citizenship and based on strict obedience and discipline (see Beirnaert 1992).

18 'Da, mit einem Mal, kam mir der rettende Gedanke! Und weil es keinen anderen Ausweg gab, führte ich den Plan aus. Liebe Leser, ich möchte mich so vornehm wie

möglich ausdrücken, um euer Feingefühl nicht zu verletzen. Nun denn: Ich tat, was kleine Jungen, wenn sie viel Limonade getrunken haben, hinterm Haus oder im Walde tun. Ihr habt es schon erraten? Ganz recht! Und was sämtlichen Löschzügen der hauptstädtischen Feuerwehr nicht gelungen war, dem Schiffsarzt Gulliver, einem einzigen Menschen, gelang es! Die Flammen wurden kleiner und kleiner. Das Feuer erlosch' (Kästner 1961: 24f.).

19 The birthday occasion for writing misspelt messages in *Pippi Långstrump* is reminiscent of this episode in *Winnie-the-Pooh*, according to Lindgren herself her 'favourite book'. Pippi is inviting her friends to a birthday party: 'En dag hittade Tommy och Annika ett brev i sin brevlåda. "TIL TMMY Å ANIKA" stod det utanpå. Oh när de öppnade det, hittade de ett kort, där det stod såhär: "TMMY Å ANIKA SKA KOMA TIL PIPPI PÅ FÖLSKALAS I MÅRRGÅN ÄFTERMIDDAG. KLEDSEL: VAR NI VIL" ' (Lindgren 1945: 152).

20 'Du kan inte proppa näsan full med ärter, för den är redan full med snor, snorung där!' (Lindgren 1960: 88).

21 'Inte för dej, din djävelunge' (Lindgren 1960: 89).

22 A detailed discussion of this and other issues in the translations of Erich Kästner's novels for children can be found in O'Sullivan (2002b); Gillian Lathey (2002) has also examined the translation, adaptation and reception of *Emil* in England.

23 These observations were expressed by the publisher Mona Henning in a discussion at the twelfth conference of the IRCSL, September 1-5, 1995.

24 A comprehensive analysis of the German translations of *Alice in Wonderland* can be found in O'Sullivan (2000: 296–378), and a summary in English in O'Sullivan (2001).

25 Antoine Zimmermann was a teacher of German living in England and an acquaintance of an aunt of Dodgson. Her German version of *Alice in Wonderland* was the first translation of the work into any language.

26 See Krutz-Arnold (1978) and Fernández López (2000).

27 Unless a little local colour lends the genre particular interest, as for instance the 'typical' English atmosphere of Edgar Wallace's detective novels, which is not only retained but to some extent even emphasized in translation. This could be one reason for the fact that these books have enjoyed longer popularity in Germany than in England, their country of origin.

28 This money-saving procedure is by no means new. Friedrich Johann Justin Bertuch, author of the encyclopaedic *Bilderbuch für Kinder* in twelve volumes (Bertuch 1792–1830), each with around 200 explanatory pages of text and one hundred plates with 500 engravings, prepared it for export with partial editions set with translations into English, French and Italian.

5 The implied translator and the implied reader in translated children's literature

1 The terms 'the implied reader of the translation' and 'the implied translator' were introduced by Giuliana Schiavi (1996) who, working from observations made by Raymond van den Broeck (1986) and Kitty van Leuven-Zwart (1989 and 1990), theoretically located these agencies in the translated text. She did not, however, provide examples of the discursive presence of the implied translator in actual translations.

2 Theo Hermans speaks of the translator 'ruptur[ing] the narrative frame by means of paratextual Notes' (1996: 34).

3 Quite often myths about the author and creation of a book are passed on in these paratexts. Paratextual information about the author, for instance, is particularly inaccurate in German translations of *Alice's Adventures in Wonderland*. They attempt to address the phenomenon of nonsense through the image of Dodgson/Carroll as a gifted lover of children and mathematical genius, combined with accounts of English drollery.

4 'Irgendwann später in dieser Geschichte kommen *Marshmallows* vor, und wenn man nicht weiss, was Marshmallows sind, hat die ganze Geschichte ziemlich wenig Sinn (jedenfalls an den Stellen, wo Marshmallows vorkommen.) Marshmallows spricht man *Marschmällos* aus, und sie sind rund und so gross wie ein Zweimarkstück und so dick wie ein gutes Buch und ziemlich ekelhaft süss und klebrig, und man kriegt schlechte Zähne davon. Wenn man ein Lagerfeuer hat, kann man sie auf einen Stock pieken und in das Lagerfeuer halten, bis sie schwarz und eklig sind, aber immer noch genauso süss und eher noch klebriger und nur noch so gross wie ein Zweipfennigstück und immer noch so dick wie ein gutes Buch, und schlechte Zähne kriegt man immer noch davon, sowie höchstwahrscheinlich auch Krebs. Marshmallows gibt es in Weiss und in Rosa; die in Rosa schmecken genauso wie die weissen, aber viel besser. Jetzt wissen wir alle, was Marshmallows sind. Die, die es immer schon wussten, wissen es jetzt noch mehr, und die, die es jetzt erst wissen, wissen es jetzt genausogut' (Silverstein 1987: unpaginated).

5 Dahl wrote the book for the London Dyslexia Institute, to which he left the rights.

6 See, for instance, the translations into Irish (Kästner 1937a) and Bengali (Kästner n.d.), and both British versions of the book (Kästner 1931a and 1959). See the analysis of Kästner translations in O'Sullivan (2002b).

7 'begannen sie, sich in freundschaftlicher Weise über dies und das zu unterhalten. Und grade als sie zu den sechs Kiefern kamen, sah sich Pu um, ob niemand anders ihn hörte, und sagte mit sehr feierlicher Stimme: "Ferkel, ich habe etwas beschlossen!" ' (Milne 1947: 75f).

8 'Eule lebte in den Kastanien in einem alten, schönen Palast, der prächtiger war als alles, was der Bär je gesehen hatte, denn vor der Tür hing ein Klopfer und ein Klingelzug' (Milne 1947: 65).

9 For a more detailed discussion of these and other elements in the translations of *Winnie-the-Pooh*, see O'Sullivan (1993). The Hebrew translation of 1943, which in its mock-epic dimension is amusing only for adults, is an example of the reduction of the multiple address of *Winnie-the-Pooh* in favour of adult rather than child readers (see Weissbrod 1999).

10 'Es ist schon eine gute Weile her, da waren einmal vier Kinder – Susi, Schlawuzi, Max und Milian –, die hatten sich in den Kopf gesetzt, die Welt zu sehen. Sie kauften sich also ein ordentliches Boot, mit dem wollten sie rund um die Welt segeln; zurück-kommen wollten sie dann von hintenherum auf dem Landweg. Das Boot war blau gestrichen und hatte grüne Tupfen, und das Segel war gelb mit roten Streifen. Als sie losfuhren, nahmen sie nichts mit ausser einer kleinen Katze, die musste steuern und das Boot versorgen, dazu einen älteren Quengelbengel, der sollte das Essen bereiten und den Tee kochen, wofür sie einen stattlichen Teekessel mit an Bord nahmen.' (Lear 1973: 5f.).

11 'Nachdem sie mehrere Tage friedlich weitergesegelt waren, erreichten sie ein anderes Land, wo sie etwas Wunderhübsches entdeckten. Es sassen dort nämlich unzählige weisse Mäuse mit roten Augen in einem grossen Kreis und assen stillvergnügt und mit feinstem Benehmen Vanillepudding. Die vier Reisenden ... verspürten einen Riesenappetit. Sie hielten daher eine Beratung ab, wie sie den Mäusen am schicklich-sten etwas Pudding abbetteln könnten. ... Max sollte gehen und anfragen. Das tat er auch sofort. Was aber war das Ergebnis? Eine Walnussschale, nur zur Hälfte mit Pudding gefüllt, und der war noch mit Wasser verdünnt! Na, da wurde Max aber wütend! "Bei der Menge Pudding, die ihr da habt," so schrie er, "hättet ihr uns ruhig ein bisschen mehr abtreten können!" ' (Lear 1973: 33ff.)

12 The following analysis of the translation of *Papa Vroum* was first published in *Signal* (O'Sullivan 1999).

13 'Il ouvre la portière et regarde. "Moins de bruit, les petits chats, Papa dort!". "C'est ta voiture? On peut monter?" demandent les petits chats. "Miam! la bonne odeur de saucisson!" ' (Gay 1986).

14 'Nun ist das Meer aber voller wunderbarer Geschöpfe, die Swimmy in seiner heimatlichen Meeresecke nie gesehen hatte. Als der grosse Ozean ihm Wunder um Wunder vorführte, wurde er bald wieder so munter wie ein Fisch im Wasser (und ein Fisch im Wasser war er ja; wenn auch nur ein kleiner). Zuerst sah Swimmy die Medusa, die Qualle. Er fand sie wunderbar. Sie sah aus, als wäre sie aus Glas, und sie schillerte in allen Farben des Regenbogens' (Lionni 1964).

15 See, for instance, the first German translations of Michael Bond's *Paddington* stories. The beginning of the first volume of the original reads: 'Mr and Mrs Brown first met Paddington on a railway platform. In fact, that was how he came to have such an unusual name for a bear, for Paddington was the name of the station' (Bond 1958: 9). In the German translation of 1968 we read: 'Paddington heisst ein grosser Bahnhof, in London. Eines Tages haben dort Herr und Frau Braun einen kleinen Bären gefunden. Darum hat der kleine Bär einen so merkwürdigen Namen. Er heisst wie der Bahnhof in dem er gefunden worden ist' [Paddington is the name of a big railway station in London. One day Mr and Mrs Brown found a little bear there. That is why the little bear has such an unusual name. He is called after the station where he was found] (Bond 1968: 7). Instead of beginning with the important point – the meeting of the characters – the text starts with a topographical explanation. The additional contrast between the 'big' station and the bear, twice described as 'little', is trivializing, the elements of the two sentences of the source text are remixed and reproduced as a more 'comprehensible' sequence of five short sentences consisting of main clauses. See, by way of contrast, the new translation of 1995 by Monika Osberghaus: 'Mr und Mrs Brown lernten Paddington in einem Bahnhof kennen. Es war, genauer gesagt, im Londoner Bahnhof Paddington, und so kam Paddington auch zu seinem für einen Bären etwas ungewöhnlichen Namen' [Mr and Mrs Brown first met Paddington at a railway station. In actual fact, it was Paddington Station in London, and that was how Paddington came to have rather an unusual name for a bear] (Bond 1995a: 5).

16 The following analysis of the translation of *Granpa* was first published in *Signal* (O'Sullivan 1999).

17 'Ich habe ein Schiff gemalt, und wir sind nach Amerika gefahren. "Willst du Kapitän sein, Opa?" "Gern, wenn ich darf." "Ich habe dich lieb, Opa." "Ich habe dich auch lieb, mein kleines Mädchen." // "Mama hat gesagt, dass du bald für immer weggehst, Opa." "Vielleicht. Ich bin schon so alt. Aber wenn ich nicht mehr da bin, musst du bloss die Augen zumachen und an mich denken. Dann siehst du mich." "Stimmt das, Opa?" "Habe ich dir schon einmal etwas vorgelogen, mein kleines Mädchen?" (Burningham 1984b).

18 'Und dann war mein Opa wirklich nicht mehr da. Zuerst war ich traurig. Aber später nicht mehr. Mein Opa hat mir nichts vorgelogen. Immer, wenn ich die Augen zumache und an ihn denke, ist er wieder bei mir. "Mein kleines Mädchen." "Ich bin gar nicht mehr so klein, Opa. Ich bin bald so gross wie du" ' (Burningham 1984b).

6 World literature and children's classics

1 Goethe countered the increasing literary nationalism in Europe of the Romantic era by cultivating international literary connections. He emphasized the importance of personal contact between authors through travel, the significance of translations for the development of a national literature, and the invaluable contribution of literary journals with an international outlook (see Koppen 1984: 816).

2 A comprehensive discussion of what 'world literature' comprises today can be found in Damrosch (2003).

3 See Peter Weiss's reception of *Struwwelpeter*: 'Struwwelpeter and his cronies acted out all my own faults, terrors and desires. The naïve, brightly coloured pictures were like

scenes from my own dreams, there were the amputated, bleeding thumbs and the huge open blades of the scissors ready to cut off yet more, there was Augustus and his words, *Not any soup for me, I say, I won't have any soup today* were my own words, it was I myself rocking back and forth on the chair and pulling the tablecloth down with all the plates and food on it as I fell. It was revenge. It served them right for all their nagging and admonishing' (trans. from Weiss 1961: 12).

4 See Jerry Griswold (1992), who sees an 'ur-story' (ibid.: xi) in the classics of North American children's literature in which children overcome their parents (symbolically as well as in fact) and thus achieve independence (see Chapter 3).

5 See the destruction of rebellious child figures in literature (for instance in Wilhelm Busch's *Max und Moritz, 1865*). A characteristic feature of the dealings of the adult author and reader with the child who is driven by his urges is the ambiguity 'that derives from the regressive pull of the child in us even as we enforce the role of responsible adults upon ourselves. Our idea of maturity and a workable social order necessitates the repression of the child whose amoral vitality and primordiality represent a threat to that idea' (Perella 1986: 48).

6 This form of serial publication determines the structure of *Pinocchio*, in which the various adventures are episodic in nature. It also explains the contradictions of characterization, caused by the long breaks in the writing of the story. It was originally to have ended with Chapter 15: Pinocchio is hung from the Great Oak by the murderers, and his last thought is for his father. This is an 'ending in the style of the cautionary tale' (trans. from D. Richter 1996: 51). But for economic and literary reasons, it was not expedient for Pinocchio to die. What follows alters the whole character of the hero, and the theme of his metamorphosis into a human becomes central; the cautionary tale becomes a novel of childhood (ibid.: 53).

7 It is interesting to compare this delayed reception with the immediate German translation of the other famous Italian children's book of this period, *Cuore* [Heart] (de Amicis 1886), whose protagonist Enrico is 'what Pinocchio became only at the end: a *ragazzo perbene*, a good boy' (trans. from D. Richter 1996: 105).

8 The straightforward title of Andrae's translation is in striking contrast to the titles of two versions for children which appeared after 1905 and stress that the adaptations are intended to teach a moral lesson. They are: *Die Geschichte vom hölzernen Bengele – lustig und lehrreich für kleine und grosse Kinder* [The story of the wooden boy – amusing and instructive for children large and small] (Collodi 1913), and *Hölzele, der Hampelmann, der schlimm ist und nicht folgen kann! Eine viellehrreiche Böse-Buben-Geschichte* [Woody the jumping-jack, who is naughty and disobedient! A very instructive story of a bad boy] (Collodi 1923).

9 Not until 1944 was Collodi's protagonist called 'Pinocchio' in a German translation (Collodi 1944). Even in 1949 one German translator was anxious 'to spare German children the foreign name Pinocchio, which would certainly only rarely be correctly pronounced Pinókkio' by calling 'the boy "Purzel" [little creature – to "purzel" literally means to tumble] because he is such a funny little thing' (trans. from Birnbaum 1949: 209f.). The influence and later familiarity of the Disney film (1939) using the Italian name in its title made the name *Pinocchio* more acceptable. The last German version to use a different name appeared in 1956 as *Die Geschichte vom hölzernen Hampelchen* [The story of the little wooden jumping-jack] (Collodi 1956). Among Pinocchio's German names are Hippeltitsch, Zäpfel Kern, das hölzerne Bengele, Kasperle, Klötzi, Larifari (with reference to Franz von Pocci's famous Munich puppet character), Purzel and Hampelchen. See, in contrast, the first English translation of 1891, which immediately uses the name Pinocchio in the title (Collodi 1891).

10 See, for instance, the episodes about Wanstphalen (*Wanst* = belly, while the full place name plays on Westfalen, Westphalia), 'the land of pot-bellies who do nothing but eat dumplings and drink thick brown beer. Happy people, clever people' (trans. from Bierbaum 1905: 215).

11 The piece of wood that will later become Zäpfel Kern is handed over by a little brownie with a long white beard and bright blue eyes, a figure straight from a fairy-tale forest in the German tradition.

12 Collodi's narrator criticizes naughty children – 'ragazzi cattivi' – in general, and says of lying that it is the worst character flaw a boy can have, and speaks out once against Pinocchio by equating him with all ignorant, heartless children ('come ... tutti i ragazzi senza un fil di guidizio e senza cuore' (Collodi 1993: 136) [Like all children who have no sense and no feeling]). Otherwise, the narrator's sympathies tend to be on Pinocchio's side; he several times speaks of him sympathetically as 'il povero Pinocchio' [poor Pinocchio] and praises his 'buon cuore' [good heart] (ibid.: 56) or 'cuore eccellente' [excellent heart] (ibid.: 224). Collodi's affection for the puppet boy explains his saying later that he could not remember writing the close of the story, particularly the last cruel, treacherous comment made by Pinocchio as a real boy just after his transformation, when he looks at the now life-less *burattino* and says, 'con grandissima compiacenza ... "Come'ero buffo, quand'ero burattino! E come ora son contento di essere diventato un ragazzino perbene!" ' (Collodi 1993: 362) [with the greatest satisfaction ... 'How funny I was when I was a puppet! And how happy I am now that I've become a proper boy.']. Collodi's uneasiness 'betrays the ambivalent attitude he had towards his wayward, unregimented puppet and the deep-rooted sympathy he had for the free-living street kid' (Perella 1986: 55).

13 'Pinocchio fuhr aus dem Bettchen hoch. "Dann bleibe ich ja auf ewig ein Kind", rief er entsetzt. "Das will ich nicht! Kinder sind übel dran! Sie werden ausgeschimpft und herumkommandiert, man hält ihnen lange Predigten. Wenn sie es schlecht treffen, werden sie sogar geprügelt und können sich dagegen nicht wehren. Und jetzt, wo ich nicht einmal mehr einen Vater habe, hätte ich doch jedes Recht darauf, erwachsen zu werden" ' (Nöstlinger 1988: 131).

14 As a sociologist, Wunderlich traces the various influences of prevailing social, political and educational norms but excludes the field of aesthetic norms in the narrower sense, ones that influence the literary form of translations.

15 The first English translation, by Mary Alice Murray, appeared in 1891 and is still well thought of today as a direct, fresh, exact version for adults and children.

16 Two further versions of *Pinocchio* produced in the 1930s – a dramatized version first performed in 1937 (Frank 1939) and a retelling, *Pinocchio: A Story for Children* (Collodi 1939) – which appeared before Disney's and very probably influenced it, display a similar tendency.

17 Something similar can be said of other characters from classics of children's litera-ture. *Peter Pan*, for instance, in transmission, changes from an egotistical, cruel boy to a fantastic flying playmate, and *Heidi* loses its disturbing psychological elements in the Japanese cartoon film, where we see an 'irrepressible Heidi leaping about in the meadows ... , a kind of laughing garden gnome in a dirndl dress' (trans. from Hurrelmann 1995b: 201).

18 This is still frequently the case. In one of the rare contributions to the study of classics of children's literature that does differentiate, J. D. Stahl distinguishes between books that have achieved classic status in their own culture, which he calls 'simple classics', and those from other cultures – which he calls 'transfer classics' – and observes that their dynamics are very different: 'Transfer classics exist in a more superficial, less conclusive relationship to their society of adoption than to their society of origin. The same works are often problematic in the country of origin because the issues they raise are still alive, though in different ways than at the time these works first appeared' (Stahl 1985: 27). The relatively unproblematic reception in Germany of *Uncle Tom's Cabin* is cited as an example, a book that Stahl says cannot be read 'undisturbedly' in America by either a black or a white child.

19 A recent example of inadequate awareness of the translation occurs in an article on *Heidi* by Maria Nikolajeva, in which the English translation is unthinkingly analysed as an original text (Nikolajeva 2000).

20 See the exhaustive list of products through which *Curious George* can currently be experienced in Daniel Hade's article (2002) on how massive changes in the publishing industry are altering the way children read today.

21 All these questions so far remain unanswered, since there are hardly any studies of 'orature for children that include examples from many cultures' (Pellowski 1996: 667).

Bibliography

Primary sources

Ahlberg, J. and Ahlberg, A. (1986) *The Jolly Postman or Other People's Letters*, London: Heinemann.

Ahlberg, J. and Ahlberg, A. (1987) *Each Peach Pear Plum*, London: Heinemann.

Ahlberg, A. and Amstutz, A. (1983) *Ten in a Bed*, London: Granada.

Aiken, J. (1993) *Rabenspass in der Regenwassergasse*, German trans. S. Gräfin Schönfeldt, Hamburg: Oetinger. (*Mortimer Says Nothing* 1985).

Alcott, L.M. (1868) *Little Women; or Meg, Jo, Beth and Amy*, Boston: Roberts Bros.

Alington, G. (1977) *Willow's Luck*, London: Heinemann.

Almog, R. (1993) *Die Silberkugel*, German trans. M. Pressler, Mölding, Vienna: St. Gabriel. [The silver ball]. (*Kadur ha-kesef* 1986).

Amicis, E. de (1886) *Cuore. Libro per i ragazzi*, Milano: Treves. [Heart].

Barrie, J.M. (1904) *Peter Pan, or the Boy Who Wouldn't Grow Up*, Play. First performance London 1904.

Barrie, J.M. (1911) *Peter and Wendy*, London: Hodder & Stoughton.

Baum, L.F. (1900) *The Wonderful Wizard of Oz*, Chicago, New York: Hill.

Belloc, H. (1907) *Cautionary Tales for Children: Designed for the Admonition of Children between the Ages of Eight and Fourteen Years*, London: Nash.

Berquin, A. (1782–3) *L'Ami des Enfants*, Paris. [The children's friend].

Bertuch, F.J.J. (1792–1830) *Bilderbuch für Kinder enthaltend eine angenehme Sammlung von Tieren, Pflanzen, Blumen, Früchten, Mineralien, Trachten und allerhand andern unterrichtenden Gegen-ständen aus dem Reiche der Natur, der Künste und Wissenschaften; alle nach den besten Originalen gewählt, gestochen, und mit einer kurzen wissenschaftlichen, und den Verstandes-Kräften eines Kindes angemessenen Erklärung begleitet*, 12 vols, Weimar: Industrie-Comptoir. [Children's picture book containing a delightful collection of animals, plants, flowers, fruits, minerals, clothing].

Bichsel, P. (1969) *Kindergeschichten*, Neuwied, Berlin: Luchterhand. [Children's stories].

Bichsel, P. (1970) *There's No Such Place as America*, English trans. M. Hamburger, New York: Delacorte. (*Kindergeschichten* 1969).

Bierbaum, O.J. (1905) *Zäpfel Kerns Abenteuer. Eine deutsche Kasperlegeschichte in dreiundvierzig Kapiteln. Frei nach Collodis italienischer Puppenhistorie Pinocchio*, Cologne: Hermann Schaffstein. [Little pine-cone's adventures].

Bojunga-Nunes, L. (1979) *Corda Bamba*, Rio de Janeiro: Editora Civilização. [Tightrope].

Bond, M. (1958) *A Bear Called Paddington*, London: Collins.

Bond, M. (1959) *More about Paddington*, London: Collins.

Bond, M. (1968) *Paddington. Unser kleiner Bär*, German trans. B. von Mechnow and P. Kent, Zurich, Einsiedeln, Cologne: Benziger. (*A Bear Called Paddington* 1958).

Bond, M. (1969) *Paddington: Neue Abenteuer des kleinen Bären*, German trans. K. Recheis, Zurich, Einsiedeln, Cologne: Benziger. (*More about Paddington* 1959).

Bond, M. (1995a) *Ein Bär mit Namen Paddington*, German trans. M. Osberghaus, Munich, Vienna: Hanser. (*A Bear Called Paddington* 1958).

Bond, M. (1995b) *Mehr von Paddington*, German trans. M. Osberghaus, Munich, Vienna: Hanser. (*More about Paddington* 1959).

Breen, E. (1975) *I stripete genser*, Oslo: Aschehoug. [In a striped jumper].

Brooks, R. and Wagner, J. (1973) *The Bunyip of Berkeley's Creek*, Harmondsworth: Longman.

Brunhoff, J. de (1931) *L'Histoire de Babar, le petit éléphant*, Paris: Édition du Jardin des Modes. [The story of Babar, the little elephant].

Brunhoff, J. de (1934) *The Story of Babar the Little Elephant*, with a preface by A.A. Milne [translator not named], London: Methuen. (*L'Histoire de Babar, le petit éléphant*, 1931).

Brunhoff, J. de (1946) *Die Geschichte von Babar*, [Translator not named], Zurich: Diogenes. [The story of Babar]. (*L'Histoire de Babar, le petit éléphant* 1931).

Burnett, F.H. (1911) *The Secret Garden*, London: Heinemann.

Burningham, J. (1984a) *Granpa*, London: Cape.

Burningham, J. (1984b) *Mein Opa und ich*, German trans. I. Korschunow, Zurich, Schwäbisch Hall: Parabel. (*Granpa* 1984).

Burningham, J. (1988) *Grosspapa*, German trans. R. Inhauser, Aarau, Frankfurt/M, Salzburg: Sauerländer. (*Granpa* 1984).

Bursch, W. (1865) *Max und Moritz. Eine Burbengeschichte in Sieben Streichen*. München: Braun und Scneider

Carroll, L. (1865) *Alice's Adventures in Wonderland*, London: Macmillan.

Carroll, L. [1869] *Alice's Abenteuer im Wunderland*, German trans. A. Zimmermann, Leipzig: Hartknoch. (*Alice's Adventures in Wonderland* 1865).

Carroll, L. (1871) *Through the Looking Glass and What Alice Found There*, London: Macmillan.

Carroll, L. (1912) *Alice im Wunderland*, German trans. H. Scheu-Riesz, Weimar: Kiepenheuer. (*Alice's Adventures in Wonderland* 1865).

Carroll, L. (1949) *Alicens Abenteuer im Wunderland*, German trans. F. Sester, Düsseldorf. (*Alice's Adventures in Wonderland* 1865).

Carroll, L. [1963] *Alice im Wunderland. Alice hinter den Spiegeln*, German trans. C. Enzensberger, Frankfurt/M: Insel. (*Alice's Adventures in Wonderland* 1865 and *Through the Looking Glass and What Alice Found There* 1871).

Carroll, L. (1967) *Alice im Wunderland*, German trans. L. Remané and M. Remané, Berlin: Alfred Holz. (*Alice's Adventures in Wonderland* 1865).

Carroll, L. (1989) *Alice im Wunderland*, German trans. B. Teutsch, Hamburg: Dressler. (*Alice's Adventures in Wonderland* 1865).

Carroll, L. (1993) *Alice im Wunderland*, German trans. S. Bublitz, Reinbek: rotfuchs. (*Alice's Adventures in Wonderland* 1865).

Chambers, A. (1982) *Dance on My Grave*, London: Bodley Head.

Chambers, A. (1987) *Now I Know*, London: Bodley Head.

Chambers, A. (1990) *Die unglaubliche Geschichte des Nik Frome*, German trans. K.H. Dürr, Ravensburg: Maier. (*Now I Know* 1987).

Collodi, C. (1883) *Le avventure di Pinocchio. Storia di un burattino*, Firenze: Paggi. [Pinocchio's adventures. The story of a puppet].

Collodi, C. (1891) *The Story of a Puppet or the Adventures of Pinocchio*, English trans. M.A. Murray, London: Fisher Unwin. (*Le avventure di Pinocchio* 1883).

Collodi, C. (1904) *Pinocchio, the Adventures of a Marionette*, English trans. W.H. Cramp, ed. S.E.H. Lockwood, Boston: Ginn. (*Le avventure di Pinocchio* 1883).

Collodi, C. (1905) *Hippeltitsch's Abenteuer. Geschichte eines Holzbuben*, German trans. E. Andrae, Chattowitz and Leipzig: Carl Siwinna. [The adventures of Hippeltitsch. The story of a wooden boy]. (*Le avventure di Pinocchio* 1883).

Collodi, C. (1913) *Die Geschichte vom hölzernen Bengele – lustig und lehrreich für kleine und grosse Kinder*, German trans. A. Grumann, Freiburg: Herder. [The story of the wooden boy – amusing and instructive for children large and small]. (*Le avventure di Pinocchio* 1883).

Collodi, C. (1923) *Hölzele, der Hampelmann, der schlimm ist und nicht folgen kann! Eine viellehrreiche Böse-Buben-Geschichte*, German trans. F. Latterer, Vienna: Steyermühl. [Woody the jumping-jack, who is naughty and disobedient! A very instructive story of a bad boy]. (*Le avventure di Pinocchio* 1883).

[Collodi, C.] (1939) *Pinocchio: A Story for Children by C. Collodi*, adapted by Roselle Ross, Akron, OH: Saalfield. (*Le avventure di Pinocchio* 1883).

Collodi, C. (1944) *Pinocchio. Die Geschichte des hölzernen Hampelmanns, der ein richtiger Junge wurde*, German trans. E. Russig, Leipzig: Wiking. [Pinocchio. The story of a wooden jumping-jack who became a real boy]. (*Le avventure di Pinocchio* 1883).

Collodi, C. (1954) *Pinocchios Abenteuer*, German trans. P. Rova [i.e. Heinz Riedt], East Berlin: Aufbau. [Pinocchio's adventures]. (*Le avventure di Pinocchio* 1883).

Collodi, C. (1956) *Die Geschichte vom hölzernen Hampelchen*, German trans. L. Dolezahl, Cologne: Atlas. [The story of a little wooden jumping-jack]. (*Le avventure di Pinocchio* 1883).

Collodi, C. (1966) *Pinocchios Abenteuer*, German trans. P. Goldschmidt, Berlin: Alfred Holz. [Pinocchio's adventures]. (*Le avventure di Pinocchio* 1883).

Collodi, C. (1967) *Le Avventure di Pinocchio. Die Abenteuer des Pinocchio*, German trans. H. Legers, Munich: Hueber. [Pinocchio's adventures]. (*Le avventure di Pinocchio* 1883).

Collodi, C. (1972) *Pinocchio*, German trans. B. Eichhorn, Bayreuth: Loewe. (*Le avventure di Pinocchio* 1883).

Collodi, C. (1986a) *Pinocchios Abenteuer. Die Geschichte einer Holzpuppe*, German trans. H. Bausch, Stuttgart: Reclam. [Pinocchio's adventures. The story of a puppet]. (*Le avventure di Pinocchio* 1883).

Collodi, C. (1986b) *The Adventures of Pinocchio. Story of a Puppet*, translated with an introductory essay and notes by Nicolas J. Perella, Berkeley, London: University of California Press. (*Le avventure di Pinocchio* 1883).

Collodi, C. (1988) *Pinocchios Abenteuer*, German trans. J. Meinert, Berlin, Weimar: Aufbau. [Pinocchio's adventures]. (*Le avventure di Pinocchio* 1883).

Collodi, C. (1993) *Le Avventure di Pinocchio. Pinocchios Abenteuer*, German trans. H. Riedt, Frankfurt, Leipzig: Insel. [Pinocchio's adventures]. (*Le avventure di Pinocchio* 1883).

Collodi, C. (1996) *The Adventures of Pinocchio*, translated with an introduction and notes by A. Lawson Lucas, Oxford etc.: Oxford University Press. (*Le avventure di Pinocchio* 1883).

Coolidge, S. (1873) *What Katy Did*, Boston: Roberts.

Dahl, R. (1989) *Matilda*, London: Puffin.

Dahl, R. (1991) *The Vicar of Nibbleswicke*, London: Century.

Dahl, R. (1992) *Der Pastor von Nibbleswick*, German trans. U.M. Gutzschhahn, Ravensburg: Maier. (*The Vicar of Nibbleswicke* 1991).

Donaldson, J. and Scheffler, A. (1993) *A Squash and a Squeeze*, London etc.: Methuen.

Donnelly, E. (1977) *Servus Opa, sagte ich leise*, Hamburg: Dressler. [Goodbye Grandad, I said softly].

Dumas, P. (1978) *Laura sur la route*, Paris: L'école des loisirs. [Laura on the road].

Dumas, P. (1981) *Laura unterwegs*, German trans. H.C. Meiser, Feldafing: Parabel. [Laura on the road]. (*Laura sur la route* 1978).

Dupont, R. (n.d.) *Bombs on Berchtesgaden*, London: W. Barton.

Edelfeldt, I. (1985) *Breven till nattens drotting*, Stockholm: Alqvist & Wiksell. [Letters to the queen of the night].

Edelfeldt, I. (1986a) *Kamalas bok*, Stockholm: Alqvist & Wiksell. [Kamala's book].

Edelfeldt, I. (1986b) *Briefe an die Königin der Nacht*, German trans. B. Kicherer, Stuttgart: Spectrum. [Letters to the queen of the night]. (*Breven till nattens drotting* 1985).

Edelfeldt, I. (1988) *Kamalas Buch*, German trans. B. Kicherer, Stuttgart: Spectrum. [Kamala's book]. (*Kamalas bok*, 1986).

Ende, M. (1973) *Momo oder Die seltsame Geschichte von den Zeit-Dieben und von dem Kind, das den Menschen die gestohlene Zeit zurückbrachte*, Stuttgart: Thienemanns. [Momo or the peculiar story of the time thieves and the child who brought stolen time back to humanity].

Enzensberger, H.M. (ed.) (1961) *Allerleirauh. 777 schöne Kinderreime. Mit 391 alten Holzschnitten geschmückt*, Frankfurt/M: Suhrkamp. [All sorts of things. 777 nice children's poems].

Ewing, J.H. (1912) 'Friedrich's Ballad: A Tale of the Feast of St. Nicholas', in *Melchior's Dream and Other Tales*. London: Bell, 47–83 (first edn 1862).

Frank, Y. (1939) *Pinocchio (A Musical Legend)*, New York: Marx Music (first performed in 1937).

Gaarder, J. (1991) *Sofies verden*, Oslo: Aschehoug. [Sophie's world].

Gay, M. (1986) *Papa Vroum*, Paris: L'école des loisirs.

Gay, M. (1987) *Night Ride*, English trans. M. Lundell, New York: Morrow. (*Papa Vroum* 1986).

Gilson, C. [1915] *A Motor-Scout in Flanders: or, Held by the Enemy etc.*, London, Glasgow, Bombay: Blackie.

Goddard, J. (1863) 'Peter's Story – The Poor Musician', in *More Stories*, London: Hall, Smart & Allan , 57–77.

Goethe, J.W. von (1774) *Die Leiden des jungen Werthers*, 2 vols, Leipzig. [The sorrows of young Werther].

Gormander, Dr. (1970) *Als die Kinder die Macht ergriffen*, Frankfurt: März. [When the children seized power].

Grahame, K. (1908) *The Wind in the Willows*, London: Methuen.

Grahame, K. (1929) *Christoph, Grossmaul und Cornelius. Die Abenteuer einer fidelen Gesellschaft am Fluss, im Wald und anderswo*, German trans. E. Steup, Stuttgart: Gundert. [Christoph, Bigmouth and Cornelius. The adventures of a jolly group by the river, in the woods, and elsewhere]. (*The Wind in the Willows* 1908).

Grahame, K. (1996) *Der Wind in den Weiden*, German trans. A. Löhr-Gössling, Stuttgart, Vienna: Thienemann. (*The Wind in the Willows* 1908).

Gripe, M. (1964) *Glasblåsarns barn*, Stockholm: Bonniers. [The glassblower's children].

Gripe, M. (1976) *The Glassblower's Children*, trans. Sheila la Farge, London: Target Books. (*Glasblåsarns barn* 1964).

Gripe, M. (1977) *Die Kinder des Glasbläsers*, German trans. A. Kutsch, Stuttgart: Thienemann. [The glassblower's children]. (*Glasblåsarns barn* 1964).

Gydal, M. and Danielsson, T. (1973) *Så var det när Olas farfar dog*, Stockholm: Sveriges Radios Förlag. [When grandad died].

Härtling, P. (1975) *Oma*, Weinheim, Basel: Beltz & Gelberg. [Grandma].

Hein, C. (1984) *Das Wildpferd unterm Kachelofen. Ein schönes dickes Buch von Jakob Borg und seinen Freunden*, Weinheim, Basel: Beltz & Gelberg. [The wild horse under the stove].

Hein, C. (1988) *Jamie and His Friends*, trans. Anthea Bell, London: Andersen Press. (*Das Wildpferd unterm Kachelofen* 1984).

Helm, C. (1863) *Backfischen's Leiden und Freuden*, Leipzig: Wigand. [The joys and sorrows of a teenage girl].

Hesse, H. (1906) *Unterm Rad*, Berlin: Fischer. [Under the wheel].

Hoffmann, E.T.A. (1816) 'Nussknacker und Mausekönig', in *Kindermärchen von C.W. Contessa, Friedrich Baron de la Motte Fouqué und E.T.A. Hoffmann*, Berlin: Realschulbuchhandlung. [Nutcracker and mouse-king].

Hoffmann, H. (1845) *Der Struwwelpeter. Lustige Geschichten und drollige Bilder*, Frankfurt/M: Literarische Anstalt. [Shock-headed Peter. Funny stories and merry pictures].

Hutchins, P. (1968) *Rosie's Walk*, London: Bodley Head.

Janosch (1985) *The Curious Tale of Hare and Hedgehog*, English trans. A. Bell, London: Andersen. (*Der Wettlauf zwischen Hase und Igel* 1984).

Kästner, E. (1929) *Emil und die Detektive. Ein Roman für Kinder*, Berlin: Williams & Co. (1984 edition cited, see below). [Emil and the detectives].

Kästner, E. (1930) *Emil and the Detectives*, English trans. M. Massee, New York: Doubleday. (*Emil und die Detektive* 1929).

Kästner, E. (1931a) *Emil and the Detectives*, [English trans. M. Goldsmith], with an introduction by Walter de la Mare, London: Cape. (*Emil und die Detektive* 1929).

Kästner, E. (1931b) *Pünktchen und Anton. Ein Roman für Kinder*, Berlin: Williams & Co. [Little Dot and Anton].

Kästner, E. (1936a) *Emil und die drei Zwillinge. Die zweite Geschichte von Emil und den Detektiven*, Berlin: Dressler. [Emil and the three twins].

Kästner, E. (1936b) *Petit Point et ses amis*, French trans. S. Hugh, Paris: Bourrelier. [Little Dot and her friends]. (*Pünktchen und Anton* 1931).

Kästner, E. (1937a) *Emil agus na lograirí*, Irish trans. S. MacGiollarnáth, Baile Átha Cliath (Dublin): Oifig Díolta Foillseacháin Rialtais. [Emil and the detectives]. (*Emil und die Detektive* 1929).

Kästner, E. (1937b) *Emil ve Hateomim*, Hebrew trans. M.Z. Wolfowski, Jerusalem: Achiasaf. [Emil and the detectives]. (*Emil und die Detektive* 1929).

Kästner, E. (1959) *Emil and the Detectives*, English trans. E. Hall, London: Jonathan Cape. (*Emil und die Detektive* 1929).

Kästner, E. (1961) *Gullivers Reisen*, Vienna, Heidelberg: Ueberreuter. (*Gulliver's Travels* 1726).

Kästner, E. (1980) *Émile et les détectives*, French trans. Mme. L. Faisans-Maury, revised edn, Paris: Hachette le livre de poche jeunesse (first edn 1931). [Emil and the detectives]. (*Emil und die Detektive* 1929).

Kästner, E. (1982) *Petit Point et ses amis*, French trans. S. Hugh, Paris: Le Livre de Poche. [Little Dot and her friends]. (*Pünktchen und Anton* 1931).

Kästner, E. (1984) *Emil und die Detektive. Ein Roman für Kinder*, Hamburg: Dressler. [Emil and the detectives].

Kästner, Erich (n.d.) [*Emil und die Detektive (Bengali)*], Bengali trans. S. Baru, Bipani Bitan, Chittagong: Boi-Ghar/Tuebingen: Horst Erdman. [Emil and the detectives]. (*Emil und die Detektive* 1929).

Krüss, J. (ed.) (1972) *Seifenblasen zu verkaufen. Das grosse Nonsens-Buch mit Versen aus aller Welt*, Gütersloh: Bertelsmann. [Bubbles for sale. The big book of nonsense poems from all over the world].

Lear, E. (1949) *The Complete Nonsense of Edward Lear*, edited and introduced by H. Jackson, London, Boston: Faber & Faber.

Lear, E. (1964) *Edward Lears Nonsense Verse*, German trans. H. Artmann, Frankfurt/M: Insel.

Lear, E. (1965) *Wie nett, Herrn Lear zu kennen. Reime und Geschichten*, German trans. G. Fischer, Munich: Heimeran. [How nice to meet Mr Lear. Rhymes and stories].

Lear, E. (1973) *Phantastische Reise*, German trans. J. Guggenmos, Weinheim, Basel: Beltz & Gelberg. (*The Story of the Four Little Children Who Went Round the World* 1871).

Lear, E. (1977) *Edward Lears Kompletter Nonsens*, German trans. H.M. Enzensberger, Frankfurt/M: Insel. [Edward Lear's complete nonsense].

Lear, E. (1991) *Die Geschichte von vier Kindern, die um die Welt segelten*, German trans. V. Pohl, Weinheim, Basel: Beltz & Gelberg. (*The Story of the Four Little Children Who Went Round the World* 1871).

Lear, E. (1992) *Die Geschichte von den vier kleinen Kindern, die rund um die Welt zogen*, German trans. G. Dahne, Berlin: Altberliner Verlag. (*The Story of the Four Little Children Who Went Round the World* 1871).

Lindenbaum, P. (1990) *Else-Marie och småpapporna*, Stockholm: Bonniers. [Else-Marie and her little papas].

Lindenbaum, P. (1991) *Else-Marie and Her Seven Little Daddies*, adapted by G. Charbonnet, New York: Holt. (*Else-Marie och småpapporna* 1990).

Lindgren, A. (1945) *Pippi Långstrump*, Stockholm: Rabén & Sjögren. [Pippi Longstocking].

Lindgren, A. (1949) *Pippi Langstrumpf*, German trans. C. Heinig, Hamburg: Oetinger. [Pippi Longstocking]. (*Pippi Långstrump* 1945).

Lindgren, A. (1954) *Pippi Longstocking*, English trans. E. Hurup, London etc.: Oxford University Press. (*Pippi Långstrump* 1945).

Lindgren, A. (1960) *Madicken*, Stockholm: Rabén & Sjögren.

Lindgren, A. (1961) *Madita*, German trans. A.L. Kornitzky, Hamburg: Oetinger. (*Madicken* 1960).

Lindgren, A. (1965) *Pippi Langstrumpf*, German trans. C. Heinig. Hamburg: Oetinger. [Pippi Longstocking]. (*Pippi Långstrump* 1945).

Lindgren, A. (1973) *Bröderna Lejonhjärta*, Stockholm: Rabén & Sjögren. [The Brothers Lionheart].

Lindgren, A. (1979) *Mardie*, English trans. P. Crampton, London: Methuen. (*Madicken* 1960).

Lindgren, A. (1986) *Pippi Langstrumpf*, German trans. C. Heinig, new edition, Hamburg: Oetinger. [Pippi Longstocking]. (*Pippi Långstrump* 1945).

Lindgren, A. (1987) *Pippi Langstrumpf*, German trans. C. Heinig, new edition, Hamburg: Oetinger. [Pippi Longstocking]. (*Pippi Långstrump* 1945).

Lindquist, M. (1969) *Malena och glädjen*, Stockholm: Bonnier. [Malena and her joy].

Lindsay, N. (1918) *The Magic Pudding: Being the Adventures of Bunyip Bluegum and His Friends Bill Barnacle and Sam Sawnoff*, Sydney: Angus & Robertson.

Lingard, J. (1989) *Für schuldig befunden*, German trans. C. Krutz-Arnold, Stuttgart: Spectrum. (*The Guilty Party* 1986).

Lionni, L. (1963) *Swimmy*, New York: Pantheon.

Lionni, L. (1964) *Swimmy*, German trans. J. Krüss, Cologne: Middelhauve.

Lowry, L. (1982) *Anastasia at Your Service*, New York: Houghton Mifflin.

Lucas, A. (1902) *Leonie: A Tale of the Franco-German War*, London, Edinburgh, New York: Nelson & Son.

Maar, P. (1968) *Der tätowierte Hund*, Hamburg: Oetinger. [The tattooed dog].

McCutcheon, E. (1983) *Summer of the Zeppelin*, London, Melbourne: Dent.

MacDonald, G. (1871) *At the Back of the North Wind*, London: Blackie & Son.

Miller, W. (1959) *The Cool World*, London: Secker & Warburg.

Miller, W. (1979) *Kalte Welt – Ein Bandenchef aus Harlem berichtet*, German trans. H. Rowohlt, Weinheim, Basel: Beltz & Gelberg. (*The Cool World* 1959).

Milne, A.A. (1926) *Winnie-the-Pooh*, London: Methuen (1965 edition cited, see below).

Milne, A.A. (1928) *Pu der Bär*, German trans. E.L. Schiffer, Berlin: Williams & Co. (1947 edition cited, see below). (*Winnie-the-Pooh* 1926).

Milne, A.A. (1947) *Pu der Bär*, German trans. E.L. Schiffer, Berlin: Williams & Co. (*Winnie-the-Pooh* 1926).

Milne, A.A. (1965) *Winnie-the-Pooh*, London: Methuen.

Milne, A.A. (1987) *Pu der Bär*, German trans. H. Rowohlt, Hamburg: Dressler. (*Winnie-the-Pooh* 1926).

Moritz, K.P. (1785–94) *Anton Reiser*, 5 vols, Berlin.

Musil, R. (1906) *Die Verwirrungen des Zöglings Törless*, Vienna, Leipzig. [The confusions of the pupil Törless].

Needle, J. (1977) *Albeson and the Germans*, London: Deutsch.

Nesbit, E. (1899) *The Story of the Treasure Seekers: Being the Adventures of the Bastable Children in Search of a Fortune*, London: Fisher Unwin.

Nesbit, E. (1901) *The Wouldbegoods: Being the Further Adventures of the Treasure Seekers*, London: Fisher Unwin.

Nesbit, E. (1907) *The Enchanted Castle*, London: Fisher Unwin.

Newbery, E. [1774] *Vice in Its Proper Shape. Containing prose accounts of the wonderful and melancholy transformation of several naughty masters and misses into those contemptible animals which they most resemble in disposition*, London.

Newbery, J. (1744) *A Little Pretty Pocket-Book, Intended for the Instruction and Amusement of Little Master Tommy and Pretty Miss Polly*, London: Newbery.

Nöstlinger, C. (1974) *Ilse Janda, 14*, Hamburg: Oetinger.

Nöstlinger, C. (1988) *Der neue Pinocchio*, Weinheim, Basel: Beltz & Gelberg. [The new Pinocchio].

Nöstlinger, C. (1993) *Ilse Janda*, Turkish trans. S. Dilidüzgün, Istanbul: Düzlem. (*Ilse Janda, 14*).

Park, B. (1991) *Charly und drei Nervensägen*, German trans. U. Neckenauer, Würzburg: Arena. (*My Mother Got Married (and Other Disasters)* 1989).

Plenzdorf, U. (1978) *Die neuen Leiden des jungen W.*, Rostock: VEB Hinstorff. [New sorrows of young W.].

Pohl, P. (1985) *Janne min vän*, Stockholm: Almqvist & Wiksell. [Johnny, my friend].

Pohl, P. (1991) *Johnny, My Friend*, English trans. L. Thompson, London: Turton & Chambers. (*Janne min vän* 1985).

Potter, B. (1902) *The Tale of Peter Rabbit*, London: Warne.

Rauter, E.A. (1971) *Wie eine Meinung in einem Kopf entsteht. Über das Herstellen von Untertanen*, Munich: Weismann. [How an opinion forms in the mind. On creating subject people].

Rees, D. (1976) *The Missing German*, London: Dobson.

Rhoden, E. von (1885) *Der Trotzkopf. Eine Pensionsgeschichte für erwachsene Mädchen*, Stuttgart: Weisse. [The defiant girl].

Roberts, M. [1877] *Fair Else, Duke Ulrich, and Other Tales*, London: Frederick Warne.

Rowling, J.K. (1997) *Harry Potter and the Philosopher's Stone*, London: Bloomsbury.

Saint-Exupéry, A. de (1943) *Le Petit Prince*, New York: Reynal & Hitchcock. [The little prince].

Salinger, J.D. (1951) *The Catcher in the Rye*, London: Hamish Hamilton.

Sánchez-Silva, J.M. (1953) *Marcelino pan y vino*, Madrid: Editorial Cigüeña. [Marcelino bread and wine].

Sheppard, G. and Rozier, J. (1971) *The Man Who Gave Himself Away*, New York: Harlin Quist.

Sherwood, M.M. (1818–47) *The History of the Fairchild Family or the Child's Manual*, 3 vols, London: J. Hatchard.

Silverstein, S. (1963) *Uncle Shelby's Story of Lafcadio, the Lion Who Shot Back*, New York: Evil Eye Music.

Silverstein, S. (1987) *Lafcadio. Ein Löwe schiesst zurück*, German trans. H. Rowohlt, Cologne: Middelhauve. (*Uncle Shelby's Story of Lafcadio, the Lion Who Shot Back* 1963).

Sixtus, A. and Koch-Gotha, F. (1924) *Die Häschenschule*, Leipzig: Hahn. [The school for hares].

Spillner, W. (1977) *Gänse überm Reiherberg*, Berlin: Kinderbuchverlag. [Geese over the Reiherberg].

Spyri, J. (1880) *Heidis Lehr- und Wanderjahre. Eine Geschichte für Kinder und auch für Solche, welche die Kinder lieb haben*, Gotha: Perthes. [Heidi's years of wandering and learning. A story for children and those who love children].

Spyri, J. (1883) *Wo Gritlis Kinder hingekommen sind. Eine Geschichte für Kinder und auch für Solche, welche die Kinder lieb haben*, Gotha: Perthes. [Gritli's children. A story for children and those who love children].

Stow, R. (1967) *Midnite. The Story of a Wild Colonial Boy*, London: Macdonald.

Stow, R. (1972) *Käpt'n Mitternacht*, German trans. S. Gräfin Schönfeldt, Baden-Baden: Signal. (*Midnite* 1967).

Strauss, E. (1902) *Freund Hein. Eine Lebensgeschichte*, Berlin: Fischer. [The grim reaper].

Strobl, J.B. (1788) *Unglücksgeschichten zur Warnung für die unerfahrene Jugend*, Munich: Strobl. [Tales of misfortune as a warning to inexperienced youth].

Swift, J. (1726) *Travels into Several Remote Nations of the World. By Lemuel Gulliver, First a Surgeon, and then a Captain of Several Ships*, 2 vols, London: Motte.

Swift, J. (1986) *Gulliver's Travels*, Oxford, New York: Oxford University Press.

Tolkien, J.R.R. (1937) *The Hobbit*, London: Allen & Unwin.

Tolstoy, A. (1936) *Zolotoy Klyuchik*, Moscow: Raduga. [The golden key].

Twain, M. (1876) *The Adventures of Tom Sawyer*, London: Chatto & Windus.

Twain, M. (1884) *The Adventures of Huckleberry Finn*, London: Chatto & Windus.

Varley, S. (1984) *Badger's Parting Gifts*, London: Andersen.

Watts, I. (1715) *Divine Songs Attempted in Easy Language for the Use of Children*, London: Lawrence.

Weiss, P. (1961) *Abschied von den Eltern*, Frankfurt: Suhrkamp. [Taking leave of my parents].

Weisse, C.F. (1776–82) *Der Kinderfreund. Ein Wochenblatt*, Leipzig: Crusius. [The children's friend. A weekly magazine].

Westall, R. (1975) *The Machine-Gunners*, London: Macmillan.

Wiggin, K.D. (1903) *Rebecca of Sunnybrook Farm*, London, Cambridge, MA: Gay & Bird.

Wilde, O. (1888) *The Happy Prince and Other Tales*, London: Nutt.

Wilde, O. (1891) *A House of Pomegranates*, London: Osgood, McIlvaine & Co.

Wilkes, A. and Schindler, N. (1992) *Mein erstes Wörterbuch*, Mannheim etc.: Duden. [My First Dictionary]

Winter, A. (1840) *Memoiren einer Berliner Puppe für Kinder von fünf bis zehn Jahren und für deren Mütter*, Leipzig: Baumgärtner. [Memoirs of a Berlin doll].

Secondary sources

Adoum, J.E. (1983) 'Der Stachel im Märchen. Über die kulturelle Kolonisierung lateinamerikanischer Jugend', in K. Doderer (ed.) *Über Märchen für Kinder von heute. Essays zu ihrem Wandel und ihrer Funktion*, Weinheim, Basel: Beltz, 47–56.

Allsobrook, M. (1996) 'Major Authors' Work for Children', in P. Hunt (ed.) *International Companion Encyclopedia of Children's Literature*, London, New York: Routledge, 410–21.

Appleton, T. (1991) 'Saurer Pudding. Provozierende Randbemerkungen zu angelsächsischen Kinderbuch-Klassikern und deutscher Ignoranz', *Die Zeit* 46, 8 November, 30.

Apseloff, M.F. (1989) *They Wrote for Children Too: An Annotated Bibliography of Children's Literature by Famous Writers for Adults*, Westport, London: Greenwood Press.

Ariès, P. (1962) *Centuries of Childhood: A Social History of Family Life*, trans R. Baldick, New York: Knopf.

Ariès, P. (1975) *Western Attitudes towards Death from the Middle Ages to the Present*, trans. Patricia M. Ranum, Baltimore: Johns Hopkins University Press.

Assmann, A. (1983) 'Schriftliche Folklore. Zur Entstehung und Funktion eines Überlieferungstyps', in A. Assmann, J. Assmann and C. Hradmeier (eds) *Schrift und Gedächtnis. Beiträge zur Archäologie der literarischen Kommunikation*, Munich: Fink, 175–93.

Bachmann-Medick, D. (1994) 'Multikultur oder kulturelle Differenzen? Neue Konzepte von Weltliteratur und Übersetzung in postkolonialer Perspektive', *Deutsche Vierteljahrsschrift für Literaturwissenschaft und Geistesgeschichte* 68, 585–612.

'"Baden wir in unserem Ruhm"' (1997), in *Der Spiegel* 36, 160–73

Bakhtin, M. (1984a) *Problems of Dostoevsky's Poetics*, ed. and trans. by C. Emerson, Minneapolis: University of Minnesota Press.

Bakhtin, M. (1984b) *Rabelais and His World*, trans. H. Iswolsky, Bloomington, London: Indiana University Press.

Balakian, A. (1990) 'Literary Theory and Comparative Literature', in M.J. Valdés (ed.) *Towards a Theory of Comparative Literature: Selected Papers Presented in the Division of Theory of Literature at the XIth International Comparative Literature Congress*, New York etc.: Lang, 17–24.

Bamberger, R. (1961) 'Das Jugendbuch in aller Welt. Europa im Spiegel der Jugendbuchübersetzungen im deutschen Sprachraum', *Jugend und Buch* 10, 1, 28–43.

Bamberger, R. (1978) 'Die Bedeutung der Übersetzung in der Entwicklung der nationalen Jugendliteratur zur Weltliteratur der Jugend', in L. Binder (ed.) *Weltliteratur der Jugend. Trends, Autoren, Übersetzungen*, Vienna: Internationales Institut für Jugendliteratur und Leseforschung, 3–20.

Barth, S. (1998) 'La poupée Vermeille – Puppe Wunderhold. Zur Rezeption französischer Puppengeschichten für Mädchen in Deutschland zwischen 1800 und 1850', in B. Hurrelmann and K. Richter (eds) *Das Fremde in der Kinder- und Jugendliteratur. Interkulturelle Perspektiven*, Weinheim, Munich: Juventa, 29–44.

Bassnett, S. (1993) *Comparative Literature: An Introduction*, Oxford, Cambridge MA: Blackwell.

Bassnett-McGuire, S. (1991) *Translation Studies*, revised edn, London, New York: Routledge.

Baumgärtner, A.C. (ed.) (1992) *Deutsch-französische Beziehungen in Jugendliteratur und Volksdichtung*, Würzburg: Königshausen & Neumann.

Becher, J. (1992) *Kindermädchen. Ihre Bedeutung als Bezugspersonen für Kinder in bürgerlichen Familien des Zweiten Deutschen Kaiserreichs (1871–1918)*, Frankfurt/M. etc.: Lang.

Beckett, S. (1995) 'From the Art of Rewriting for Children to the Art of Crosswriting Child and Adult: The Secret of Michel Tournier's Dual Readership', in M. Nikolajeva (ed.) *Voices from Far Away: Current Trends in International Children's Literature Research*, Stockholm: Centrum för barnkulturforskning vid Stockhoms universitet, 9–34.

Beirnaert, C. (1992) 'Spuren der Schwarzen Pädagogik in Kinderliteratur und Kinderprogrammen in Marokko', unpublished thesis, University Mohammed V. Rabat.

Bekkering, H. and Heimeriks, N. (eds) (1989) *De hele Bibelebontse berg. De geschiedenis van het kinderboek in Nederland & Vlaanderen van de middeleeuwen tot heden*, Amsterdam: Querido.

Bell, A. (1979) 'Children's Books in Translation', *Signal* 28, 47–53.

Bell, A. (1985a) 'Translator's Notebook: The Naming of Names', *Signal* 46, 3–11.

Bell, A. (1985b) 'Translator's Notebook: On Approaching the Traditional Tales', *Signal* 48, 139–47.

Bell, A. (1986) 'Translator's Notebook: Delicate Matters', *Signal* 49, 17–26.

Ben-Ari, N. (1992) 'Didactic and Pedagogic Tendencies in the Norms Dictating the Translation of Children's Literature: The Case of Postwar German–Hebrew Translations', *Poetics Today* 13, 1, 221–30.

Benton, M. (1980) 'Children's Responses to the Text', in G. Fox and G. Hammond (eds) *Responses to Children's Literature: Proceedings of the Fourth Symposium of the International Research Society for Children's Literature*, New York etc.: Saur, 13–33.

Bernheimer, C., Arac, J., Hirsch, M., Jones, A.R., Judy, R., Krupat, R., La Capra, D., Nichols, S. and Suleri May, S. (1995) 'Bernheimer Report 1993: Comparative Literature at the Turn of the Century', in C. Bernheimer (ed.) *Comparative Literature in the Age of Multiculturalism*, Baltimore, London: Johns Hopkins University Press, 39–48.

Beuchat, C. and Valdiviseo, C. (1992) 'Translation of Children's Literature: Intercultural Communication', *Bookbird* 30, 1, 9–14.

Birkeland, T. and Storaas, F. (1993) *Den norske biletboka*, Oslo: Landslaget for norskundervisning.

Birnbaum, C. (1949) 'Nachwort', in Carlo Collodi *Purzels Abenteuer. Die Geschichte von Pinocchio*, German trans. C. Birnbaum, Munich: Detsch, 209f.

Boie, K. (1995) 'Vom Umgang mit der Sprache beim Schreiben', *Beiträge Jugendliteratur und Medien* 47, 1, 2–17.

Booth, W. (1961) *The Rhetoric of Fiction*, Chicago, London: University of Chicago Press.

Bottigheimer, R. (1987) *Grimms' Bad Girls and Bold Boys: The Moral and Social Visions of the Tales*, New Haven, London: Yale University Press.

Bottigheimer, R. (1993) 'Recent Scholarship in Children's Literature, 1980 to the Present', *Eighteenth Century Life*, 17, n.s.3, 89–103.

Bouckaert-Ghesquière, R. (1992) 'Cinderella and Her Sisters', *Poetics Today* 13, 1, 85–95.

Bradford, C. (2001) *Reading Race: Aboriginality in Australian Children's Literature*, Carlton: Melbourne University Press.

Bratt, I. (1996) *Barnböcker utgivna i Sverige 1890–1899. En kommenterad bibliografi*, Lund: Lund University Press.

Bravo-Villasante, C. (1971) *Historia de la literatura infantil universal*, Madrid: Ministerio de Cultura.

Bredsdorff, E. (1993) *Hans Christian Andersen: The Story of His Life and Work 1805–75*, London: Souvenir Press.

Bühler, K. (1965) *Sprachtheorie. Die Darstellungsfunktion der Sprache*, Stuttgart: G. Fischer.

Carpenter, H. and Prichard, M. (1984) *The Oxford Companion to Children's Literature*, Oxford, New York: Oxford University Press.

Cech, J. (1986) 'The Triumphant Transformations of "Pinocchio" ', in F. Butler and R. Rotert (eds) *Triumphs of the Spirit in Children's Literature*, Hamden: Lib. Professional Pub, 171–7.

Chambers, A. (2001) 'In Spite of Being a Translation', in A. Chambers, *Reading Talk*, Stroud: Thimble Press, 113–37.

Charlton, M. and Neumann-Braun, K. (1992) *Medienkindheit – Medienjugend. Eine Einführung in die aktuelle kommunikationswissenschaftliche Forschung*, Munich: Quintessenz.

Chatman, S. (1978) *Story and Discourse: Narrative Structure in Fiction and Film*, Ithaca, London: Cornell University Press.

Chatman, S. (1990) *Coming to Terms: The Rhetoric of Narrative in Fiction and Film*, Ithaca, London: Cornell University Press.

Christadler, M. (1978) *Kriegserziehung im Jugendbuch. Literarische Mobilmachung in Deutschland und Frankreich vor 1914*, Frankfurt/M: Haag und Herchen.

Coghlan, V. (in press) 'Ireland', in P. Hunt (ed.) *International Companion Encyclopedia of Children's Literature*, revised edition, London, New York: Routledge.

Colin, M. (1995) 'Children's Literature in France and Italy in the Nineteenth Century: Influences and Exchanges', in M. Nikolajeva (ed.) *Aspects and Issues in the History of Children's Literature*, Westport, London: Greenwood Press, 77–88.

Craig, I. (2001) *Children's Classics under Franco: Censorship of the William Books and the Adventures of Tom Sawyer*, Bern etc.: Peter Lang.

Cunningham, H. (1995) *Children and Childhood in Western Society since 1500*, London, New York: Longman.

Damrosch, D. (2003) *What Is World Literature?*, Princeton: Princeton University Press.

Dankert, B. (1991) 'Internationalism in Children's Literature Research Today', in International Youth Library (ed.) *Children's Literature Research, International Resources and Exchange*, Munich etc.: Sauer, 21–30.

Darton, F.H.H. (1914) 'Children's Books in England', in A.W. Ward and A.R. Waller (eds) *The Cambridge History of English Literature*, 15 vols, Cambridge: Cambridge University Press, vol. 9.

Darton, F.H.H. (1932) *Children's Books in England: Five Centuries of Social Life*, Cambridge: Cambridge University Press.

DeLuca, G. and Natov, R. (1986) 'The State of International Research in Children's Literature: An Interview with James Fraser', *The Lion and the Unicorn*, 10, 1, 139–45.

Desmet, M. (2002) 'Babysitting the Reader: Translating English Narrative Fiction for Girls into Dutch (1946–1995)', unpublished PhD thesis, University College London.

Dierks, M. and Nottebohm, B. (1975) 'Josef Guggenmos', in K. Doderer (ed.) *Lexikon der Kinder- und Jugendliteratur. Personen-, Länder- und Sachartikel zur Geschichte und Gegenwart der Kinder- und Jugendliteratur*, 4 vols, Weinheim, Basel: Beltz, vol. 1, 508f.

Dillsworth, G. (1988) 'Children's and Youth Literature in Sierra Leone', in *African Youth Literature Today and Tomorrow*, Bonn: Deutsche UNESCO-Kommission, 11–24.

Dixon, B. (1977) *Catching Them Young*, 2 vols, London: Pluto Press.

Doderer, K. (ed.) (1969) *Klassische Kinder- und Jugendbücher. Kritische Betrachtungen*, Weinheim, Basel: Beltz.

Doderer, K. (ed.) (1972) *Internationales Symposium für Kinder- und Jugendliteratur*, Frankfurt/M: International Forschungsgesellschaft für Kinderliteratur.

Doderer, K. (ed.) (1975–82) *Lexikon der Kinder- und Jugendliteratur. Personen-, Länder- und Sachartikel zur Geschichte und Gegenwart der Kinder- und Jugendliteratur*, 4 vols, Weinheim, Basel: Beltz.

Doderer, K. (1986) 'Wie sollte ein internationales Netzwerk der Kinder- und Jugendliteratur aussehen?', *Mitteilungen des Instituts für Jugendbuchforschung*, 3, 10–17.

Doderer, K. (1992) *Literarische Jugendkultur. Kulturelle und gesellschaftliche Aspekte der Kinder- und Jugendliteratur in Deutschland*, Weinheim, Munich: Juventa.

Dolle-Weinkauff, B. (1996) 'The German Democratic Republic', in P. Hunt (ed.) *International Companion Encyclopedia of Children's Literature*, London, New York: Routledge, 734–47.

Dolle-Weinkauff, B. and Ewers, H.-H. (eds) (1996) *Theorien der Jugendlektüre. Beiträge zur Kinder- und Jugendliteraturkritik seit Heinrich Wolgast*, Weinheim, Munich: Juventa.

Dolle-Weinkauff, B. and Ewers, H.-H. (eds) (2002) *Erich Kästners weltweite Wirkung als Kinderschriftsteller. Studien zur internationalen Rezeption des kinderliterarischen Werks*, Frankfurt etc.: Peter Lang.

Dollerup, C. (2003) 'Translating for Reading Aloud', *Meta*, 48, 1–2, 81–103.

Dorfman, A. (1983) *The Empire's Old Clothes: What the Lone Ranger, Barbar and Other Innocent Heroes Do to Our Minds*, trans. C. Hansen, London: Pluto.

Duijx, T. (ed.) (1994) *Taal in Vertaling. Het Nederlandstalige kinder- en juegdboek binnen en over de grenzen*, Leiden: Rijksuniversiteit Leiden.

Dunbar, R. (1997) 'Rarely Pure and Never Simple: The World of Irish Children's Literature', *The Lion and the Unicorn* 21, 3, 309–21.

Dyserinck, H. (1980) 'Die Quellen der Negritude-Theorie als Gegenstand komparatistischer Imagologie', *Komparatistische Hefte* 1, 31–40.

Eco, U. (1979) *The Role of the Reader: Explorations in the Semiotics of Texts*, Bloomington, London: Indiana University Press.

Edström, V. (1995) '*Pippi Longstocking*, an essay. Humour and farce. A chapter from *Campfire Rebel*', English translation by Eivor Cormack. Manuscript. From V. Edström (1992) *Astrid Lindgren – vildtoring och lägereld*, Stockholm: Rabén & Sjögren.

Eggert, H. and Garbe, C. (1995) *Literarische Sozialisation*, Stuttgart, Weimar: Metzler.

Emmrich, C. (1988) 'Zur Diskussion um die Kinderbuch-Klassiker: Kritische Anmerkungen', in *Schauplatz* 2. *Aufsätze zur Kinder- und Jugendliteratur und zu anderen Medienkünsten*, Berlin: Kinderbuchverlag, 58–66.

Erdheim, M. (1984) *Die gesellschaftliche Produktion von Unbewusstheit*, Frankfurt/M: Suhrkamp.

Erdogan, F. (1994) 'Luftballons für die ganz Kleinen, für die Kinder Bücher. Anmerkungen zum türkischen Kinderbuchmarkt', *Buch und Bibliothek* 46, 6/7, 575–9.

Escarpit, D. (1981) *La littérature d'enfance et de jeunesse en Europe. Panorama historique*, Paris: Presses Universitaires.

Even-Zohar, B. (1992) 'Translation Policy in Hebrew Children's Literature: The Case of Astrid Lindgren', *Poetics Today* 13, 1, 231–45.

Even-Zohar, I. (1978) 'The Position of Translated Literature within the Literary Polysystem', in J. Holmes, J. Lambert and R. van den Broeck (eds) *Literature and Translation: New Perspectives in Literary Studies*, Leuven: Acco, 117–27.

Even-Zohar, I. (1979) 'Polysystem Theory', *Poetics Today* 1, 1–2, 287–310.

Even-Zohar, I. (1990) *Polysystem Studies*, Durham: Duke University Press.

Ewers, H.-H. (1990) 'Das doppelsinnige Kinderbuch', in D. Grenz (ed.) *Kinderliteratur – Literatur auch für Erwachsene? Zum Verhältnis von Kinderliteratur und Erwachsenenliteratur*, Munich: Fink, 15–24.

Ewers, H.-H. (1992) 'Der Adoleszenzroman als jugendliterarisches Erzählmuster', *Der Deutschunterricht* 45, 6, 291–7.

Ewers H.-H. (1995) 'Themen-, Formen- und Funktionswandel der westdeutschen Kinderliteratur seit Ende der 60er, Anfang der 70er Jahre', *Zeitschrift für Germanistik* 2, 257–78.

Ewers, H.-H. (1996a) 'Kinder- und Jugendliteratur', in U. Ricklefs (ed.) *Fischer Lexikon Literatur*, 2 vols, Frankfurt/M: Fischer, 2nd vol., 842–77.

Ewers, H.-H. (1996b) 'Germany', in P. Hunt (ed.) *International Companion Encyclopedia of Children's Literature*, London, New York: Routledge, 735–43.

Ewers, H.-H. (1997) 'Deutschsprachige Kinderliteratur zwischen eigenkultureller literarischer Wertschätzung und Mißachtung', in H.-H. Ewers, U. Nassen, K. Richter and R. Steinlein (eds) *Kinder- und Jugendliteraturforschung 1996/97*, Stuttgart, Weimar: Metzler, 69–85.

Ewers, H.-H. (2000) *Literatur für Kinder und Jugendliche. Eine Einführung in grundlegende Aspekte des Handlungs- und Symbolsystems Kinder- und Jugendliteratur*, Munich: Fink.

Ewers, H.-H., Lehnert, G. and O'Sullivan, E. (eds) (1994) *Kinderliteratur im interkulturellen Prozess. Studien zur Allgemeinen und Vergleichenden Kinderliteraturwissenschaft*, Stuttgart, Weimar: Metzler.

Fadimann, C. (1994) 'Children's Literature', in *The New Encyclopaedia Britannica*, 15th edn, Chicago etc.: Encyclopaedia Britannica, 23rd vol., 198–211.

Fayose, P.O. (1991) 'Children's Literature Research in Africa: Problems and Prospects', in International Youth Library (eds) *Children's Literature Research: International Resources and Exchange*, Munich etc.: Sauer, 73–8.

Fernández López, M. (2000) 'Translation Studies in Contemporary Children's Literature: A Comparison of Intercultural Ideological Factors', *Children's Literature Association Quarterly*, 25, 1, 29–37.

Feuerhahn, N. (1992) 'Das Lachen des Kindes', in H.-H. Ewers (ed.) *Komik im Kinderbuch. Erscheinungsformen des Komischen in der Kinder- und Jugendliteratur*, Weinheim, Munich: Juventa, 33–43.

Fisher, M. (1986) *Classics for Children and Young People: A Signal Bookguide*, Stroud: Thimble Press.

Flugge, K. (1994) 'Crossing the Divide: Publishing Children's Books in the European Context', *Signal* 75, 209–14.

Fox, C. (1993) *At the Very Edge of the Forest: The Influence of Literature on Storytelling by Children*, London: Cassell.

Frank, A.P. (1988) 'Einleitung', in H. Kittel (ed.) *Die literarische Übersetzung. Stand und Perspektiven ihrer Erforschung*, Berlin: Erich Schmidt, ix–xiii.

Freese, H.-L. (1989) *Kinder sind Philosophen*, Weinheim, Berlin: Quadriga.

Frey, C. and Griffith, J. (1987) *The Literary Heritage of Childhood: An Appraisal of Children's Classics in the Western Tradition*, New York, Westport, London: Greenwood Press.

Furuland, L. (1978) 'Sweden and the International Children's Book Market: History and Present Situation', in G. Klingberg, M. Ørvig and S. Amor (eds) *Children's Books in Translation*, Stockholm: Almqvist & Wiksell International, 60–76.

Galtung, J. (1983) 'Struktur, Kultur und intellektueller Stil. Ein vergleichender Essay über sachsonische, teutonische, gallische und nipponische Wissenschaft', *Leviathan* 11, 303–38.

Garrett, J. (1996) 'The Many Republics of Childhood', in Byron Preiss (ed.) *The Best Children's Books in the World: A Treasury of Illustrated Stories*, New York: Abrams, 3–5.

Genette, G. (1997) *Paratexts: Thresholds of Interpretation*, trans. J. E. Lewin, Cambridge: Cambridge University Press.

Gentzler, E. (1993) *Contemporary Translation Theories*, London, New York: Routledge.

Goldthwaite, J. (1997) 'The Further Adventures of Pinocchio. Chapter XXXVII, in which Pinocchio returns to school to study Gresham's Law', *Signal* 82, 67–74.

Griswold, J. (1992) *Audacious Kids: Coming of Age in America's Classic Children's Books*, New York, Oxford: Oxford University Press.

Grotzer, P. (1991) *Die zweite Geburt. Figuren des Jugendlichen in der Literatur des 20. Jahrhunderts*, 2 vols, Zurich: Ammann.

Grützmacher, J. (1985) 'Vorwort', in J. Grützmacher (ed.) *Rabenschwarze Geschichten von Joan Aiken, Roald Dahl u.a.*, Stuttgart: Klett, 4f.

Gumbrecht, H.U. (1995) 'The Future of Literary Studies?', in H. Birus (ed.) *Germanistik und Komparatistik, DFG Symposium 1993*, Stuttgart, Weimar: Metzler, 399–416.

Hade, D. (2002) 'Storytelling: Are Publishers Changing the Way Children Read?', *The Horn Book Magazine*, 78, September/October, 509–17.

Hagfors, I. (2003) 'The Translation of Culture-Bound Elements into Finnish in the Post-War Period', *Meta* 48, 115–27.

Hazard, P. (1932) *Les livres, les enfants et les hommes*, Paris: Flammarion.

Hazard, P. (1944) *Books, Children and Men*, trans. M. Mitchell, Boston: The Horn Book.

Hazard, P. (1955) *Böcker, barn och vuxna*, trans. E. v. Zweigbergk, Stockholm: Rabén & Sjögren.

Heale, J. (1996) 'English-Speaking Africa', in P. Hunt (ed.) *International Companion Encyclopedia of Children's Literature*, London, New York: Routledge, 795–801.

Heidtmann, H. (1993) 'Kinder- und Jugendbücher in anderen Medien. Oder: Auswirkungen der Mediatisierung auf die Kinderkultur', *Tausend und ein Buch* 5, 7–14.

Henning, M. (1990) 'Alfons Åberg och arabisk barnlitteratur', *Barnboken* 2, 20–5.

Hermans, T. (ed.) (1985a) *The Manipulation of Literature: Studies in Literary Translation*, London, Sydney: Croom Helm.

Hermans, T. (1985b) 'Translation Studies and a New Paradigm', in T. Hermans (ed.) *The Manipulation of Literature: Studies in Literary Translation*, London, Sydney: Croom Helm, 7–15.

Hermans, T. (1996) 'The Translator's Voice in Translated Narrative', *Target* 8, 1, 23–48.

Heydebrandt, R. von (1993) 'Probleme des "Kanons" ' – Probleme der Kultur und Bildungspolitik', in J. Janota (ed.) *Kultureller Wandel und die Germanistik in der Bundesrepublik: Vorträge des Augsburger Germanistentages 1991*, Tübingen: Niemeyer, 3–22.

Hickey, T. (1982) '… And after Lynch?', in *Loughborough '81: Conference Proceedings 14th Loughborough International Conference on Children's Literature, Dublin 1981*, Dublin: Dublin Public Libraries, 32–7.

Hollindale, P. (1988) *Ideology and the Children's Book*, Stroud: Thimble Press.

Hönig, H.G. and Kussmaul, P. (1982) *Strategie der Übersetzung. Ein Lehr- und Arbeitsbuch*, Tübingen: Narr.

Honsza, N. and Kunicki, W. (1987) 'Zur Interkulturalität Karl Mays. Die Rezeption Karl Mays in Polen', in A. Wierlacher (ed.) *Perspektiven und Verfahren interkultureller Germanistik*, Munich: iudicium, 437–45.

Hunt, P. (1991) *Criticism, Theory, and Children's Literature*, Oxford, Cambridge MA: Blackwell.

Hunt, P. (1995) 'Dragons in the Department and Academic Emperors: Why Universities Are Afraid of Children's Literature', *Compar(a)ison* 2, 19–31.

Hunt, P. (ed.) (1996) *International Companion Encyclopedia of Children's Literature*, London, New York: Routledge.

Hürlimann, B. (1959) *Europäische Kinderbücher aus drei Jahrhunderten*, Zurich, Freiburg/B: Atlantis.

Hurrelmann, B. (ed.) (1995a) *Klassiker der Kinder- und Jugendliteratur*, Frankfurt/M: Fischer.

Hurrelmann, B. (1995b) 'Was heißt hier "klassisch"?', in B. Hurrelmann (ed.) *Klassiker der Kinder- und Jugendliteratur*, Frankfurt/M: Fischer, 9–20.

Hurrelmann, B. (1995c) 'Mignons erlöste Schwester. Johanna Spyris "Heidi" ', in B. Hurrelmann (ed.) *Klassiker der Kinder- und Jugendliteratur*, Frankfurt/M: Fischer, 191–215.

Hurrelmann, B. (1996) 'Klassiker der Kinder- und Jugendliteratur', *Praxis Deutsch* 23, 135, 18–25.

Ipsiroglu, Z. (1992) 'Kinder- und Jugendliteratur im Schatten des islamischen Fundamentalismus', *Diyalog* 1, 115–30.

Irish Books Marketing Group (ed.) (1987) *The Book Market in the Republic of Ireland*, Dublin: IBMG.

Isensee, R. (1993) 'Gewalt in der US-amerikanischen Kinder- und Jugendliteratur. Übersetztes und Nicht-Übersetztes', *JuLit Informationen* 19, 3, 32–41.

Jafa, M. (1991) 'Children's Literature and Research in India, Bangladesh, Sri Lanka and Nepal', in International Youth Library (ed.) *Children's Literature Research: International Resources and Exchange*, Munich etc.: Sauer, 123–38.

Kaminski, W. (1990) 'Zur Einführung', in *Von Marx/smenschen und Superbirnen. Vor zwanzig Jahren: Kinderliteratur und Studentenbewegung*, Frankfurt/M: Institut für Jugendbuchforschung, 4f.

Karrenbrock, H. (1995) 'Das stabile Troittoir der Großstadt. Zwei Kinderromane der Neuen Sachlichkeit: Wolf Durians "Kai aus der Kiste" und Erich Kästners "Emil und die Detektive"', in S. Becker and C. Weiß (eds) *Neue Sachlichkeit im Roman. Neue Interpretationen zum Roman der Weimarer Republik*, Stuttgart, Weimar: Metzler, 176–94.

Kinderbuchfonds Baobab (ed.) (2003) *Fremde Welten. Kinder- und Jugendbücher zu den Themen: Afrika, Asien, Lateinamerika, ethnische Minderheiten und Rassismus empfohlen von den Lesegruppen des Kinderbuchfonds Baobab*, 15th edn, Basel: Kinderbuchfonds Baobab.

Kinnell, M. (1987) 'Cross-Cultural Futures: Research and Teaching in Comparative Children's Literature', *International Review of Children's Literature and Librarianship* 2, 3, 161–73.

Kittel, H. (1988) 'Kontinuität und Diskrepanzen', in H. Kittel (ed.) *Die literarische Übersetzung. Stand und Perspektiven ihrer Erforschung*, Berlin: Erich Schmidt, 158–79.

Klausemeier, R. (1963) *Völkerpsychologische Probleme in Kinderbüchern. Vergleichende Untersuchungen an englischer, französischer und deutschschweizerischer Kinderliteratur*, Bonn: Bouvier.

Klingberg, G. (1964) *Svensk barn- och ungdomslitteratur 1591–1839. En pedagogisk och bibliografisk översik*, Stockholm: Natur och Kultur.

Klingberg, G. (1967a) 'Die Gattungen des Kinder- und Jugendbuches. Ein Programm für die geschichtliche Kinder- und Jugendliteraturforschung', *Wirkendes Wort* 17, 5, 329–40.

Klingberg, G. (1967b) *Kronologisk bibliografi över barn- och ungdomslitteratur utgiven i Sverige 1591–1839*, Stockholm: Föreningen för svensk undervisningshistoria.

Klingberg, G. (1973) *Das deutsche Kinder- und Jugendbuch im schwedischen Raum. Ein Beitrag zum Studium der Verbreitungswege der Kinder- und Jugendliteratur*, Weinheim, Basel: Beltz.

Klingberg, G. (1986) *Children's Fiction in the Hands of the Translators*, Lund: Gleerup.

Klingberg, G. (1994) 'Die west-nordeuropäische Kinderliteraturregion im 19. Jahrhundert. Einige vergleichende Beobachtungen', in H.-H. Ewers, G. Lehnert and E. O'Sullivan (eds) *Kinderliteratur im interkulturellen Prozess. Studien zur Allgemeinen und Vergleichenden Kinderliteraturwissenschaft*, Stuttgart, Weimar: Metzler, 65–71.

Klingberg, G. and Bratt, I. (1988) *Barnböcker utgivna i Sverige 1840–1889: en kommenterad bibliografi*, Lund: Lund University Press.

Klingberg, G., Ørvig, M. and Amor, S. (eds) (1978) *Children's Books in Translation*, Stockholm: Almqvist & Wiksell International.

Klotz, A. (1990–2000) *Kinder- und Jugendliteratur in Deutschland 1840–1950. Gesamtverzeichnis der Veröffentlichungen in deutscher Sprache*, 6 vols, Stuttgart, Weimar: Metzler.

Köberle, S. (1972) *Jugendliteratur zur Zeit der Aufklärung. Ein Beitrag zur Geschichte der Jugendschriftenkritik*, Weinheim, Basel: Beltz.

Koelb, C. and Noakes, S. (1988) 'Introduction: Comparative Perspectives', in C. Koelb and S. Noakes (eds) *The Comparative Perspective on Literature: Approaches to Theory and Practice*, Ithaca, London: Cornell University Press, 3–17.

Koppe, S. (1992) 'Die Pilgerväter schnappen zu. Die Auswirkungen internationaler Koproduktion: Kinderbücher wie Fast Food', *Die Zeit* 46, 8 November, 21.

Koppen, E. (1980) 'Pinocchio im Reich des Simplicissimus. Otto Julius Bierbaum als Bearbeiter Collodis', in G. Schmidt and M. Tietz (eds) *Stimmen der Romania. Festschrift für W. Theodor Elwert zum 70. Geburtstag*, Wiesbaden: Heymann, 225–41.

Koppen, E. (1984) 'Weltliteratur', in Klaus Kanzog and Achim Masser (eds) *Reallexikon der deutschen Literaturgeschichte*, 2nd edn, vol. 4, Berlin, New York: de Gruyter, 815–27.

Köstlin, K. (1949) 'Vorwort', in L. Carroll *Alices Abenteuer im Wunderland*, trans. K. Köstlin, Stuttgart: Riederer, 4.

Kristeva, J. (1969) *Sémeiotiké – Recherches pour une sémanalyse*, Paris: Éditions du Seuil.

Krüger, A. (1968) 'Antilaudatien? Literaturkritische Analysen der mit Preisen ausgezeichneten Bilder- und Kinderbücher', *Zeitschrift für Jugendliteratur* Beiheft 1, 37–54.

Krusche, D. (1985) *Literatur und Fremde. Zur Hermeneutik kulturräumlicher Distanz*, Munich: iudicium.

Krusche, D. (1993) 'Erinnern, Verstehen und die Rezeption kulturell distanter Texte', in A. Wierlacher (ed.) *Kulturthema Fremdheit. Leitbegriffe und Problemfelder kulturwissenschaftlicher Fremdheitsforschung*, Munich: iudicium, 433–49.

Krutz-Arnold, C. (1978) 'Die deutschen Übersetzungen der Blyton-Bücher', *Informationen des Arbeitskreises für Jugendliteratur* 4, 3, 53–67.

Kuivasmäki, R. (1995) 'International Influence on the Nineteenth Century Finnish Children's Literature', in M. Nikolajeva (ed.) *Aspects and Issues in the History of Children's Literature*, Westport, London: Greenwood Press, 97–102.

Kümmerling-Meibauer, B. (1997) 'Internationale Kinderbuchklassiker. Definition und Standortbestimmung', *Eselsohr* 2, 5–9.

Kümmerling-Meibauer, B. (1999) *Klassiker der Kinder- und Jugendliteratur. Ein internationales Lexikon*, 2 vols, Stuttgart, Weimar: Metzler.

Künnemann, H. (1994) 'Die Seite Drei', *Bulletin Jugend + Literatur 25*, 5, 3.

Kurultay, T. (1994a) 'Probleme und Strategien bei der kinderliterarischen Übersetzung im Rahmen der interkulturellen Kommunikation', in H.-H. Ewers, G. Lehnert and E. O'Sullivan (eds) *Kinderliteratur im interkulturellen Prozess. Studien zur Allgemeinen und Vergleichenden Kinderliteraturwissenschaft*, Stuttgart, Weimar: Metzler, 191–201.

Kurultay, T. (1994b) 'Kulturelle Begegnungen durch Übersetzung – Fragen und Überlegungen zur Übersetzung der deutschsprachigen Mädchenliteratur ins Türkische', paper presented at the 7th annual conference of the Arbeitsgemeinschaft Kinderliteraturforschung, Falkenstein, June 1994.

Ladenthin, V. (1991) 'Viktorianischer Reisebericht', *Bulletin Jugend + Literatur* 22, 8, 22.

Lambert, J. (1991) 'In Quest of Literary World Maps', in H. Kittel and A.P. Frank (eds) *Interculturality and the Historical Study of Literary Translations*, Berlin: Erich Schmidt, 133–51.

Lathey, G. (2002) '"Emils in England" – the mediation of a modern classic', in B. Dolle-Weinkauff and H.-H. Ewers (eds) *Erich Kästners weltweite Wirkung als Kinderschriftsteller. Studien zur internationalen Rezeption des kinderliterarischen Werks*, Frankfurt etc.: Peter Lang, 154–67.

Lathey, G. (2003) 'Time, Narrative Intimacy and the Child: Implications of the Transition from the Present to the Past Tense in the Translation into English of Children's Texts', *Meta* 48, 233–40.

Laurentin, M. (1996) 'French-Speaking Africa', in P. Hunt (ed.) *International Companion Encyclopedia of Children's Literature*, London, New York: Routledge, 801–6.

Leerssen, J. (1996) 'National Stereotypes and Literature: Canonicity, Characterization, Irony', in M. Beller (ed.) *L'immagine dell'altro e l'identità nazionale: metodi di ricerca letteraria. Il confronto letterario. Supplemento al numero 24*, Fasano: Schena, 49–60.

Leerssen, J. (2000) 'The Rhetoric of National Character: A Programmatic Survey', *Poetics Today* 21, 2, 267–92.

Lehnert, G. (1988) 'Kinder- und Jugendliteraturforschung komparatistisch. Anmerkungen zu einem Desiderat', *Fundevogel* 51, 3–5.

Lehnert, G. (1995) 'Phantastisches Erzählen seit den 1970er Jahren. Zu einem kinderliterarischen Paradigmenwechsel', *Zeitschrift für Germanistik* 2, 279–89.

Lepman, J. (2002) *A Bridge of Children's Books*, trans. E. McCormick, Dublin: O'Brien Press/IBBY.

Lesnik-Oberstein, K. (1996) 'Defining Children's Literature and Childhood', in P. Hunt (ed.) *International Companion Encyclopedia of Children's Literature*, London, New York: Routledge, 17–31.

Lévi-Strauss, C. (1963) *Structural Anthropology*, trans. C. Jacobson and B. Grundfest Schoepf, New York: Basic Books.

Lewis, N. (1989) 'Preface', in T. Chevalier (ed.) *Twentieth-Century Children's Writers*, 3rd edn, London, Chicago: St. James Press, vii–xi.

Lindgren, A. (1969) 'Traduire des livres d'enfant – est-ce possible?', *Babel* 15, 2, 98–100.

Lucas, A.L. (1996) 'Introduction', in Carlo Collodi, *The Adventures of Pinocchio*, trans. A.L. Lucas, Oxford etc.: Oxford University Press, vii–xlv.

Lundqvist, U. (1974) 'Ur-Pippi. Pippi Långstrumps väg från första manuskriptet ut till kritik och publik', *Litteratur och samhälle* 10, 5.

Lypp, M. (1984) *Einfachheit als Kategorie der Kinderliteratur*, Frankfurt/M: dipa.

Lypp, M. (1986) 'Lachen beim Lesen. Zum Komischen in der Kinderliteratur', *Wirkendes Wort* 36, 6, 439–55.

Maar, P. (1994) *Meine beiden Biographien. Rede in der Johann Wolfgang Goethe-Universität Frankfurt am 8. Juli 1994*, Frankfurt/M: Freundeskreis des Instituts für Jugendbuchforschung.

McCallum, R. and Stephens, J. (1998) *Retelling Stories, Framing Culture: Traditional Story and Metanarratives in Children's Literature*, New York, London: Garland.

McGillis, R. (ed.) (1999) *Voices of the Other: Children's Literature and the Postcolonial Context*, New York, London: Garland.

McGillis, R. (1999) 'Introduction', in R. McGillis (ed.) *Voices of the Other: Children's Literature and the Postcolonial Context*, New York, London: Garland, xix–xxxii.

Mackey, M. (1998) *The Case of Peter Rabbit: Changing Conditions of Literature for Children*, New York: Garland Press.

Mackey, M. (1999) 'Playing in the Phase Space: Contemporary Forms of Fictional Pleasure', *Signal* 88, 16–33.

Mackey, M. (2002) *Literacies across Media: Playing the Text*, London: Routledge.

Mählqvist, S. (1977) *Böcker för svenska barn 1870–1950. En kvantitativ analys av barn- och ungdomslitteratur i Sverige*, Stockholm: Gidlund.

Mählqvist, S. (1983) *Biggles i Sverige. En litteratursociologisk studie av W.E. Johns Bigglesböcker*, Stockholm: Gidlund.

Mähne, S. and Rouvel, C. (1994) 'Magischer Realismus. Gespräch mit Ana Maria Machado und Ziraldo Alves Pintos', *Eselsohr* 9, 8f.

Mahony, B.E. (1944) 'Publisher's Preface', in P. Hazard, *Books, Children and Men*, trans. M. Mitchell, Boston: The Horn Book, v–vii.

Marx, S. (1987) *Le Avventure tedesche di Pinocchio*, Padova: Università di Padova.

Massee, M. (1930) 'This Explains about Some of the Names', in E. Kästner, *Emil and the Detectives*, trans. M. Massee, New York: Doubleday, ix–x.

Matsuoka, K. (1996) 'Ost und West, Nord und Süd. Was für einen Eindruck voneinander vermittelt unsere Kinderliteratur?', *Tausend und ein Buch* 2, 4–13.

Mecklenburg, N. (1987) 'Über kulturelle und poetische Alterität. Kultur- und literatur-theoretische Grundprobleme einer interkulturellen Germanistik', in A. Wierlacher (ed.) *Perspektiven und Verfahren interkultureller Germanistik*, Munich: iudicium, 563–84.

Meckling, I. (1975) 'Gemüt statt Solidarität. Ein englisches Kinderbuch und seine deutsche Übersetzung', *Der Deutschunterricht* 27, 5, 42–52.

Meek, M. (1996) 'Introduction', in P. Hunt (ed.) *International Companion Encyclopedia of Children's Literature*, London, New York: Routledge, 1–13.

Miller, A. (1990) *For Your Own Good: Hidden Cruelty in Child-Rearing and the Roots of Violence*, trans. H. and H. Hannum, New York: Noonday Press.

Mooser, A.-L. (1993) 'Heidi et son adaptation française ou l'aliénation d'une liberté', in J. Perrot and P. Bruno (eds) *La littérature de jeunesse au croisement des cultures*, Paris: CRDP de l'Académie de Créteil, 101–16.

Moss, G. (1992) 'Metafiction, Illustration, and the Poetics of Children's Literature', in P. Hunt (ed.) *Literature for Children: Contemporary Criticism*, London, New York: Routledge, 44–66.

Müller, H.M. (ed.) (2001) *Migration, Minderheiten und kulturelle Vielfalt in der europäischen Jugendliteratur.* Bern etc.: Lang.

Neubauer, P. (ed.) (2002) *Children in Literature – Children's Literature: Proceedings of the XX International Congress of F.I.L.L.M. 1996*, Regensburg, Frankfurt am Main etc.

Neumann, K. and Charlton, M. (1988) 'Massenkommunikation als Dialog. Zum aktuellen Diskussionsstand der handlungstheoretisch orientierten Rezeptions-forschung', *Communications* 14, 3, 7–37.

Nières, I. (1988) 'Lewis Carroll en France (1870–1985); les ambivalences d'une réception littéraire', unpublished doctoral thesis, Université de Picardie.

Nières, I. (1992) 'Une Europe des livres de l'enfance?', in Agence de Cooperation des Bibliotheques de Bretagne (ed.) *Livres d'enfants en Europe*, Pontivy: COBB, 9–17.

Nières, I. (1994) 'Kinderliteratur in Frankreich. Neuere Forschungsansätze', in H.-H. Ewers, G. Lehnert and E. O'Sullivan (eds) *Kinderliteratur im interkulturellen Prozeß. Studien zur Allgemeinen und Vergleichenden Kinderliteraturwissenschaft*, Stuttgart, Weimar: Metzler, 217–23.

Nikolajeva, M. (1996) *Children's Literature Comes of Age: Towards a New Aesthetic*, New York, London: Garland.

Nikolajeva, M. (2000) 'Tamed Imagination: A Re-reading of "Heidi" ', *Children's Literature Association Quarterly* 25, 2, 68–75.

Nikolajeva, M. (2002) *The Rhetoric of Character in Children's Literature*, Lanham: Scarecrow.

Nist, J.S. (1980) 'Patterns of Cultural Interchange in Children's Literature: Data from the Mildred L. Batchelder Award', in *Proceedings of the Sixth Annual Conference of the Children's Literature Association*, Villanova: Villanova University, 136–45.

Noaves, N.C. (1991) *Panorama historico da literatura infantil/juvenil*, São Paulo: Ática.

Nodelman, P. (1985) 'Introduction: Matthew Arnold, a Teddy Bear, and a List of Touchstones', in P. Nodelman (ed.) *Touchstones: Reflections on the Best in Children's Literature. Volume One*, West Lafayette: Children's Literature Association Publishers, 1–12.

Nodelman, P. (ed.) (1985–9) *Touchstones: Reflections on the Best in Children's Literature*, 3 vols, West Lafayette IN: Children's Literature Association Publishers.

Nord, C. (1991) *Textanalyse und Übersetzen*, 2nd edn, Heidelberg: Groos.

Nord, C. (1993) 'Alice im Niemandsland. Die Bedeutung von Kultursignalen für die Wirkung von literarischen Übersetzungen', in J. Holz-Mänttäri and C. Nord (eds) *Traducere Navem. Festschrift für Katherina Reiss zum 70. Geburtstag*, Tampere: University of Tampere, 395–416.

Oittinen, R. (1993) *I Am Me – I Am Other: On the Dialogics of Translating for Children*, Tampere: University of Tampere.

Oittinen, R. (2000) *Translating for Children*, New York: Garland Publishing.

Oittinen, R. (2003) 'Where the Wild Things Are: Translating Picture Books', *Meta* 48, 1–2, 128–41.

O'Neill, P. (1981) *German Literature in English Translation: A Select Bibliography*, Toronto, Buffalo, London: University of Toronto Press.

Ørvig, M. (1981) 'Some International Aspects of Children's Books', in B. Hearne and M. Kaye (eds) *Celebrating Children's Books: Essays on Children's Literature in Honor of Zena Sutherland*, New York: Lothrop, 218–40.

Osa, O. (1995) *African Children's and Youth Literature*, New York: Twayne.

Osberghaus, M. (1996) 'Widewidewie sie mir gefällt. Hej, Pippi Langstrumpf: eine deutsche Übersetzungsgeschichte', *Frankfurter Allgemeine Zeitung*, 23 December, 27.

Osberghaus, M. (1997) 'Die Zeitgebundenheit kinderliterarischer Übersetzungspraxis. Analyse eines exemplarischen Falles', unpublished MA thesis, J.W. Goethe-Universität, Frankfurt/M.

O'Sullivan, E. (1989) *Das ästhetische Potential nationaler Stereotypen in literarischen Texten. Auf der Grundlage einer Untersuchung des Englandbildes in der deutschsprachigen Kinder- und Jugendliteratur nach 1960*, Tübingen: Stauffenburg.

O'Sullivan, E. (1990) *Friend and Foe: The Image of Germany and the Germans in British Children's Fiction from 1870 to the Present*, Tübingen: Narr.

O'Sullivan, E. (1993) 'The Fate of the Dual Addressee in the Translation of Children's Literature', *New Comparison* 16, 109–19.

O'Sullivan, E. (1996) 'The Development of Modern Children's Literature in Late Twentieth-Century Ireland', in *Signal* 81, 189–211.

O'Sullivan, E. (1998) 'Losses and Gains in Translation: Some Remarks on the Translation of Humour in the Books of Aidan Chambers', *Children's Literature* 26, 185–204.

O'Sullivan, E. (1999) 'Translating Pictures', in *Signal* 90, 167–75.

O'Sullivan, E. (2000) *Kinderliterarische Komparatistik*, Heidelberg: Universitätsverlag C. Winter.

O'Sullivan, E. (2001) 'Alice in Different Wonderlands: Varying Approaches in the German Translations of an English Children's Classic', in M. Meek (ed.) *Children's Literature and National Identity*, London: Trentham, 23–32.

O'Sullivan, E. (2002a) 'Comparing children's literature', *GFL. German as a Foreign Language* 2, 33–56 (http://www.gfl-journal.de/).

O'Sullivan, E. (2002b) 'Erich und die Übersetzer. Eine komparatistische Analyse der Übersetzungen von Kästners Kinderromanen', in B. Dolle-Weinkauff and H.-H. Ewers (eds) *Erich Kästners weltweite Wirkung als Kinderschriftsteller. Studien zur internationalen Rezeption des kinderliterarischen Werks*, Frankfurt etc.: Peter Lang, 79–114.

Ottevaere-van Praag, G. (1987) *La littérature pour la jeunesse en Europe occidentale (1750–1925).
Histoire sociale et courants d'idées.* Angleterre, France, Pays-Bas, Allemagne, Italie, Berne etc.:
Lang.

Pape, W. (1981) *Das literarische Kinderbuch. Studien zur Entstehung und Typologie,* Berlin, New
York: de Gruyter.

Pedersen, V.H. (1990) *Translation or Paraphrase? An Evaluation of Various Versions of 'The Tinder
Box', 'The Ugly Duckling' and 'The Little Mermaid',* Odense: H.C. Andersen-Centret.

Pellowski, A. (1968) *The World of Children's Literature,* New York, London: Bowker.

Pellowski, A. (1996) 'Culture and Developing Countries', in P. Hunt (ed.) *International
Companion Encyclopedia of Children's Literature,* London, New York: Routledge, 663–75.

Peltsch, S.â__(1990) 'Zeiten, von Bäumen zu sprechen. Umweltthema in der DDR-Prosa
für Kinder', *Eselsohr* 5, 24.

Perella, N.J. (1986) 'An Essay on Pinocchio', in Carlo Collodi, *The Adventures of Pinocchio.
Story of a Puppet. Translated with an Introductory Essay and Notes by N.J. Perella,* Berkeley,
London: University of California Press, 1–69.

Perrot, J. (1991) *Art baroque, art d'enfance,* Nancy: Presse Universitaires.

Perrot, J. and Bruno, P. (eds) (1993) *La littérature de jeunesse au croisement des cultures,* Paris:
CRDP de l'Académie de Créteil.

Petzold, D. (1997) 'Anglistik und Kinderliteratur', *Anglistik* 8, 1, 75–90.

Plotz, J. (1995) 'Literary Ways of Killing a Child: the 19th Century Practice', in M. Nikolajeva (ed.) *Aspects and Issues in the History of Children's Literature,* Westport, London:
Greenwood Press, 1–24.

Prawer, S.S. (1973) *Comparative Literary Studies: An Introduction,* London: Duckworth.

Preiswerk, R. (ed.) (1980) *The Slant of the Pen: Racism in Children's Books,* Geneva: World
Council of Churches.

Preuss-Lausitz, U. (1995) 'Kindheit 2000. Entwicklungstendenzen zwischen Risiken und
Chancen', in H. Daubert and H.-H. Ewers (eds) *Veränderte Kindheit in der aktuellen Kinderliteratur,* Braunschweig: Westermann, 7–22.

Prieger, A. (1982) *Das Werk Enid Blytons. Eine Analyse ihrer Erfolgsserien in westdeutschen
Ausgaben,* Frankfurt/M: dipa.

Puurtinen, T. (1989) 'Assessing Acceptability in Translated Children's Books', *Target* 1, 2,
201–13.

Puurtinen, T. (1994) 'Dynamic Style as a Parameter of Acceptability in Translated Children's Books', in M. Snell-Hornby, F. Pöchhacker and K. Kaindl (eds) *Translation
Studies: An Interdiscipline,* Amsterdam, Philadelphia: Benjamins, 83–90.

Ray, S. (1996) 'The Far East', in P. Hunt (ed.) *International Companion Encyclopedia of Children's Literature,* London, New York: Routledge, 823–9.

Reiss, K. (1971) *Möglichkeiten und Grenzen der Übersetzungskritik. Kategorien und Kriterien für eine
sachgerechte Beurteilung von Übersetzungen,* Munich: Hueber.

Reiss, K. (1982) 'Zur Übersetzung von Kinder- und Jugendbüchern. Theorie und Praxis',
Lebende Sprachen 27, 1, 7–13.

Reiss, K. (2000) 'Type, Kind and Individuality of Text: Decision Making in Translation',
trans. S. Kitron, in L. Venuti (ed.) *The Translation Studies Reader,* London, New York:
Routledge, 160–71.

Reiss, K. and Vermeer, H.J. (1984) *Grundlegung einer allgemeinen Translationstheorie,* Tübingen:
Niemeyer.

Reynolds, K. (1990) *Girls Only? Gender and Popular Children's Fiction in Britain 1880–1910,*
New York etc: Harvester Wheatsheaf.

Reynolds, K. (2000) 'Fatal Fantasies: The Death of Children in Victorian and Edwardian Fantasy Writing', in G. Avery and K. Reynolds (eds) *Representations of Childhood Death*, London: Macmillan, 169–88.

Richter, D. (1996) *Pinocchio oder vom Roman der Kindheit*, Frankfurt/M: Fischer.

Richter, K. (1992) 'Die wahren Abenteuer sind im Kopf. Anmerkungen zu Christoph Heins "Wildpferd unterm Kachelofen" ', in H.-H. Ewers (ed.) *Komik im Kinderbuch. Erscheinungsformen des Komischen in der Kinder- und Jugendliteratur*, Weinheim, Munich: Juventa, 135–49.

Richter, K. (1996) 'Kinderliteratur und Kinderliteraturforschung in der DDR', in B. Dolle-Weinkauff and H.-H. Ewers (eds) *Theorien der Jugendlektüre. Beiträge zur Kinder- und Jugendliteraturkritik seit Heinrich Wolgast*, Weinheim, Munich: Juventa, 191–209.

Rose, J. (1994) *The Case of Peter Pan or The Impossibility of Children's Fiction*, revised edn, London: Macmillan.

Rosebrock, C. (1998) 'Kinderliteratur im Kanonisierungsprozess. Eine Problemskizze', in K. Richter and B. Hurrelmann (eds) *Kinderliteratur im Unterricht. Theorien und Modelle zur Kinder- und Jugendliteratur im pädagogisch-didaktischen Kontext*, Weinheim, Munich: Juventa, 89–108.

Rudd, D. (2000) *Enid Blyton and the Mystery of Children's Literature*, Houndmills: Macmillan Press.

Rutschky, K. (1983) *Deutsche Kinder-Chronik. Wunsch- und Schreckensbilder aus vier Jahrhunderten*, Cologne: Kiepenheuer & Witsch.

Rutschmann, V. (ed.) (1992) *BilderBuchReisen. Kinderliteratur in Brasilien. Wegleitung zur Ausstellung im Schweizerischen Jugendbuch-Institut in Zürich und in der Internationalen Jugendbibliothek in München*, Text: Evelin Höhne, Bibliographie: Ruth Fassbind-Eigenheer, Redaktion: Zurich: Schweizerisches Jugendbuch-Institut.

Rutschmann, V. (1994) *Fortschritt und Freiheit. Nationale Tugenden in historischen Jugendbüchern der Schweiz seit 1880*, Zurich: Chronos.

Saif, W. (1995) 'Astrid Lindgren in the Arabic Context', paper presented at the 12th IRSCL Conference, Stockholm, September.

Santucci, L. (1958) *Letteratura Infantile*, Milan: Fratelli Fabbri.

Schär, H. (1994) 'Von vergifteten Sachbüchern. Sachvermittlung für Kinder und Jugendliche in Afrika, Asien und Lateinamerika', *Jugendliteratur* 3, 3–8.

Scherf, W. (1976) 'From "Mio Cid" to "El Polizon del Ulises". Some Remarks on the Influence of the Spanish Literary Tradition on German Children's Literature', in *Libros infantiles y juveniles en España 1960–1975*, Madrid: Instituto Nacional del Libro Español, 62–6.

Scherf, W. (1978) 'Zur Aufnahme der schwedischen Kinder- und Jugendliteratur im Ausland', paper presented at a meeting of Swedish–German publishers at the Frankfurt Book Fair, October.

Scherf, W. (1981) 'The influence of Great Britain on German Children's Literature', in D. Ader *et al.* (eds) *Sub tua platano. Festschrift für Alexander Beinlich*, Emsdetten: Lechte, 255–65.

Schiavi, G. (1996) 'There Is Always a Teller in a Tale', *Target* 8, 1, 1–21.

Schmidt, N.J. (1981) *Children's Fiction about Africa in English*, New York: Conch Magazine.

Schneehorst, S. (1994) 'Für einen Dialog der Kulturen. Fremdsprachige Kinderliteratur in öffentlichen Bibliotheken', *Buch und Bibliothek* 46, 6/7, 573–84.

Schön, E. (1990) 'Die Entwicklung literarischer Rezeptionskompetenz. Ergebnisse einer Untersuchung zum Lesen bei Kindern und Jugendlichen', *SPIEL* 9, 2, 229–76.

Schultz, J. (1994) 'Für Kinder oder Erwachsene: Luigi Malerbas Kindergeschichten in Italien und Deutschland', in H.-H. Ewers, G. Lehnert and E. O'Sullivan (eds) *Kinderliteratur im interkulturellen Prozess. Studien zur Allgemeinen und Vergleichenden Kinderliteraturwissenschaft*, Stuttgart, Weimar: Metzler, 172–80.

Seibert, E. (1987) *Jugendliteratur im Übergang vom Josephinismus zur Restauration*, Vienna, Cologne, Graz: Böhlau.

Seifert, M. (forthcoming) 'The Image Trap: the Translation of English-Canadian Children's Literature into German', in E. O'Sullivan, K. Reynolds and R. Romøren (eds) *Children's Literature Global and Local: Social and Aesthetic Perspectives*, Kristiansand: Hoyskoleforlaget AS – Norwegian Academic Press.

Shavit, Z. (1981) 'Translation of Children's Literature as a Function of Its Position in the Literary Polysystem', *Poetics Today* 2, 4, 171–9.

Shavit, Z. (1986) *Poetics of Children's Literature*, Athens, GA, London: University of Georgia Press.

Shavit, Z. (1994) 'Israelische Kinderliteratur', in M. Morad (ed.) *Begegnung mit Kinder- und Jugendliteratur aus Israel*, Vienna: Zirkluar, 10–27.

Simons, A. (1926) 'Das englische Kinderbuch', *Die literarische Welt* 2, 49, 3 December, 9.

Snell-Hornby, M. (ed.) (1986) *Übersetzungswissenschaft – eine Neuorientierung. Zur Integrierung von Theorie und Praxis*, Tübingen: Francke.

Sønsthagen, K. and Eilstrup, L. (1992) *Danske bornelitteraturhistorie*, Copenhagen: Host & Son.

Spinner, K.H. (1993) 'Entwicklung des literarischen Verstehens', in O. Beisbart, U. Eisenbeiss, G. Koss and D. Marenbach (eds) *Leseförderung und Leseerziehung. Theorie und Praxis des Umgangs mit Büchern für junge Leser*, Donauwörth: Auer, 55–64.

Stach, R. (1996) *Robinsonaden. Bestseller der Jugendliteratur*, Baltmannsweiler: Schneider Verlag Hohengehren.

Stahl, J.D. (1985) 'Cross-cultural Perceptions: Images of Germany in America and of America in Germany Conveyed by Children's and Youth Literature', *Phaedrus* 11, 25–37.

Stahl, J.D. (1992) 'Canon Formation: A Historical and Psychological Perspective', in G.E. Sadler (ed.) *Teaching Children's Literature: Issues, Pedagogy, Resources*, New York: MLA, 12–21.

Steiner, G. (1975) *After Babel: Aspects of Language and Translation*, Oxford, New York: Oxford University Press.

Steiner, G. (1989) *Real Presences: Is There Anything in What We Say?*, London: Faber.

Steinlein, R. (1996) 'Neuere Geschichtsschreibung der deutschen Kinder- und Jugendliteratur seit den 70er Jahren', in B. Dolle-Weinkauff and H.-H. Ewers (eds) *Theorien der Jugendlektüre. Beiträge zur Kinder- und Jugendliteraturkritik seit Heinrich Wolgast*, Weinheim, Munich: Juventa, 239–62.

Stephens, J. (1992) *Language and Ideology in Children's Fiction*, London, New York: Longman.

Stephens, J. (1995) 'Representations of Place in Australian Children's Picture Books', in M. Nikolajeva (ed.) *Voices from Far Away: Current Trends in International Children's Literature Research*, Stockholm: Centrum för barnkulturforskning vid Stockholms universitet, 97–118.

Stolt, B. (1978) 'How Emil Becomes Michel – on the Translation of Children's Books', in G. Klingberg, M. Ørvig and S. Amor (eds) *Children's Books in Translation*, Stockholm: Almqvist & Wiksell International, 130–46.

Sunindyo (1980) 'Publishing and Translating in Indonesia', in S. Lees (ed.) *A Track to Unknown Water: Pacific Rim Conference on Children's Literature*, Carlton, Victoria: Melbourne State College, 44–54.

Surmatz, A. (1992) 'Astrid Lindgrens "Pippi Långstrump". Übersetzung und Rezeption als Indikatoren einer Veränderung der schwedischen und deutschen Kinderbuchlandschaft', unpublished MA thesis, Georg-August-Universität Göttingen.

Surmatz, A. (1996) 'Markering av könsroller inom barnlitteraturen och hur de översätts – Astrid Lindgren: "Pippi Långstrump" och "Bullerby" ', in H. Kress (ed.) *Litteratur og kjønn i Norden. Publications from the IASS Biannual Conference in Iceland 7–12 August 1994*, Reykjavík, 569–75.

Swierczynska-Jelonek, D. (1995–6) 'What Polish Children Actually Read', *Bookbird* 33, 3–4, 45f.

Tabbert, R. (1989) 'Australien für junge Leserinnen und Leser', in R. Tabbert (ed.) *Kinderbuchanalysen. Autoren – Themen – Gattungen*, Frankfurt/M: dipa, 122–40.

Tabbert, R. (1991a) 'Bilderbücher zwischen zwei Kulturen', in R. Tabbert (ed.) *Kinderbuchanalysen II. Wirkung – Kultureller Kontext – Unterricht*, Frankfurt/M: dipa, 130–48.

Tabbert, R. (1991b) 'Nationale Mythen in drei klassischen Bilderbüchern', in R. Tabbert (ed.) *Kinderbuchanalysen II. Wirkung – Kultureller Kontext – Unterricht*, Frankfurt/M: dipa, 117–29.

Tabbert, R. (1992) 'The Surprising Career of Wolf Spillner's "Wild Geese" ', *Poetics Today* 13.1, 247–58.

Tabbert, R. (1995) 'Umweltmythen in Kinderbüchern verschiedener Nationen', in U. Nassen (ed.) *Naturkind, Landkind, Stadtkind. Literarische Bilderwelten kindlicher Umwelt*, Munich: Fink, 135–51.

Tabbert, R. (1996a) 'Forschungen zur Übersetzung von Kinderliteratur (1975–1995)', in H.-H. Ewers, U. Nassen, K. Richter and R. Steinlein (eds) *Kinder- und Jugendliteraturforschung 1995/96*, Stuttgart, Weimar: Metzler, 97–107.

Tabbert, R. (1996b) 'Swimmy, the BFG und Janne min vän: Prämierte Bücher aus fremden Sprachen', in H. Peetz and D. Liesenhoff (eds) *40 Jahre Deutscher Jugendliteraturpreis. Eine Dokumentation über 40 Jahre*, Munich: Arbeitskreis für Jugendliteratur, 49–67.

Tabbert, R. (2002) 'Approaches to the Translation of Children's Literature: A Review of Critical Studies since 1960', *Target* 14, 2, 303–51.

Tähtiin, M. (1993) *Venäläinen lasten – ja nuortenkirjallisuus ja sen suomennokset*, Tampere: TOIM.

Thomson-Wohlgemuth, G. (2003) 'Children's Literature and Translation under the East German Regime', *Meta* 48, 1–2, 241–9.

Thwaite, A. (1991) *A. A. Milne: His Life*, London, Boston: Faber & Faber.

Thwaite, M. (1972) *From Primer to Pleasure in Reading*, 2nd edn (first edn published 1963), London: Library Association.

Tomlinson, C. (1998) *Children's Books from Other Countries*, Lanham and London: The Scarecrow Press.

Tötemeyer, A.-J. (1994) 'Transfer of De-recorded Information to the Information Starved', *IFLA Journal* 20, 4, 410–18.

Toury, G. (1980) *In Search of a Theory of Translation*, Tel Aviv: Porter Institute.

Toury, G. (1995) *Descriptive Translation Studies and Beyond*, Amsterdam, PA: Benjamins.

Ulrich, A.K. (1998a) '"Und wenn Du das nicht glaubst … ". Anthologien als Wegbereiter moderner lesedidaktischer Konzepte', in K. Richter and B. Hurrelmann (eds) *Kinderliteratur im Unterricht. Theorien und Modelle zur Kinder- und Jugendliteratur im pädagogisch-didaktischen Kontext*, Weinheim, Munich: Juventa, 61–74.

Ulrich, A.K. (1998b) 'Die Kinderliteratur geht fremd. Gedanken zur Herausgabe aussereuropäischer Kinder- und Jugendbücher für deutschsprachige junge Menschen', in B. Hurrelmann and K. Richter (eds) *Das Fremde in der Kinder- und Jugendliteratur. Interkulturelle Perspektiven*, Weinheim, Munich: Juventa, 115–29.

van den Broeck, R. (1986) 'Contrastive Discourse Analysis as a Tool for the Interpretation of Shifts in Translated Texts', in J. House and S. Blum-Kulka (eds) *Interlingual and Intercultural Communication: Discourse and Cognition in Translation and Second Language Acquisition Studies*, Tübingen: Narr, 37–47.

van Leuven-Zwart, K. (1989) 'Translation and Original: Similarities and Dissimilarities I', *Target* 1, 2, 151–81.

van Leuven-Zwart, K. (1990) 'Translation and Original: Similarities and Dissimilarities II', *Target* 2, 1, 69–95.

van Uffelen, H. (1993) *Bibliographie der niederländischen Kinder- und Jugendliteraur in deutscher Übersetzung 1830–1990*, Münster etc.: Zentrum für Niederlande-Studien.

Veeser, H.A. (1989) 'Introduction', in H.A. Veeser (ed.) *The New Historicism*, London: Routledge, ix–xvi.

Venuti, L. (1995) *The Translator's Invisibility: A History of Translation*, London, New York: Routledge.

Venuti, L. (ed.) (2000) *The Translation Studies Reader*, London, New York: Routledge.

Wakabayashi, H. (1990) 'Warum japanische Kinder- und Jugendbücher kaum ins Deutsche übersetzt werden', *Eselsohr* 9, 20f.

Wall, B. (1991) *The Narrator's Voice: The Dilemma of Children's Fiction*, London: Macmillan.

Webb, J. (ed.) (2000) *Text, Culture and National Identity in Children's Literature*, Helsinki: Nordinfo.

Weissbrod, R. (1999) 'Mock-Epic as a Byproduct of the Norm of Elevated Language', *Target* 11, 2, 245–62.

Weisstein, U. (1968) *Einführung in die Vergleichende Literaturwissenschaft*, Stuttgart: Kohlhammer.

White, M. (1990) 'Translated Children's Books: A Study of Successful Translations and a Comprehensive Listing of Books Available in the United States', unpublished thesis, Texas Woman's University, Denton, Texas.

Wild, R. (1987) *Die Vernunft der Väter. Zur Psychographie von Bürgerlichkeit und Aufklärung in Deutschland am Beispiel ihrer Literatur für Kinder*, Stuttgart: Metzler.

Wilkending, G. (1984) 'Der Widerspruch in der klassischen Kinder- und Jugendliteratur. Grenzüberschreitung und Erziehungsfunktion', *Informationen des Arbeitskreises für Jugendliteratur* 10, 1, 52–69.

Wilkending, G. (1994) 'Einleitung', in G. Wilkending (ed.) *Kinder- und Jugendliteratur. Mädchenliteratur. Vom 18. Jahrhundert bis zum Zweiten Weltkrieg. Eine Textsammlung*, Stuttgart: Reclam, 7–70.

Wilkending, G. (1996) 'Mädchenlektüre und Mädchenliteratur. "Backfischliteratur" im Widerstreit von Aufklärungspädagogik, Kunsterziehungs- und Frauenbewegung', in B. Dolle-Weinkauff and H.-H. Ewers (eds) *Theorien der Jugendlektüre. Beiträge zur Kinder- und Jugendliteraturkritik seit Heinrich Wolgast*, Weinheim, Munich: Juventa, 105–25.

Wilkie, C. (1996) 'Intertextuality', in P. Hunt (ed.) *International Companion Encyclopedia of Children's Literature*, London, New York: Routledge, 131–7.

Wolfenstein, M. (1955) 'French Parents Take Their Children to the Park', in M. Mead and M. Wolfenstein (eds) *Childhood in Contemporary Culture*, Chicago: University of Chicago Press, 99–177.

Wolgast, H. (1896) *Das Elend unserer Jugendliteratur. Ein Beitrag zur künstlerischen Erziehung der Jugend*, Hamburg: Selbstverlag.

Wunderlich, R. (1992) 'The Tribulations of "Pinocchio": How Social Change Can Wreck a Good Story', *Poetics Today* 13, 1, 197–219.

Wunderlich, R. and Morrissey, T.J. (2002) *Pinocchio Goes Postmodern: Perils of a Puppet in the United States*, New York, London: Routledge.

Zima, P. (1992) *Komparatistik. Einführung in die Vergleichende Literaturwissenschaft*, with the assistance of Johann Strutz, Tübingen: Francke.

Zipes, J. (1979) *Breaking the Magic Spell: Radical Theories of Folk and Fairy Tales*, London: Heinemann.

Zipes, J. (1983) *Fairy Tales and the Art of Subversion*, London: Heinemann.

Zipes, J. (1994) 'Neue kritische Ansätze zur englischen und amerikanischen Kinderliteratur seit 1980. Eine Bestandsaufnahme', in H.-H. Ewers, G. Lehnert and E. O'Sullivan (eds) *Kinderliteratur im interkulturellen Prozess. Studien zur Allgemeinen und Vergleichenden Kinderliteraturwissenschaft*, Stuttgart, Weimar: Metzler, 205–16.

Ziv, A. (1988) 'Introduction', in A. Ziv (ed.) *National Styles of Humor*, New York, Westport, London: Greenwood, vii–xiii.

Index